No-Nonsense
RESUMES

The Essential Guide to
Creating Attention-Grabbing
Resumes That Get
Interviews & Job Offers

Wendy S. Enelow
Master Resume Writer

Arnold G. Boldt
Certified Professional Resume Writer

CAREER
PRESS
Franklin Lakes, NJ

NO-NONSENSE RESUMES
EDITED BY KARA REYNOLDS
TYPESET BY EILEEN DOW MUNSON
Cover design by DesignConcept
Printed in the U.S.A. by Book-mart Press

To order this title, please call toll-free 1-800-CAREER-1 (NJ and Canada: 201-848-0310) to order using VISA or MasterCard, or for further information on books from Career Press.

CAREER PRESS

The Career Press, Inc., 3 Tice Road, PO Box 687,
Franklin Lakes, NJ 07417
www.careerpress.com

Library of Congress Cataloging-in-Publication Data

Enelow, Wendy S.
    No-nonsense resumes : the essential guide to creating attention-grabbing resumes that get interviews & job offers / by Wendy S. Enelow and Arnold G. Boldt.
        p. cm.
    Includes bibliographical references and index.
    ISBN-13: 978-1-56414-905-3
    ISBN-10: 1-56414-905-6
    1. Résumés (Employment) I. Boldt, Arnold G. II. Title.

HF5383.B548 2006
650.14'2—dc22

                                                                2006012474

Contents

Introduction..5

Chapter 1: Simple Truths About **Resume Writing**..................................7

  The Six Simple Truths About Resume Writing................................. 7

    Truth #1: Write To the Future.. 8
    Truth #2: Know Who You Are.. 9
    Truth #3: Strategy and Positioning Are Key.............................15
    Truth #4: Sell It; Don't Tell It...16
    Truth #5: Keywords Rock!..17
    Truth #6: There Are No Rules for Resume Writing....................20

  Top 10 Critical Mistakes to Avoid..22

Chapter 2: Simple Truths About **Resume Formatting and Design**.................25

  Resume Formats... 2 5

    Chronological Resumes.. 26
    Functional Resumes... 28
    Hybrid Resumes.. 30

  Resume Designs... 32

  Top 10 Critical Formatting and Design Mistakes to Avoid.......................34

Chapter 3: Simple Truths About **Writing Your Resume**............................ 39

  Step-by-Step Process.. 39

  The Key Resume Elements..40

    Contact Information... 40
    Career Summary.. 42
    Professional Experience.. 45
    Education.. 48
    The Extras... 50

  Age *Does* Matter.. 52

  Streamlining Your Writing Process... 53

Chapter 4: Simple Truths About **Electronic Resumes**............................. 55

  Electronic Resumes..56

    E-mail Attachments.. 56
    ASCII Text Files.. 58
    Scannable Resumes.. 60
    Web Resumes... 61

Chapter 5: Resumes for **Accounting, Banking, and Finance** Careers............ 69
    Keywords and Keyword Phrases.. 70
    Sample Resumes 71

Chapter 6: Resumes for **Administrative and Clerical** Careers..................... 82
    Keywords and Keyword Phrases.. 83
    Sample Resumes 84

Chapter 7: Resumes for **Government** Careers... 93
    Keywords and Keyword Phrases.. 94
    Sample Resumes 95

Chapter 8: Resumes for **Healthcare and Social Service** Careers................. 106
    Keywords and Keyword Phrases.. 107
    Sample Resumes 108

Chapter 9: Resumes for **Hospitality and Food Service** Careers................... 120
    Keywords and Keyword Phrases.. 121
    Sample Resumes 122

Chapter 10: Resumes for **Human Resources and Training** Careers.............. 135
    Keywords and Keyword Phrases.. 136
    Sample Resumes 137

Chapter 11: Resumes for **Law Enforcement and Legal** Careers.................... 148
    Keywords and Keyword Phrases.. 149
    Sample Resumes 150

Chapter 12: Resumes for **Manufacturing and Operations** Careers.............. 160
    Keywords and Keyword Phrases.. 161
    Sample Resumes 162

Chapter 13: Resumes for **Sales, Marketing, and Customer Service** Careers........ 175
    Keywords and Keyword Phrases.. 176
    Sample Resumes 177

Chapter 14: Resumes for **Skilled Trades** Careers..................................... 188
    Keywords and Keyword Phrases.. 189
    Sample Resumes 190

Chapter 15: Resumes for **Teaching and Education** Careers....................... 197
    Keywords and Keyword Phrases.. 198
    Sample Resumes 199

Chapter 16: Resumes for **Technology, Science, and Engineering** Careers...... 207
    Keywords and Keyword Phrases.. 208
    Sample Resumes 209

Appendix A: Resume Writing Worksheet.. 223

Appendix B: Professional Keyword List... 227

Appendix C: Contributors... 229

Index.. 233

About the Authors.. 237

If you're currently in the job market, we've got some great news for you! According to the U.S. Bureau of Labor Statistics (*www.bls.gov*), total employment in the United States is expected to increase by 14.7 percent between the years 2004 and 2014. What's more, not only is the number of opportunities expanding, but the composition of the workforce is also changing. Service-producing industries such as healthcare, technology, engineering, transportation, social services, and others are growing at a much stronger pace (nearly 20 percent over the same period of time) than goods-producing industries such as manufacturing and construction.

As the numbers indicate, it's a great time to be looking for a job, whatever your particular situation (for example, graduating college student, skilled tradesperson, mid-level professional, senior-level executive, return-to-work mom, or military veteran). Opportunities are everywhere, and your challenge is to position yourself in the best way possible to capture those opportunities and land a great new job.

The first and perhaps most vital step in preparing yourself for a successful job search is to create a powerful resume that will open doors and generate interviews. Bottom line: That's the real purpose of your resume. Resumes do not get jobs; people do. Your resume is simply your calling card, designed to clearly communicate *who* you are, *what* you can do, and *how well* you do it. If you're equipped with a powerful resume, you will instantly give yourself a measurable advantage over your similarly qualified competition.

To help you achieve that competitive edge, we've created a one-of-a-kind resume book that clearly and concisely guides you through the resume-writing process. To be sure that this book is easy to use, we've cut through all the confusion and gotten right down to brass tacks—hence our *no-nonsense* approach. We've given you the information you need, provided you with the worksheets to assemble all your information, demonstrated how and where to use that information, and given you close to 100 resume samples to review. When you're finished with this book, you should have a resume that is well-polished, well-positioned, and powerful—a true *no-nonsense* resume.

Chapter 1

▶ Simple Truths About

Resume Writing

Professional resume writers know that resume writing is a unique combination of art and science; careful attention to detail and creative use of language; substance and style; and strategy and implementation. They understand that resumes are not just listings of past work experience and educational credentials, but rather they are documents designed to *sell* job seekers into their next jobs.

As professional resume writers ourselves, we follow a very systematic, no-nonsense approach to resume writing that has opened the doors to new opportunities for tens of thousands of job seekers. Now, we're going to share that information with you in the first-ever, no-nonsense guide to resume writing that gives you insider secrets to writing well-polished, well-positioned, and powerful resumes. If you follow the steps, activities, and strategies outlined in this book, you'll be able to craft a resume that is sharp, distinctive, on-target, and effective in generating interviews and offers.

The Six Simple Truths About Resume Writing

Before you begin to write your resume, there are six strategic concepts you must understand. Professional resume writers live by these truths and understand how critical they are in positioning a candidate for the *right* opportunity.

Truth #1: Write to the Future

Truth #2: Know *Who* You Are

Truth #3: Strategy and Positioning Are Key

Truth #4: Sell It; Don't Tell It

Truth #5: Keywords Rock!

Truth #6: There Are No Rules for Resume Writing

If you can truly grasp what these concepts mean and how they apply to your particular job-search situation, you will be able to write a strong and effective resume that will open doors and generate interviews. Let's explore each of these simple truths.

Truth #1: Write to the Future

Resume writing is about writing *toward* your next job; it's not about rehashing your past experience. That is, perhaps, the single most important strategy for resume writing. If you understand it, then you'll be well prepared to write your resume. If you do not, you'll find that your resume-writing process becomes much more difficult than it needs to be.

To best illustrate this concept, let's examine the resumes of two sales professionals with similar backgrounds, but very different objectives. The first candidate, Sam, has been in sales for 12 years and now wants to move into a sales management position. To write toward his new career goal, Sam is going to place a heavy emphasis on activities such as sales recruitment, sales training, region/territory management, product positioning, sales budgeting, forecasting, and all the other management-related functions he has performed. These items, in combination with his sales achievements, become the foundation on which Sam's entire resume is written. He needs to put a heavier emphasis on his sales management qualifications, as opposed to his field sales experience, to better position himself as an individual who is *already* well-qualified for his targeted management position.

Our other sales candidate, Leslie, wants to transition from her 12-year field-sales career into an accounting position, and her resume will be totally different from Sam's. To write toward her future career goals, Leslie is going to highlight her experience in budgeting, forecasting, revenue planning, profit projection, cost control, and other related skills. Most likely, these functions were not Leslie's primary job responsibilities as a field sales representative; however, they were ancillary responsibilities that she managed. As such, she needs to bring them to the forefront of her resume so that she is able to effectively position herself to make her desired transition into her future accounting career.

To further demonstrate this concept, let's examine the resume-writing process for an insurance agent who now wants to work as a crisis intervention counselor. Employed in the insurance industry for more than 15 years, Jim has also been an active volunteer in several community-based counseling organizations. He's been doing this for more than 10 years, although he's never been paid for his time and expertise in this area. Because Jim's goal is to transition into a counseling career, the primary focus of his resume will be the skills and experiences he's acquired through his volunteer efforts, with just a brief mention of his insurance career at the very end of his resume. The terms you'll see on his resume will include crisis intervention, one-on-one counseling, group counseling, treatment planning, inter-agency relations, and more. If prepared effectively, Jim's resume will communicate that he is a well-qualified counselor and not an "insurance guy." In turn, he will have created a document that appropriately positions him for his desired career move.

This concept is what is referred to as *re-weighting,* or shifting the emphasis of your resume from one set of skills to another in order to support your current career objectives. Decide what it is you want to do at this point in your career and then highlight all of your relevant skills, experiences, and qualifications—whether from paid work experience, training, volunteer activities, or community service. Each of these experiences is important, because each equipped you with different skills that may be pertinent to your current career goals.

Re-weighting is an acceptable practice in resume writing. It's what gives you the power to transform yourself into *who* you want to be to successfully pursue your new career goals. A word of caution, however: Don't overstate your qualifications. If you are granted an interview, you'll discover that you're neither adequately prepared nor qualified for the job. Rather, always write with our motto in mind: *Stay in the realm of reality!*

Truth #2: Know *Who* You Are

It's not possible to write a truly effective resume without knowing what your objective is—the type of position you're interested in or the industry in which you want to work. This concept ties directly into Truth #1—Write to the Future—and in order to do that, you *must* have a job goal in mind. This goal may be as specific as a network engineering position or it may be more general, such as a position in marketing, public relations, or corporate communications. Either way, in order to write *toward* your future goals, you must know *who* you are and *how* you want to be perceived by prospective employers and recruiters.

Many people reading this book may, indeed, already have a particular job objective in mind, or at least a good idea of the types of positions in which they're interested. If this describes your situation, you may want to jump to Truth #3, starting on page 15.

For others of you who may be uncertain as to where you're headed next in your career, we recommend you take some time to explore your core skills and competencies, the things you enjoy doing and the things that motivate and inspire you. It's also important to have a clear awareness of the things you truly *dis*like doing. If you assemble a list of these items, you should begin to see patterns of interest that will help you in identifying your career goals.

To help you with that process, we've designed a few simple exercises that should guide you in further clarifying your career goals and highlighting particularly relevant strengths. Take your time when completing these exercises and think carefully about your responses.

Capturing Your Core Skills

Directions: Think about all of your skills—work-related and otherwise—and include them in the column "What I Do Well." Maybe you're great with organizing things, good with numbers, effective in staff training, successful in increasing revenues; the list goes on and on.

In the column, "What I Don't Do Well," list all the things you're not so good at (dealing with irate customers, interpreting written instructions, or maybe researching data). Be honest with yourself; no one but you is ever going to see this list.

What I Do Well	What I Don't Do Well

Identifying Your Optimal Working Environment

Directions: In the left-hand column, list all the things you enjoy about your current job. If you're not currently employed, think back to your last job. This column might include things such as flexibility, autonomy, decision-making responsibility, and people interaction.

Then, in the right-hand column, list all the things you did not like about that job. These items might include a difficult boss, an isolated working environment, or poor staff communication.

What I Love About My Job	What I Hate About My Job
_____	_____
_____	_____
_____	_____
_____	_____
_____	_____
_____	_____
_____	_____
_____	_____
_____	_____
_____	_____
_____	_____
_____	_____
_____	_____

Identifying Your Key Interests and Motivators

Directions: Forget about work for a few moments and focus on your personal interests and activities. In the left-hand column, list things you enjoy doing outside of work (for example, baseball, cycling, or stamp collecting).

Then, in the right-hand column, list things you dislike doing outside of work, such as household chores, errands, and volunteering.

What I Like Doing Away From Work	What I Don't Like Doing Away From Work

Once you've completed the previous three exercises, you should immediately begin to see certain patterns and be able to identify four distinct areas:

▶ Things you do well and like doing.

▶ Things you do well, but dislike doing.

▶ Things you enjoy, but don't do well.

▶ Things you dislike and don't do well.

Take a look at the following chart to better understand how this works.

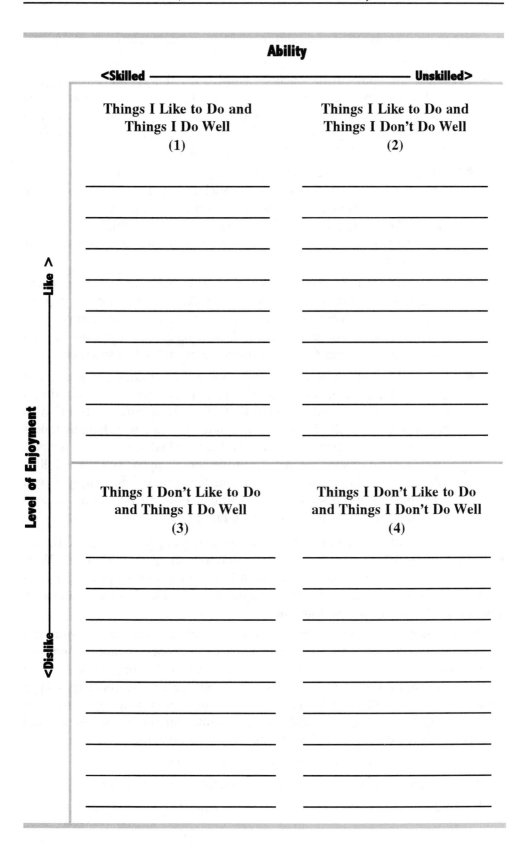

Ability

<Skilled ———————————————————— Unskilled>

Things I Like to Do and
Things I Do Well
(1)

Things I Like to Do and
Things I Don't Do Well
(2)

Things I Don't Like to Do
and Things I Do Well
(3)

Things I Don't Like to Do
and Things I Don't Do Well
(4)

Level of Enjoyment

Like >

<Dislike

To help you interpret your results, we've labeled the sections in the chart 1 through 4:

Box #1: These are your "proficiencies." They're the things you're really good at doing and you also particularly enjoy. Perhaps you're a purchasing agent who is excellent at negotiating with vendors. You take pride in this capability and genuinely enjoy the interaction with each supplier. This type of skill definitely belongs in Box #1.

Box #2: Things listed here are "development opportunities." You really enjoy these activities, but aren't very "proficient" at them. Perhaps you've always wanted to be a master woodworker and cabinetmaker, but have little skill or experience. With extra training, you might be able to develop this skill and transform woodworking into one of your "proficiencies."

Box #3: These are your "burnout skills." You're probably very good at doing these things, but don't *enjoy* doing them. At work, you may be repeatedly asked to perform a task that you do very well, but that you perceive as unchallenging and unrewarding. Exploring career opportunities that move you away from these tension points is probably a smart choice.

Box #4: "Avoid like the plague." You hate doing these things *and* you're not good at doing them. For example, many bank tellers were hired at a time when the valued skills for that job were accuracy, attention to detail, and a friendly demeanor. In today's banking world, many tellers are now expected to sell products and are evaluated on their sales performance. Gradually, the nature of the job changed, and many tellers felt they were being forced to do something they didn't enjoy. If you find yourself in this situation, or a similar one, the best thing to do is start looking for a different position more suited to your proficiencies.

Once you identify what you do well, what you truly enjoy, and what motivates you to do a good job, you will have a better understanding of *who* you are. With this enhanced self-awareness, you're much better prepared to put together a resume that tells an employer what's unique and valuable about you, and how you can contribute to the bottom line.

If, after doing the previous exercises, you're still uncertain as to your next career move, we recommend you consult with a career coach or career counselor who can offer more comprehensive career assessment and testing services. Some of the more well-known career assessment tools are the Myers-Briggs Type Indicator (MBTI), DISC, O*NET, Keirsey Temperament, and TypeFocus. To find a qualified career professional who can administer these assessments and help you set your career direction, check out these resources:

▶ Career Masters Institute (*www.cminstitute.com*).

▶ National Career Development Association (*www.ncda.org*).

▶ International Coach Federation (*www.coachfederation.org/ICF*).

Truth #3: Strategy and Positioning Are Key

Your resume needs to present you as the best candidate for the position you are applying for in order to capture job interviews and offers. You can achieve this by using the right strategy to communicate *who* you are and by positioning yourself as you want to be perceived. Think of resume writing just as you would portrait painting; the only difference is you're using words on the page instead of paint on a canvas.

In *no-nonsense* terms, your resume must portray the best *you* for the position you seek. If you're targeting a senior management position, you need a resume that looks sharp and upscale, clearly highlights your achievements and contributions, and demonstrates the depth of your management and leadership experience. If you create a resume that is less sophisticated in its presentation and wording, you will not have positioned yourself effectively for the senior-level positions you are pursuing.

The opposite can also happen. If you're a recent college graduate who is anxious to land your first professional position, don't overdo it! Your resume should reflect the fact that you *are* a graduating student (with great skills, training, and internships) and not misrepresent you in any way. If a company is recruiting recent college graduates, it wants college-graduate resumes and not resumes for CEOs! Here are a few more examples that will help show you how to accomplish this:

▶ If you consider yourself an up-and-coming candidate ready for your next big step, your strategy should be to emphasize the significant responsibilities and achievements of your last few positions, and how you have responded successfully to the demands of increased responsibility.

▶ If you're an older worker with management experience who wants to "smell the roses" and pursue a job with less pressure, then your approach might be to create a resume that highlights your people skills, your capacity to work independently, and the diversity of your experience over the course of your career (while shifting the focus away from all of your hard-core management experience).

▶ If you were a stay-at-home mom who is now ready to re-enter the workforce, a resume that features the skills you gained from your earlier work experience and volunteer activities, along with your educational credentials, will be the foundation on which you build your resume.

Every job seeker's situation is different and, as such, every resume is unique. You must be certain to create a resume that strategically positions you for the type of job you are seeking. The words, the format, the design, and the presentation are all key factors that we'll explore in greater depth as we move through this book.

Truth #4: Sell It; Don't Tell It

When it comes right down to it, resume writing is really all about sales, marketing, and brand positioning. Think of yourself as a unique and special product that's just the right solution for employers who desperately need the *features* and *benefits* you have to offer. Your goal is to develop the best plan for *marketing* yourself to those employers who have a *demand* for the skills and qualifications you offer. If you think about it, this is the fundamental principle that drives our supply/demand economy—buyers with a need (in this case, the employer who needs skilled workers) and a seller with a solution (in this case, you!).

When you submit your resume to a prospective employer, think of it as a piece of direct-mail advertising. We've all received direct-mail ads—they're the envelopes that say, "You May Have Already Won!" Truly effective direct-mail campaigns get your attention and prompt you to act—namely, by opening the envelope and reading the enclosed material.

The *no-nonsense* approach to resume writing is more subtle than the cliched slogans used by mass advertisers in direct-mail campaigns. However, the underlying strategy is the same: specifically, prompting the recipient to read and respond to the material. In the case of a job search, you must prepare a resume that markets your unique skills and encourages the reader (HR director or hiring manager) to decide, "I've got to talk to this candidate!"

A humdrum listing of job duties doesn't accomplish this. Your resume needs to highlight accomplishments that show your value to the company you work for now (and the companies you've worked for in the past), and how these accomplishments make you a potential asset to a new employer.

Using the "Sell It; Don't Tell It" concept is a great way to communicate your value and the benefits you bring to the workforce. And it's a relatively easy thing to achieve. Compare the two statements that follow—one that *tells* what you did; the other that *sells* what you did—and you'll easily see what we mean.

➤ **Telling It**

Responsible for managing sales and customer service throughout Michigan, Ohio, Indiana, and Illinois.

➤ **Selling It**

Planned, staffed, budgeted, and directed regional sales and customer relationship management programs for 200+ corporate accounts in the $35 million Midwestern sales region. Increased product sales by 45% in two years, captured 22 new accounts, and exceeded performance goals by 30%.

Can you see the difference in the impact of these two examples? It should be obvious that the second example is a much better representation of that individual's talents and responsibilities and, in turn, a more compelling statement of the value he or she brings to a new employer.

Unfortunately, job seekers often don't believe they have real successes that translate into benefits they can sell to a prospective employer. For example, many assembly-line workers think their most notable achievement is reliably showing up for work every day. Not true! If you've ever worked in manufacturing, did you suggest to your supervisor that a safety guard be added to the line to prevent accidents? Did you figure out a way to reduce scrap by making a change that prevented pieces from being damaged on the line? Even if the company didn't formally acknowledge your suggestion, you know what your contribution was and it's legitimate to mention it on your resume.

Now, think about your accomplishments—small and large—and how they positively impacted a company's operating efficiency, productivity, customer satisfaction, or overall profitability. Including these types of noteworthy attributes and achievements on your resume will identify you as someone who brings immediate value to an organization and is well worth hiring.

Truth #5: Keywords Rock!

Let's start our discussion of keywords with a clear definition of what they are and why they're so important. If you've ever used a search engine on the Internet to find something, then you've used keywords. If you were to type in "Chicago Cubs + Wrigley Field + Box Seats," you'd probably find a link that would take you to a Website where you could buy tickets for the next time the Mets are in Chicago. Now imagine you're searching a database of job candidates. You type in "Process Engineer + Lean Manufacturing + Six Sigma Black Belt." When you click on "Search," you should come up with a list of process engineering candidates with lean manufacturing and Six Sigma experience. Your results will be ranked by how many times the search engine found those particular keywords in each person's resume.

Simply put, keywords are those *buzz words* found in each and every profession. They identify the essential skills, knowledge, and expertise that distinguish someone in a particular field. You probably know what they are for your job—you use them every day—but they've become so second nature to your day-to-day activities that you might not recognize their importance. If your resume is entered into one of a variety of scanning systems, or the electronic version of your resume gets uploaded to a database, the potential employer will use specialized software, which functions as a search engine does, to scour the database looking for keywords that are relevant to a particular position.

In the early days of the Internet (way back in 1995!), it was common to see a "Keyword Summary" at the beginning or end of a resume intended for posting on the Internet. This approach was designed to improve the chances that a search tool would *hit* on the job seeker's resume and identify him or her as a qualified candidate. As technology has become more sophisticated, it's become much less common (or necessary) to have a distinctly separate keyword summary. Today, you can incorporate your keywords into various sections throughout your resume; scanning technology will identify them in any location. To help you get started, here are a few examples.

Example 1: Keywords included in summary:

CAREER SUMMARY

Ten years of progressively responsible experience in **Accounting**, **Auditing**, and **Finance** with Dow Chemical Company. Excellent qualifications in:

* General Accounting	* Financial Analysis
* Cost Accounting	* Financial Reporting
* Internal Auditing	* Budget Administration
* Expense Reduction	* Information Technology
* Investor Reporting	* Staff Training & Supervision

Example 2: Keywords integrated into job description:

Social Studies Teacher – Brooks High School, Midland, MI   2002 to 2006
*Teach European History, Political Science, and Government to junior and senior **high-school** students. Develop **course curricula**, design **instructional materials**, select **textbooks**, write **student exams**, evaluate **academic performance**, and train **student teachers**.*

Example 3: Keywords integrated into accomplishments:

Sales Representative   2004 to Present
IBM, Menlo Park, CA

- Closed $22.8 million in sales in 2004 and $32.6 million in 2005 through solid performance in **new account development** and **territory expansion**.
- Negotiated and closed a $4.8 million **sales contract** with UCLA, the company's first-ever sale into the academic market.
- Built academic market to 68% of **total revenues** for the region (22% over projections).
- Led **sales presentations** and **executive briefings** to major corporate accounts throughout the western U.S.

Although we have put the keywords in bold in the examples so you could easily identify them, we do not recommend that you bold them when preparing your resume.

Don't be concerned if you don't have experience in the career field you are targeting. You can still benefit by incorporating some of the most important keywords from that field into your resume by using a Career Objective. Here's an example:

CAREER OBJECTIVE: Investigative Research

Desired job emphasis to include the following:

Background Checks / Fraud Investigations / Insurance Claims

Fact-Finding / Investigative Report Writing / Legal Research

This is one of the few instances when we recommend an objective (see Truth #6, below, and a more in-depth discussion in Chapter 3). Note that in the previous example it is clearly communicated that this candidate is looking for a position that will include those specific functions. Nowhere does it state that this individual already possesses those skills and qualifications. Rather, this is simply a strategy to allow you to integrate appropriate keywords into your resume to meet the needs of scanning technology, so that a real person will eventually look at your resume.

Believe it or not, in this age of technology and electronic-based job search, individual human beings still do read resumes! In fact, many have trained themselves to scan the document with their eyes, looking for keywords that will identify candidates who meet the company's search criteria. Whether a conscious process or not, when readers see the *right* keywords, there is instant recognition that this is a well-qualified candidate.

Keywords can be powerful in another way. With a single keyword or keyword phrase, you communicate that you possess a broad range of skills in a particular area of expertise. The keyword phrase "customer relationship management" conveys to the reader that your skills and experience most likely encompass sales, customer service, lead generation, account management, order processing, customer satisfaction, customer retention, and more. A few simple words can truly communicate a wealth of information.

In the resume sample chapters in this book (Chapters 5–16), you'll find the top 20 keywords for each of the professions we've highlighted. Then, if you want additional keyword resources, pick up a copy of *Best Keywords for Resumes, Cover Letters, and Interviews* by Wendy Enelow (at *www.wendyenelow.com*). There are also extensive lists of keywords available online. Our favorites include:

www.careers.ucr.edu/Students/JobSearch/nouns.html

www.enetsc.com/ResumeTips26.htm

www.free-resume-example.com/free-resume-builder.html

www.quintcareers.com/researching_resume_keywords.html

www.westwords.com/GUFFEY/inter.html

Truth #6: There Are No Rules for Resume Writing

The fact that there are no rules for resume writing is both an advantage and a potential obstacle. On the one hand, because you aren't bound by a prescribed set of rules, you have tremendous flexibility in *what* information you include in your resume, *how* you include it, *why* you include it, and *where* you include it. On the other hand, without a prescribed set of rules, you may find yourself floundering, uncertain of how and where to start and what to include.

Have no fear! Although there aren't hard and fast rules, there *are* generally accepted guidelines you should follow to ensure that you're preparing a resume that will meet the needs and answer the questions of prospective employers. These guidelines are outlined here.

1. **Include a work experience section on your resume.** Your resume *must* include your work experience, if for no other reason than to demonstrate to prospective employers that you have, in fact, held a job at some point in your life. It may be that you've been working for 20 years and most, if not all, of your work experience is related to your current career goals. On the other hand, it may be that you haven't worked in 10 years or what you did in the past is not what you want to do now. Either way, it is expected by employers that you will include your work experience, but *how* that experience is included may differ widely from one job seeker to another, depending on the particular situation. Use the sample resumes in this book to find a format for work experience that best suits you. (The only circumstance in which you would not follow this guideline is if you have *never* worked before.)

2. **Include an education section on your resume.** Just as with your work experience, a prospective employer will expect to see an education section on your resume. Sometimes, that section will have a great deal of information about college degrees, professional training, licenses, and certifications. Other times (for example, if the training is not relevant to your current career goal), that section may be very sparse with just a brief mention of high-school graduation, a few courses at a community college, or a technical certification. Whatever your level of education, this section is an important component of a well-prepared resume.

3. **Highlight your technical skills and qualifications.** Whatever type of position you're pursuing, the majority of jobs these days require an individual to be technology-savvy. For some professions, for instance an IT manager, network analyst, or technology sales representative, this is a primary requirement, and you should include your technology skills in detail. For most other professions, basic computer knowledge is expected so be sure to include a brief listing of your specific hands-on skills.

4. **Start your resume with a career summary.** Believe it or not, most resumes these days (and most of the samples you'll see in this book) don't have what you might consider a traditional "Career Objective." With the exception of special cases, such as career changers who are trying to refocus and re-weight their qualifications (as with the example from earlier in this chapter), objectives have been replaced by career summaries. Typically, an objective will state the type of position and/or industry a candidate is seeking. Basically, the objective states what the job seeker *wants from* the employer.

   In the modern resume, chances are you'll see a "Career Summary" at the top, highlighting a job seeker's key skills, qualifications, competencies, and achievements. The summary may be as brief as a few short sentences or a list of bulleted items, or it can be as long as most of the first page. Whatever the length, the purpose of the summary is to communicate the value a job seeker *brings to* a prospective employer; namely, the benefits the employer will gain by hiring that candidate.

5. **Write in the first person.** At the risk of sounding like your grade-school English teacher, first-person pronouns are *I, me, we,* and *mine*. In your resume, you should *never* include these pronouns, yet every sentence you write should be constructed as if it started with the word "I." These examples should help you to understand this concept:

What you should be thinking as you write:	*How these phrases should appear in your resume:*
I supervised a team of 12 clerical employees.	Supervised a team of 12 clerical employees.
I achieved 127% of **my** sales quota for the third quarter of 2007.	Achieved 127% of sales quota for the third quarter of 2007.
I reduced production costs by 20% year-over-year by implementing Lean Manufacturing principles.	Reduced production costs by 20% year-over-year by implementing Lean Manufacturing principles.

6. **Beware of absolutes!** Here's a great example: Have you ever been told that a resume MUST fit on one page? In decades past, that was sage advice, but in today's job search market, that "golden rule" is obsolete. The *no-nonsense* truth is an emphatic "it depends"—in fact, that's the answer to many resume questions. It all depends on your particular situation.

The answer to the question, "How long should your resume be?" is that your resume should be as long as it needs to be in order to tell your story. For recent college graduates or skilled trades people, that may be one page. For a mid-level professional, it's likely to be two pages, and for a senior executive, it may be three or four pages.

Top 10 Critical Mistakes to Avoid

Now that we've outlined the most important strategies and concepts for writing powerful resumes, let's explore the things you should *never* do when writing and distributing your resume.

1. **Never overstate the truth on your resume.** If you do, you'll find that you'll have to defend yourself and your resume in an interview. Even if you get past the interview, your resume may become part of your permanent employee record, if you're hired, and inaccurate information could come back to haunt you.

2. **Never include negative information on your resume.** Your resume is not a job application, nor a life history. Only include information that is positive, and save any negatives for discussion during the interview. Don't give a prospective employer a reason to immediately exclude you from consideration by including information that may reflect negatively on you, such as layoffs, incarceration, or being fired.

3. **Never include salary information on your resume.** It is not the appropriate place. If you're responding to an advertisement that asks for your salary history (what you have earned in the past) and/or your salary requirements (your current salary expectations), and you choose to provide that information, put it in your cover letter instead. However, countless surveys have shown that if a company is interested in you, you will be contacted, regardless of whether or not you have included the requested salary information.

4. **Never present a resume with errors.** Your resume is your personal calling card, and chances are a prospective employer is going to "meet" your resume before actually meeting you in person. If your resume has errors—spelling, punctuation, wording, and so forth—it immediately communicates a negative message to an employer. Who wants to hire someone who produces important documents that contain careless errors? The answer? No one!

5. **Never include reasons for leaving a job on your resume.** This is information that should be shared during an interview, and *only* during an interview. Whether you left your last position on a positive note or a not-so-positive note is information that should only be shared in a one-on-one discussion during your interview. Note that prior to or immediately after your interview, you'll probably be asked to complete an employment application. Most applications will include a section that asks why you left each position. Be sure to complete this information with a brief response (for example, "seeking better career opportunities," "seeking increased management responsibilities," or "company downsizing"). If you were fired, we recommend that you do not include that on the application; rather, include a statement that reads, "To be discussed during interview."

6. **Never submit a resume that is difficult to read.** If you do, no one will read it! Be sure to use a font and type size that are easy to read, and select a format and design that are attractive and leave lots of white space to enhance readability.

7. **Never include a vague or unclear objective on your resume.** We discussed objectives and career summaries earlier in this chapter. If, after reading that information, you choose to include an objective on your resume, make certain it is specific—for example, "Position as a Chemical Engineer"—and not simply a vague statement such as "Seeking a position offering training and advancement opportunities." The latter is useless information and only detracts from the rest of your resume.

8. **Never send a resume with handwritten comments.** Believe it or not, this happens all the time: A job seeker takes a nicely designed resume, jots down a few notes about a change of address, a change in employer, or some other update, and then sends it to a prospective employer. There is *never* any time when this is acceptable. If changes or updates are necessary, edit the resume and print a fresh copy before you send it!

9. **Never send along supporting documentation with your resume.** You may think it will give you a competitive edge, but sending excess documentation such as college transcripts, performance evaluations, awards, letters of recommendation, customer testimonials, and the like is not recommended. Unless you have been specifically asked to supply this information, simply send your resume along with a cover letter. You don't want to overwhelm someone with a stack of papers that they have to go through to learn about you. That becomes a project and, on many occasions, projects get set aside, and you certainly don't want your resume set aside! Save all of that additional information to share during your actual job interviews.

10. **Never send a resume without a cover letter.** Whatever the position you're applying for, always send a cover letter. It's expected and, more importantly, appropriate job-search etiquette. Cover letters are powerful tools that, when well written, can give you a competitive edge within the market. Let your cover letter complement your resume and *sell* you into your next position. (For more information on cover letters, refer to our companion book, *No-Nonsense Guide to Cover-Letter Writing*, due to hit the market in December 2006, or *Cover Letter Magic* by Wendy Enelow and Louise Kursmark, available at *www.wendyenelow.com*).

Chapter 2

▶ ## Simple Truths About

Resume Formatting and Design

Two of the most important decisions you'll make when writing your resume have to do with formatting and design. Begin by asking yourself these key questions:

▶ What resume format am I going to use? Chronological, functional, or hybrid?

▶ What resume design am I going to use? Standard and conservative? Unique and avant-garde? What do I want my resume to look and feel like?

One huge advantage you can give yourself is to have a resume that *doesn't* look the same as everyone else's. You want to write, format, and design a document that stands out from the crowd and gives you a serious competitive edge.

Now that doesn't mean you want to do anything "over the top"; rather, you simply want to make your resume look sharp, professional, and *distinctive*. As you review all the resume samples in this book, you'll see dramatic differences in presentation, from resumes that are very conservative to ones that are quite distinctive. Later in this chapter, we'll help you decide where on that continuum—from conservative to very unique—it's best for your resume to be positioned.

Resume Formats

With very few exceptions, resumes are produced in one of three distinct formats: chronological, functional, or hybrid. Each has its own unique characteristics, advantages, and disadvantages; which is best for you will depend entirely on your current career goals.

Following is a detailed discussion of each of these formats and how they are best used. Read all three sections carefully before deciding which format is right for you.

Chronological Resumes

The chronological resume is the most commonly used resume format and the simplest to create. In fact, chronological resumes are probably what come to mind when you think of a traditional resume. And it may be the way you were taught to write resumes when you were in high school or college.

Chronological resumes are ideal for candidates who want the emphasis to be on the strength of their work experience, particularly if they've had a *linear* career. In other words, this resume format and structure works best if you've followed a logical progression from one job to the next, with no serious detours or lengthy gaps in between. This also assumes that your goal is to obtain a job that is either a lateral move (similar duties and responsibilities) or a vertical move in the same field (move up to the next "rung on the ladder").

When writing a chronological resume, you want to list your jobs in reverse chronological order, starting with your current or most recent position and then working backwards. Your goal is to write comprehensive job descriptions that clearly communicate the responsibilities and achievements of each of your positions. Then, as you move further back in time, you can shorten and summarize your job descriptions, being sure to highlight any notable contributions, projects, responsibilities, and/or awards.

The infrastructure of the chronological resume consists of two distinct sections:

▶ **Work experience**

▶ **Education**

There are, of course, other sections you may include, but these two are the most important for a chronological resume. You'll learn much more about each of these sections and all the other possible resume components in Chapter 3.

It should be noted that recruiters and human resources professionals often prefer chronological resumes because they are systematic, easy to follow, and easy to interpret. However, before you make the decision that a chronological resume is the right resume for *you,* be sure to read the section on hybrid resumes, which have many similar characteristics.

The following page features a chronological resume.

LINDA R. LAWSON

12 Clover Place   Phone: 434-228-3827
Lynchburg, VA 24503   lawsonlindar@aol.com

CAREER OBJECTIVE:

Seeking a position as a **Nurse Manager of a Labor & Delivery Unit** of a large urban hospital with the opportunity to develop and implement best-in-class nursing and patient care programs. Offer extensive clinical nursing and nurse management qualifications in combination with years of experience teaching and training other nursing professionals.

PROFESSIONAL EXPERIENCE:

CENTRA HEALTH, Lynchburg, Virginia   1996 to Present

RN III / Charge Nurse – Labor & Delivery – Virginia Baptist Hospital (1997 to Present)

Charge Nurse for 47-bed Labor & Delivery Unit. In addition to direct patient care responsibilities, coordinate nurse staffing and on-the-job training, precept newly hired nursing staff and rotating nursing students, represent the Unit at professional conferences, and serve as a resource person to all nursing staff.

Member: *Lifecare Committee, Caesarean Section Committee, Council for Excellence, Interdisciplinary Team*

RN II / Charge Nurse – Orthopedics – Lynchburg General Hospital (1996 to 1997)

Charge Nurse on a 45-bed Orthopedic Unit. Coordinated patient care with physicians, nursing staff, allied health care professionals, and other clinical care/clinical support personnel. Provided general nursing care and instruction, maintained patient documentation, coordinated medication administration, and provided specialized nursing care to meet patients' specific orthopedic requirements.

LYNCHBURG COLLEGE, Lynchburg, Virginia   2002 to Present

Clinical Instructor

Plan, schedule, assign and instruct college-level nursing students rotating through the Labor and Delivery Unit at Virginia Baptist Hospital. Maintain student records of performance, provide one-on-one training in specific nursing skills, and facilitate successful completion of 16-week clinical rotations. Qualified ACLS and BLS Instructor.

EDUCATION:

MS in Science and Nursing, 2002
LYNCHBURG COLLEGE, Lynchburg, VA

BS in Nursing, 1993
PIERCE COLLEGE, Richmond, VA

Certified in ACLS, CPR and NRP (Neonatal Resuscitation Program)

VOLUNTEER CONTRIBUTIONS:

- Disaster Relief Nurse, El Salvador and Mexico
- Volunteer Nurse, United Way of Central Virginia
- Volunteer Coach, Youth Soccer Teams

Functional Resumes

The true advantage of the functional resume is that it places a greater emphasis on skills, qualifications, and accomplishments than on your chronological work history. You may want to consider a functional format if:

➤ You're changing careers and want to highlight your transferable skills—those skills that can easily transfer from one industry to another, or from one position to another.

➤ Your most recent job is not the most relevant to the position you are targeting. With the functional format, you can emphasize your skills and accomplishments from a position you held years ago, and not have to bury that information at the end of your resume as you would with a chronological format.

➤ You're a stay-at-home mom who's ready to return to work. You may have been away from the workforce for an extended period of time, but you can use a functional resume format to highlight skills from your previous work experience, your volunteer activities, and your education.

➤ You're an *older* worker (55+ years) and want to de-emphasize your age, while focusing on your skills and qualifications that are most related to your current career objectives.

➤ You've been out of the workforce for a year or more, for reasons such as unemployment, illness, or incarceration, or you've had a *non-linear* career in which you moved around without a clear pattern of advancement or consistent employment in a single industry or job function. This scenario seems to occur more and more often in today's labor market with frequent layoffs, downsizings, and mergers/acquisitions.

The structure of the functional resume consists of three distinct sections:

▸ **Summary:** the longest and most detailed section in the resume; used to highlight your skills, experiences, qualifications, and accomplishments as they relate to your current career goals.

▸ **Work experience:** very brief; generally only a listing with no detailed information.

▸ **Education.**

There are, of course, other sections you may include, but these three are considered the foundation of every functional resume. You'll learn much more about each of these sections and all the other possible resume sections in Chapter 3.

It should be noted that some recruiters and human resources professionals are less receptive toward functional resumes. In the past, these documents gained a reputation as the format of choice for a candidate who was trying to *hide something* (usually age or employment gaps). However, if you load your resume—at the beginning—with great skills and accomplishments that meet the employer's needs, and follow that with a brief but complete work history, the functional resume can be very effective in grabbing attention and getting interviews.

The following page is a good example of a functional resume.

JOHN R. WILLIAMSON
jrwill29209@msn.com

12 Decatur Avenue
Atlanta, GA 39283

Cell: 525-555-9923
Home: 525-666-3928

CONSTRUCTION INDUSTRY PROFESSIONAL

Over 20 years' experience as a **General Contractor / Contractor / Superintendent / Project Manager** of residential (single-family and multi-family), commercial and light industrial properties. Excellent hands-on construction skills and technical qualifications in combination with strong general management, communication, supervisory and problem-solving capabilities. Proficient with Word and Excel. Highlights of qualifications and experience include:

- Managing projects from design through development and construction to completion and final occupancy.
- Interfacing with owners, developers, realtors, investors, subcontractors, field crews, regulatory agency personnel, utility representatives, buyers, tenants and others.
- Reading and interpreting blueprints, architectural drawings, project specifications and other documents.
- Managing a $1.5+ million portfolio of rental properties (multi-family residential units, 1,800 SF office building, small restaurant) and coordinating property rentals, tenant relations, maintenance and repair.
- Hiring, training, scheduling and supervising field crews and subcontractor crews (e.g., masonry, electrical, HVAC, plumbing, landscaping).

PROJECT HIGHLIGHTS

- $3.5 million Smyth Canyon Residential Development (50 single family homes), Atlanta, GA
- $1.2 million, 12,500 SF addition, Martinsburg Baptist Church, Decatur, GA
- $800,000, 10,000 SF Rembrandt Commercial Center, Atlanta, GA
- Two $500,000 Great Dane Mini-Storage Facilities (total of 700+ units), Atlanta, GA
- Fifteen-plus custom and spec homes (valued from $125,000 to $500,000+)
- Seventy-plus production homes (valued from $75,000 to $250,000+)

CAREER HISTORY:

Contractor / Project Manager	Tom Conrad Construction, Atlanta, GA	1996 to Present
Superintendent	Treton Corporation, Atlanta, GA	1995 to 1996
General Contractor	Williams Construction, Inc., Decatur, GA	1987 to 1994
Subcontractor	Roy Cumins Construction, Decatur, GA	1978 to 1987
Carpenter	Various Home Builders, Atlanta, GA	1975 to 1978

EDUCATION:

Graduate – Home Inspection Training Program – 2002
Training Learning Certification, Inc. (subsidiary of HomePro)

Graduate – Estimating and Business Management – 2000
National Association of Home Builders

Liberal Arts Major – Atlanta Community College, Atlanta, GA – 1973 to 1975

Graduate – E.C. Meyerson High School, Atlanta, GA, 1973

Hybrid Resumes

The hybrid resume gives you the advantages of both the chronological and the functional formats, and is our preferred resume format for most job seekers. As the chronological resume does, the hybrid emphasizes your work history, responsibilities, and accomplishments, combining these elements with the powerful skills focus of the functional resume. This offers you the best of both worlds, allowing you to highlight your notable work history along with your core skills, competencies, and qualifications.

Hybrid resumes can be effectively used in a variety of job-search situations. Most notably, they're an excellent format if:

➤ You're looking for a position similar to the one you hold now, or held most recently. Use the summary section to highlight your skills and qualifications that are most applicable to your targeted position.

➤ You're looking to advance within your established career track. Use the summary section to highlight all the skills and qualifications gained throughout your work history that demonstrate success within your chosen career, industry, or profession, and have prepared you to advance to the next level of responsibility.

➤ You're looking to change careers. Use the summary section to highlight all the skills and qualifications that are transferable from your previous position into your new, targeted career field.

The structure of the hybrid resume consists of three distinct sections:

▶ **Summary**: a high-impact summary of your most notable skills and competencies as they relate to your current career objective.

▶ **Work experience**: detailed, with an emphasis on key responsibilities and notable achievements.

▶ **Education.**

There are, of course, other sections you may include, but these three are considered the foundation of every hybrid resume. You'll learn much more about each of these sections and all of the other possible resume sections in Chapter 3.

The hybrid format is currently the resume style preferred by most recruiters and human resources professionals because of its dual emphasis on both employment history and skills. Someone can read the summary section of your resume and quickly understand what you offer to an employer. That information is then immediately followed by a strong presentation of your work experience, which should clearly support the skills and qualifications you've highlighted in your summary section. In essence, you're stating, "This is what I do best" (summary) and "This is the proof I know how to do it" (experience). If you can accomplish this with your hybrid resume, you will definitely have made the recruiter's or human resource professional's job much easier in identifying you as a quality candidate.

The following page features a hybrid resume.

DOLORES DUKE, J.D.

12 Pioneer Way
Cincinnati, Ohio 48937

Phone: 513.222.9382
attorneyduke@hotmail.com

PROFESSIONAL PROFILE:

Legal Experience – Four years of progressively responsible legal experience including two years as a Senior Associate. Outstanding legal research, writing, mediation and client management skills.

Bar Admissions – Licensed to practice law in the State of Ohio. United States District Court application currently pending and anticipated for award in 2007.

Languages – Fluent in English and French. Semi-fluent in Spanish and German. Extensive international experience.

Technology – PC proficient with Word, Excel and PowerPoint. Extensive Internet experience.

LEGAL EXPERIENCE:

Associate   1997 to Present
LAW OFFICES OF JOHN J. SULLIVAN, Cincinnati, OH

Senior Associate with well-established law firm specializing in personal injury litigation, inheritance, trusts, wills and estate planning. Independently manage client caseload, from initial intake through legal research, writing and submission of legal documents; coordination with third parties; and dispute resolution. Draft pleadings and motions, and submit to State and Federal courts. Negotiate with insurance companies to facilitate payment obligations. Prepare wills, trusts and other estate documents. Manage client billings. Concurrently, serve as Office Manager.

- Developed and implemented new client intake and maintenance systems. Created client database and updated all client documentation, records and reports. Resulted in a significant improvement in the firm's marketing ability and in the quality/consistency of client service.

Legal Assistant   1995 to 1997
LAW OFFICES OF JOHN J. SULLIVAN, Cincinnati, OH

Two years of intense experience drafting, preparing and submitting pleadings and appeals to State and Federal courts. Honed legal research skills and expanded use of technology-based legal research tools.

Research Assistant   1994 to 1995
LAW OFFICES OF C. GARY WAINWRIGHT, Dayton, OH

Extensive legal research and writing projects for a criminal defense attorney. Wrote first writ to the Court of Appeals.

EDUCATION:

LOYOLA UNIVERSITY SCHOOL OF LAW
Juris Doctorate / Certificate of International Law / Certificate of Clinic Experience, 1996

NOTRE DAME UNIVERSITY
Bachelors of Business Administration, 1994

PROFESSIONAL ASSOCIATIONS:

American Bar Association
Louisiana Bar Association

World Trade Center
Federalist Society

Resume Designs

Now that you've decided which resume format is right for you, it's time to start thinking about resume design and visual presentation. At this point, you might be asking yourself whether or not design is really a key consideration of the resume process. Shouldn't design concerns be limited to job seekers in artistic and creative career fields? The answer to that question is a resounding no!

Design is important because it gives you competitive distinction. Put yourself in the shoes of someone looking to hire a purchasing manager. You advertised the position on several major online job boards and in several regional newspapers. Within a week, you've collected more than 200 resumes for the position, all of which are sitting in a pile on your desk. Most likely, you're going to flip through the resumes very quickly, selecting those that catch your eye. As a job seeker, to catch someone's eye without being *over the top,* you want your resume to be sharp and clean, but distinctive enough to stand out from the crowd and get you noticed, not passed over.

Now, don't misinterpret what we're saying. We are not recommending that you prepare a resume in an unusual font or print it on purple paper. Such choices definitely qualify as *over-the-top* and are not recommended. Rather, we're recommending that you take the time necessary to prepare a resume that *doesn't* look quite the same as everyone else's.

One of the easiest ways to accomplish this is by using a font or typestyle other than Times New Roman (the most widely used typestyle in business and on resumes). For every 100 resumes we see, more than 80 of them are in Times New Roman and, as such, they all look very similar. Consider some of the following fonts to help distinguish your resume from the rest of the pack. They're still clear and easy to read, common to most word processing software, but subtly different from Times New Roman:

Georgia	Garamond
Tahoma	Verdana
Arial	Schoolbook

Once your resume is written, try placing it in several different fonts to see which one looks best, fills the page best, and most accurately reflects your profession. There are some cautions about using these different fonts if you are planning to send your resume electronically, which will be thoroughly addressed in Chapter 4.

The most commonly used design enhancements are **bold**, *italics,* and underlining. When used appropriately, these elements can effectively highlight section headings, job titles, employer names, college degrees, notable achievements, and other information you want to draw special attention to. However, be forewarned: These enhancements only work to your advantage when they're not *overused.* For example, if you put half of your resume in bold print, you've defeated the purpose, because nothing will stand out.

Comparison of Common Resume Typestyles and Sizes

Size	Roman	Bold	*Italic*
10 pt.	Arial	**Arial**	Arial
	Bookman Old Style	**Bookman Old Style**	*Bookman Old Style*
	Garamond	Garamond	*Garamond*
	Tahoma	**Tahoma**	*Tahoma*
	Times New Roman	**Times New Roman**	*Times New Roman*
	Verdana	**Verdana**	*Verdana*
10.5 pt.	Arial	**Arial**	Arial
	Bookman Old Style	**Bookman Old Style**	*Bookman Old Style*
	Garamond	Garamond	*Garamond*
	Tahoma	**Tahoma**	*Tahoma*
	Times New Roman	**Times New Roman**	*Times New Roman*
	Verdana	**Verdana**	*Verdana*
11 pt.	Arial	**Arial**	Arial
	Bookman Old Style	**Bookman Old Style**	*Bookman Old Style*
	Garamond	**Garamond**	*Garamond*
	Tahoma	**Tahoma**	*Tahoma*
	Times New Roman	**Times New Roman**	*Times New Roman*
	Verdana	**Verdana**	*Verdana*
11.5 pt.	Arial	**Arial**	Arial
	Bookman Old Style	**Bookman Old Style**	*Bookman Old Style*
	Garamond	Garamond	*Garamond*
	Tahoma	**Tahoma**	*Tahoma*
	Times New Roman	**Times New Roman**	*Times New Roman*
	Verdana	**Verdana**	*Verdana*
12 pt.	Arial	**Arial**	Arial
	Bookman Old Style	**Bookman Old Style**	*Bookman Old Style*
	Garamond	Garamond	*Garamond*
	Tahoma	**Tahoma**	*Tahoma*
	Times New Roman	**Times New Roman**	*Times New Roman*
	Verdana	**Verdana**	*Verdana*

Other design enhancements you might consider using to give your resume a distinctive look include lines, boxes, columns, and other graphics. You'll see many of these design enhancements used in the sample resumes at the end of this section and in Chapters 5–16. However, be careful if you decide to utilize graphics. "Cute" does not work on a resume! Rather, your graphics must be appropriate to your profession and your industry, and enhance the overall presentation.

That's twice we've mentioned that the design must *match* your profession. To better understand this concept, consider the resumes of two unique job seekers—an accountant and a fashion designer.

The accountant's resume, as you would suspect, should be on the conservative end of the design spectrum. The font should be very easy to read, such as Tahoma or Arial, only simple lines or boxes should be used to offset any text, and the paper should be white, ivory, or light gray. Anything else would be overstated and inappropriate. The accounting profession is straightforward and conservative, and the resume should represent that.

On the other hand, the fashion designer's resume should look entirely different and demonstrate the designer's artistic capabilities. Fonts can be less conservative, such as **Century Schoolbook** or Garamond, and designer lines, boxes, columns, and/or graphics can be used throughout. Paper should be unique, such as blue, dusty rose, or even pinstripe. The reader should be just as impressed with the visual presentation as with the content of the resume.

The various ways you can design your resume to give yourself a competitive advantage within the market are infinite, limited only by your imagination. Take a look at the three resumes on the following pages to get an idea of what you can do creatively to capture a reader's interest and entice him or her into action—offering you an interview.

Example #1 on page 35 is a fairly conservative, straightforward approach used by an accountant; Example #2 on page 36 is a "middle-of-the-road" approach, which incorporates some design elements, in this case for a marketing executive; Example #3 on page 37 shows how you can use graphic design elements, columns, text boxes, and more to create a really eye-catching design.

Top 10 Critical Formatting and Design Mistakes to Avoid

1. **Don't let your resume fail to present you in the most positive light** because it's prepared in the wrong format. If you haven't taken the time necessary to determine which format is right for you, based on your background and current career objectives, chances are that you may make a poor selection. If this happens, you've immediately short-changed yourself and have not put your best foot forward.

LUCIEN ODELL

6586 Hamlin Beach Road • Kendall, New York 14470 • 585-239-5925 • odell@hotmail.com

DIRECTOR OF FINANCE / COMPTROLLER
Property Management • Real Estate Partnerships • Business Growth & Transition

- General Accounting (A/P, A/R, General Ledger)
- Budgeting, Forecasting, Financial Projections
- Bank Financing Packages
- Employee Payroll & Benefits Administration
- Property Tax Abatements
- Economic Development Funding
- Financial Controls / Cash Flow Management
- Staff Supervision & Development

PROFESSIONAL EXPERIENCE

PALACE REAL ESTATE, LLC, Rochester, NY   1987 – Present
A multi-million dollar firm engaged in the purchase, renovation, leasing, and management of commercial and industrial real estate in the Greater Rochester area.

Comptroller / Director of Finance
Accountable for all aspects of financial management and accounting for 28 distinct operating entities owned and controlled by the firm. Supervise staff of three accountants.

- Serve on senior management team accountable for all real estate management and development issues.
- Participate in real estate closings from both purchase and sale sides of transactions.
- Control cash flow management, including monitoring short-term and long-term investments.
- Prepare financial statements and cash-flow projections for each operating company.
- Develop financing packages for presentation to banks and other investors.
- Petition City of Rochester for reassessments and tax abatements on properties.
- Negotiate, review, and approve work outs and repayment plans to resolve tenant delinquencies.
- Manage approximately 50 bank accounts for the various companies.
- Oversee accounts payable, general ledger, payroll, tenant accounts (including charge-backs), and year-end closing activities.
- Identify and implement improvements to accounting procedures that provide ongoing cost savings.
- Direct payments on loans and mortgages.

Key Accomplishments:
Managed key aspects of transition from one operating entity to 28 separate LLCs during the firm's 500% growth over a 14-year period. Set up accounting and finance systems for each of the new companies and recruited, hired, and trained accounting staff.

Implemented company's first computerized accounting system in 1987 and managed the transition from manual bookkeeping to the new automated system. In 2005, managed the firm's implementation of new Timberline accounting package, including data migration and staff training.

EDUCATION

B.S., Accounting, State University of New York, Geneseo, NY

COMPUTER LITERACY / SPECIAL SKILLS

Microsoft Office (Word, Excel, Outlook), Timberline, Libra

DAVID WASHBURN

SENIOR EXECUTIVE

Marketing & Business Development Strategist

Senior marketing executive experienced in building and nurturing successful organizations, mission-critical initiatives, and pioneering programs. Track record of accelerating growth by revitalizing business models, orchestrating beneficial strategic alliances, and creating acceptance for original concepts, new product categories, and innovative partnerships.

PROFESSIONAL EXPERIENCE

GoNet.com, Santa Clara, CA   **2001–2006**

VICE PRESIDENT OF MARKETING / GENERAL MANAGER OF VERTICAL BUSINESS UNIT

Recruited to provide marketing and business leadership to start-up business unit focusing on industry verticals; delivered immediate impact ($5MM sales in first 6 months) through successful strategic partnerships and vigorous market development. Guided business strategy, product direction and development, brand positioning, product marketing, advertising, online/offline direct marketing, and public relations. Managed $9.4MM budget.

- Chief architect of the business unit's Growth Management Plan to reach ambitious revenue goal.
  - Drove rapid-penetration initiatives, concentrating efforts on high-volume industries (e.g., financial services).
  - Directed technology-enabled marketing programs for customer acquisition, loyalty, and retention.
- Built a talented and versatile staff who were able to capitalize on new learning and rapid shifts in the market.

Semitech, Santa Clara, CA   **1998–2001**

GROUP MANAGER, MARKET DEVELOPMENT / SEMICONDUCTOR

Defined and built the Windows CE market development department. Assessed market opportunities, created strategy, and launched initiatives encompassing competitive positioning, key messages, channel partnership plans, and performance metrics. Directed all related aspects of marketing communications and market research.

- Key contributor to several "skunk works" projects to position Semitech in next wave of chip application—worked with Apple to support Microsoft NT and built PowerPC NT support within Semitech and Microsoft.
- As Business Development Manager covering Asian markets, achieved design wins with multinational firms.

Software Designers, Inc. (SDI), San Francisco, CA   **1991–1998**

OEM / CORPORATE MARKETING / SALES TRAINING MANAGER, 1995-1998
THIRD-PARTY MARKETING MANAGER, 1993-1995 / **MARKETING MANAGER,** 1991-1993

Recruited as first marketing person for SDI, played a pivotal role in establishing crucial business partnerships, evangelizing the product line, and establishing SDI as the market leader in CAD design software. Involved in all facets of marketing, PR, trade shows/seminars/events, and partner development.

- Successfully positioned SDI as partner-of-choice: developed, leveraged, and managed industry-first alliances for global product launches and joint promotions.

EDUCATION

BA, English, University of California, Berkeley, 1981

david_washburn@earthlink.net   *Home 408.742.3776*
25 Vanderbilt Way, Los Gatos, CA 95032   *Mobile 408.814.2094*

OLIVER TRENT

555 Fifth Avenue
Wessley, Minnesota 55777
(218) 879-5555
Email: olivertrent@yahoo.com

EDUCATION

UNIVERSITY OF MINNESOTA, WESSLEY
Bachelor of Arts—1998
Major: **Communications**
Minor: **Marketing**

NOTTINGHAM TRENT UNIVERSITY, NOTTINGHAM, ENGLAND
Study Abroad—Summer 1997

AWARDS

- Mayo Clinic Scholarship
- Arrowhead Award: Outstanding Student in a student organization, Minnesota Board of Regents

COMPUTER SKILLS

- PageMaker
- Microsoft Word
- WordPerfect
- Lotus 1-2-3
- Microsoft Access
- PhotoShop

"Committed on a personal and professional level to set and achieve higher goals."

EXPERIENCE

May 1998–Present
ACCOUNT EXECUTIVE
Mount Rose Publishing

Sell advertising for the University of Minnesota/Wessley telephone directory. Contact potential customers by telephone and arrange appointments. Negotiate contracts, occasionally bartering services. Upsell advertising whenever possible. Service both existing and new accounts; manage all aspects of billing and account administration.

ACCOMPLISHMENTS
- Contact potential clients more than once, often resulting in a sale that otherwise would not be made, through persuasive selling.
- Achieved exceptional customer satisfaction—95% of ratings either "excellent" or "very good" as measured by post-sale surveys.

1995–1998
SALES REPRESENTATIVE
University Statesman, Wessley, MN

Sold ad space for UMW campus newspaper through cold calling and upselling to current advertisers. Negotiated how many times ad ran. Arranged graphic designs by hand. Performed billing. Trained sales people.

ACCOMPLISHMENTS
- Sold 45% more ad space than other reps during tenure.
- Most Valuable Sales Representative, 1997–1998.
- Most sales in a single week, 1997–1998.

1995–Present
(Certified Professional) SKI INSTRUCTOR
Ghost Mountain Ski Resort, Wessley, MN

Teach advanced-level classes. Persuade students to continue their ski lessons. Provide information and sell products at pro shop.

ACCOMPLISHMENTS
- Selected to participate in hiring process for all new ski instructors. Train new hires and evaluate their performance.

2. **Don't make your resume difficult to read because there is not enough white space,** the text extends from margin to margin, and there are no blank lines between sections, paragraphs, or bullets. No one is going to struggle through your resume. Instead, if they have difficulty reading it, they'll discard it and move onto the next candidate.

3. **Don't make your resume difficult to read because the font is too small** or too fancy. Again, no hiring manager is going to spend the time that is necessary to review a document that is difficult to read. Better to let it run onto two pages and improve its readability.

4. **Don't use design enhancements that are inappropriate** for the targeted profession or industry (for example, lines, boxes, columns, and graphics). Refer to the previous discussion about resume design to be sure you're preparing a document that is appropriate for your career track.

5. **Don't overuse bold,** *italics,* and underlining, which clearly defeats the purpose of these design enhancements. They only work if used sparingly throughout the document so that they can have the most impact.

6. **Don't smudge your resume with fingerprints or coffee stains, or let it be otherwise untidy.** This includes folding the resume unevenly or stapling pages together in a haphazard manner. What do you think this communicates about you to a prospective employer? Nothing positive, we can assure you.

7. **Don't let your resume look poorly reproduced.** With the electronic resources available today, there is no excuse for circulating a resume that is not well produced. If you don't have access to your own printer, visit your local library or copy center so you can print original-looking documents. Always use a laser printer to print your resume.

8. **Don't make handwritten changes to your resume.** There is never a situation in which this is acceptable! If you have to make a change to your resume, do it in the electronic computer file and then reprint the document.

9. **Don't produce your resume on odd-sized paper.** Although many job seekers may perceive this as a competitive advantage, believe us when we tell you it's not. If you're looking for a position in the United States, be sure to print your resume on 8 1/2″ x 11″ paper. If you're looking for a position outside the United States, research that country's resume preferences and recommended paper size.

10. **Don't submit a resume with typographical errors.** Again, this is never acceptable. Do you want a prospective employer to think you are careless about your work, or that you'll send out business correspondence, proposals, and reports with errors? We think not! If necessary, enlist the help of a friend with strong English skills to proofread your documents before printing them and sending them out.

Chapter 3

▶ Simple Truths About

Writing Your Resume

As discussed in Chapter 1, resume writing is a unique combination of art and science, allowing you to use a *creative* approach to present *factual* information about your career. A resume is no longer a single sheet of paper that simply lists your work experience. Rather, today's resume is a sales document that should be designed to promote the very best you have to offer to a new employer in such a way as to encourage that employer to want to meet you. Bottom line: that's the only goal of your resume—to grab someone's attention and get you job interviews!

In this chapter, we're going to introduce you to the strategies and techniques that we, as professional resume writers, use to simplify and streamline the resume-writing process while still creating unique, customized, and one-of-a-kind resumes. Follow these instructions and you too will be able to craft a resume that will portray your very *best* you!

Step-by-Step Process

Just as many other business-related activities are, resume writing is a process. In many ways, it's much like writing a technical report, in that the final document (1) has a very specific purpose, (2) must clearly and concisely convey a particular message, and (3) must appropriately communicate that message to its target audience.

With that in mind, it's easy to understand that resume writing is *not* at all similar to creative writing (for example, novels, short stories, and poems), in which you stare at a blank piece of paper waiting for inspiration. Rather, resume writing is closer to following an outline or connecting the dots. With our *no-nonsense* approach, you'll be able to connect *your* dots and write a resume using a very methodical and logical process.

The Key Resume Elements

As discussed in Chapter 2, resume format and design will vary from job seeker to job seeker depending on each individual's career goals and target audience. However, all resumes tend to share certain common elements: contact information, skills summary or career summary, employment experience, and education/training. Beyond that, there are numerous other sections you may or may not include in your own resume, depending on how relevant that particular section is to you, your experience, training, and current career goals. Those sections include: honors and awards, licenses and certifications, professional memberships, community memberships, volunteer experience, personal information, publications, and public speaking.

Contact Information

The very first thing you're going to include on your resume is your contact information—name, mailing address, phone number(s), and e-mail address. Here are three standard formats you can select from:

Format #1: Standard

MARISSA M. MASTERS

1234 Mockingbird Circle
Henrietta, New York 14467
Home (585) 555-2937 / Cell (585) 555-0972 / mmm3@msn.com

Format #2: Modified

LEON J. MARKUS

112 Monroe Parkway
Rochester, NY 14618

(585) 555-9038
ljm22922@aol.com

Format #3: College Student

MARTIN E. YOUNGMAN

youngmanme@msn.com

Permanent Address:
122 Commodore Parkway
Rush, New York 14543
Cell (909) 555-2837

Current Address:
Reagan Hall, Rm. G-22
Pacific Coast University
Inglewood, CA 95847

Although including your contact information should be a snap, sometimes there are unusual circumstances or special considerations. Pay close attention to these recommendations:

➤ If you have a gender-neutral name, consider using one of the following formats so that anyone knows how to address you:

>   Mr. Lynn F. Gundersen
>
>   Ms. Tracey S. Simpson

➤ If you have a first name that's difficult to pronounce, or go by a *call name* other than your first name, consider using one of the following formats so that anyone knows how to address you:

>   Ranguswamy "Roger" Abdellah
>
>   Melissa C. "Chris" Miller

Human resources people and hiring managers are human, and this approach helps put them at ease in contacting and communicating with you and gives them one less reason to screen you out.

➤ If you don't yet have a personal e-mail address, get one! Today's job search market has gone electronic and many prospective employers will want to communicate with you via e-mail, and it is inappropriate to use your current work e-mail account to conduct your job search. Rather, get a free e-mail account with Yahoo!, Hotmail, or any one of a number of other providers that will allow you to access your e-mail account from any computer with an Internet connection. When setting up your account, be sure to use a professional-sounding screen name (for example, AJSmith13@hotmail.com) and *not* something cute (for example, HoneyBear@yahoo.com).

➤ Be very careful if you decide to include your work phone number on your resume, and only do so if you have a direct number. Even in that situation, it's preferable to have people contact you on your private cell phone or at your home number. You're not at your current job to spend your days conducting your job search!

   While we're on the topic, make certain that your outgoing voice mail message, whether on your cell phone or home answering machine, is professional-sounding. For example, "You have reached 555-1234. I'm unable to take your call right now, so please leave a message at the tone," is *much* more acceptable than, "Hey, dude! You know the drill—if you're a telemarketer, drop dead." One person's humor is another person's poor taste.

➤ If you have an online version of your resume (see Chapter 4 for more information on Web-based resumes), be sure to include the Website address (URL) in the contact information section of your resume so people can go online to read more about you and your career.

Career Summary

Your career summary can be the most important part of your resume and therefore may be the section that takes the longest to write. Consider the following critical information as you write your career summary:

▶ For the most part, the career summary has replaced the career objective on modern resumes. Over the years, objectives have proven to be either too specific, and thus limiting to your job search (for example, "Position as an Electrical Engineer with a Fortune 100 company"), or at the other extreme, so general that they're meaningless (for example, "Seeking a professional opportunity with a well-established company"). What's more, objectives tell companies what you want *from* them; not what you can offer *to* them.

▶ The career summary immediately communicates *who* you are and the value (skills, knowledge, and experience) you offer to a company. This makes it much easier for a recruiter to *understand* your resume and make an immediate determination that you're qualified and worth interviewing.

▶ Your career summary needs to be *front-end loaded* with information that will distinguish you from other candidates. This might include your strongest skills and qualifications, notable achievements, professional licenses and credentials, honors and awards, and anything that will set you apart from the crowd. Remember that most prospective employers only review a resume for 10 to 20 seconds on the first screening. Make those few seconds count!

Your career summary can take many forms, with a variety of titles and formats. The examples that follow demonstrate four of the most common approaches many professional resume writers use when they're writing the career summary sections of *chronological* resumes.

Format #1: Headline With Combination Paragraph and Skillsets

PHARMACEUTICAL SALES REPRESENTATIVE

Nine years' experience representing the products of two global pharmaceutical industry leaders. Track record of consistently delivering double-digit revenue and profit growth within highly competitive healthcare markets. Expertise includes:

✓ **Executive Sales Presentations**	✓ **New Product Introduction**
✓ **Price & Contract Negotiations**	✓ **Key Account Management**
✓ **Sales Budgeting & Reporting**	✓ **Territory Management**
✓ **Marketing Communications**	✓ **Sales Training & Mentoring**

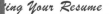

ars' experience procuring optical,
xceptional skills in vendor/supplier
of success in reducing costs,
endor quality. Experienced in ISO
es with Fortune 100 firm.

CAREER HIGHLIGHTS

- Over 12 years' counseling experience with troubled youth and adults.
- Expert in designing individualized patient care and support programs.
- Liaison with schools, clinics, and substance abuse programs.
- Outstanding communication and people skills.
- NYS Office of Mental Health *Qualified Mental Health Specialist.*

Format #4: Technical Presentation

INFORMATION TECHNOLOGY PROFESSIONAL

Ten years' increasingly responsible IT experience with strong systems integration, product development, and tele-communications skills. Outstanding customer rapport, with demonstrated ability to effectively support sales organizations in delivering customer solutions. Excellent training and leadership skills. Technical qualifications include:

Systems	Software	Languages
Windows NT	MS Project	Pascal
Windows 9x - XP	Microsoft Office	BASIC
Windows CE	Lotus 1-2-3	Assembly
DOS	VISIO	INFO/BASIC
LINUX	dBase IV	DCL
UNIX	Harvard Graphics	CPL

These are just a sampling of some of the many formats the summary section of your resume can take when you're writing a *chronological* resume. Carefully review the format, design, style, and wording of the summaries on the sample resumes in later chapters of this book to find one that fits your needs.

If, on the other hand, a *functional* resume format is best for you and your specific career objectives, then use the format that follows as a guide for writing your career summary. Remember: when using a functional format, the career summary section will be the most detailed portion of your resume and, in fact, will probably make up more than two-thirds of the entire document. This is where you're going to put the majority of your skills, experience, and accomplishments.

CAREER PROFILE

OFFICE MANAGEMENT / BUSINESS ADMINISTRATION

Highly motivated, well-organized, and hard-working professional with a record of accomplishment improving business procedures that maximize productivity while reducing costs. Strong communication, problem-solving, team-building, and coordination skills.

SELECTED ACHIEVEMENTS

Accounting: Directed all accounting functions for $12 million project. Tracked all costs, purchases, cash flow, billings, and correspondence with owners on required project paperwork. Finished project on time and under budget.

Data Management: Developed method for allocation of administrative overhead to all construction project costs throughout the year. Taught other division heads how to utilize method. Created accurate picture of true project costs.

Vendor Relations: Avoided potential problems with subcontractors caused by slow payment. Kept in touch with subcontractors, informed them of problems, secured required documentation to process payments, and notified them of anticipated payment dates. Built good vendor relations for future projects.

Training: Demonstrated exceptional ability to significantly raise the level of professionalism in accounting department. Taught employees how to cross-check data on reports to verify accuracy and expedite balancing.

Menu Selection: Career Summary Headings

(Select one of these options as a title for your career summary section.)

Career Summary	Professional Summary	Career Highlights
Career Profile	Qualifications Profile	Technical Profile
Executive Profile	Career Achievements	Skills Summary

Professional Experience

If the career summary is the *sizzle* of your resume, then the professional experience section is the *steak*. You've grabbed the attention of the reader with a powerful summary that promises the skills and experience that make you the perfect candidate for the position you are pursuing; now you need to deliver on that promise by documenting where and how you obtained those skills and experience.

The most important thing to consider when writing each of your job descriptions is that you want to communicate three distinct things about each position: (1) your responsibilities, (2) the skills you acquired, and (3) specific highlights of that job (for example, accomplishments, awards, and special projects). In essence, you want to say, "This is what I was responsible for and this is how well I did it."

The format examples that follow, along with the many resume samples in the later chapters of this book, demonstrate some of the ways you can organize the professional experience section of your resume if you're using a *chronological* resume format.

Format #1: Standard Job Description

Vice President of Manufacturing (2003-Present)
BEACON INDUSTRIES, INC., Cedar Grove, NJ
Leading manufacturer of disposable lighting products

Senior Operating Executive responsible for seven manufacturing/distribution facilities generating $350 million in annual revenues. Charged with transitioning the organization into a low-cost provider, which improved operating efficiencies and strengthened profit margins. Established performance indicators, operating goals, realignment initiatives, productivity improvements, and cost reduction programs that consistently improved production output, product quality, and customer satisfaction.

Achievements:

- Selected to lead corporate team in developing and driving forward cost-reduction initiatives; $21 million saved over three years through capital infusion and process automation.

- Saved $13 million annually by reducing fixed spending 11% and variable overhead spending 18% through effective utilization of operating resources and cost-improvement initiatives.

- Cut workers' compensation costs 40% ($750,000 annually) by implementing effective health and safety plans, employee training, management accountability, and equipment safeguarding.

- Reduced waste generation 31%, saving $1 million in material usage by optimizing manufacturing processes.

- Enhanced customer service satisfaction 3% annually during past year (measured by order fill and on-time delivery percentage) through supply chain management initiatives and flexible manufacturing practices.

Format #2: Skills-Based Job Description

PROCTOR & GAMBLE, San Francisco, CA   1995 to 2006
   Senior Accountant (2002 to 2006)
   Accountant (1998 to 2002)
   Accounting Technician (1995 to 1998)

Promoted through progressively responsible positions in Accounting Department in recognition of consistently strong performance results. Accomplishments included:

Accounting/Auditing
- Managed accounts payable disbursements totaling more than $1.7 million annually, accounts receivable processing, and over $1 million in capital assets.
- Verified and maintained GL system. Developed and implemented accounting policies/procedures.
- Instituted internal control procedures including expense account reconciliations for premium collections, reducing write-offs by $75,000 annually.

Financial Analysis & Reporting
- Coordinated and prepared NAIC financial statements in accordance with SAP and premium tax return filings for more than $1.8 million in 48 states.
- Prepared financial statements in accordance with GAAP for the Board of Directors and shareholders, and managed semiannual SEC filings for six portfolios totaling $1+ billion in net assets.
- Coordinated audits with internal/external audits and regulatory agencies. Compiled financial data for auditors. Prepared internal audit reports.

Cash Management/Budgeting
- Performed cash-management functions to meet investment objectives and prepared timely corporate cash-flow forecasts.
- Developed and implemented banking policies for accounting, premiums, commissions, and benefits.
- Coordinated $35 million budget preparation process for all departments within the business unit.

Format #3: Project-Focused Job Description

INTERNATIONAL SPIRITS COMPANY
Global producer/distributor of fine wines and spirits
GLOBAL BRAND INNOVATION GROUP—HONG KONG, CHINA
Product Innovation Senior Technologist (10/03 to 5/06)

Worked closely with Marketing and Consumer Planning on concept and proposition development. Networked and managed ingredient suppliers worldwide in product development. Served as a direct liaison with global suppliers to ensure efficient commercialization according to product specifications.

SELECTED PROJECTS & HIGHLIGHTS

- Established two liquid satellite labs (Hong Kong, United States), from start-up to user-friendly facilities that fully supported concept development and met global standards for equipment, processes, and work tools.

- Championed the development and execution of a flavored malt beverage line that became No. 2 in the category, as well as another product which received the prestigious Gold Medal in the San Francisco Spirits competition.

- Honored by ISC North America for the "Best Innovation Project" and awarded the Brand Group's Double Eagle award for "Best Product Launch" of a successful product line.

- Managed the product development of innovation projects for carbonated and non-carbonated products, from concept to commercialization in several key markets (Australia, Thailand, Taiwan, Japan, and Korea).

Format #4: Achievement-Focused Job Description

CHILI'S   2000 to Present

General Manager
- Excelling in company's training program, immediately took on general manager role in floundering Parsippany store. Turned around performance, assembling and mobilizing strong management team that stabilized operation while **growing controllable profits by 33%.**

- **Slashed annual turnover from 200% to 80%** by providing effective, hands-on leadership that fostered loyalty, while empowering and motivating staff.

- Revamped store, upgrading facility to create a better customer experience, and **internally financed $2.1 million** in renovations through effective budget management and cost controls.

- Orchestrated successful opening of new Farmingdale store, **achieving $3.5 million in sales during first year.**

- **Won award for achieving the highest average customer satisfaction ratings** in "mystery-shopper" program within 50-unit regional franchise group that ranked first in the nation.

- Took over management of Bridgeton location, a training store with $4.5 million in sales but disappointing profitability. Implemented controls that brought down costs and **restored double-digit profitability** in one year.

If the *right* format for you is a *functional* resume, writing your professional experience section is easy, because it's usually just a short listing of your job titles, employers, and dates. With a functional resume format, the majority of your experience will have already been presented in your career summary section, so there's no need to repeat it under professional experience.

Here's a perfect example of the professional experience section of a functional resume:

PROFESSIONAL EXPERIENCE

RN – Emergency Room, Elks Health System, Elm, IA (2004-Present)
RN – Intensive Care, Shore Memorial Hospital, Elm, IA (2001-2004)
Staff RN – Trauma Center, Case Hospital, Stockton, IA (1997-2001)
LPN, Turner Nursing Home, Fresco, IA (1992-1997)

Menu Selection: Professional Experience Headings

(Select one of these as a title for the experience section of your resume.)

Professional Experience	Employment Experience	Work History
Career Highlights	Experience Summary	Job History
Career Progression	Executive Experience	Experience

You'll note that two of the previous professional experience examples included brief descriptions of the companies; the other two did not. Here's the rule of thumb you can use: If the company is well-known, it is not necessary to include descriptive information. On the other hand, if you're concerned that the company is not recognizable, then we do recommend a brief description.

Education

The education section generally comes after the professional experience section on a resume. However, there are several large groups of job seekers for whom the exact opposite is most appropriate. If you're a recent college graduate, a career changer who has just earned a new degree, an educator, or anyone else for whom your educational qualifications are more important to your search than your employment background, then you'll want to position your education section immediately after your summary, and then follow up with your employment experience.

In the education section, include your college degrees, professional licenses, and certifications, as well as continuing education. If you attended college, but have not yet earned a degree, be sure to include that information. If you're a skilled-trades person or blue-collar worker, you may want to call this section "Training & Education" and include both your classroom and hands-on training related to your apprenticeship.

Examples that demonstrate several approaches to organizing information in this section follow, with many more presented in the sample resumes in later chapters of this book.

Format #1: Standard

EDUCATION:

B.S., Business Administration, Summa Cum Laude, 2006
UNIVERSITY OF VIRGINIA, Charlottesville, VA

A.A, General Studies, Academic Honors, 2004
CENTRAL VIRGINIA COLLEGE, Lynchburg, VA

Format #2: Executive

EXECUTIVE EDUCATION

MBA Degree	NORTHWESTERN UNIVERSITY (2005)
Leadership Training	WHARTON SCHOOL OF BUSINESS (2002)
BBA Degree	CHICAGO UNIVERSITY (1994)

Format #3: Certifications/Licensure

PROFESSIONAL CERTIFICATIONS and LICENSES:

Licensed Master Plumber, City of Heatherville
Certified Stick Welder, State of Ohio
Certified TIG Welder, State of Ohio
IX Brazer, ASME
6010 Installer, ASME

Format #4: Combination

EDUCATION AND TRAINING:

B.S., Marketing, Texas A&M University, 2004
A.S., Information Technology, Spring Creek College, 2001

Highlights of Continuing Professional Education:

Sales Leadership, Tom Peters & Associates, 2003
Sales Presentations, Dale Carnegie, 2002
Product Positioning, IBM, 2002
Strategic Negotiations, IBM, 2001

Menu Selection: Education Headings

(Select one of these as a title for the Education section of your resume.)

Education	Training & Development	Degrees
Executive Education	Licenses & Certifications	Credentials
Technical Training	Continuing Education	

The Extras

As mentioned earlier in this chapter, in addition to the four most important sections to include on your resume—contact information, career summary, professional experience, and education—there are several other sections you may include, depending on how relevant they are to you and your current career goals. Determine whether or not you need to include these sections on your resume and then choose from among the sample formats to most effectively present your information.

HONORS and AWARDS:

2006 Sales Representative of the Year, Dow Chemical
2005 Sales Representative of the Midwest, Dow Chemical
2004 Sales Trainee of the Year, Dow Chemical
2002 Business Student of the Year, Purdue University

LICENSES and CERTIFICATIONS

Power Plant Operator License   Boiler Mechanic License
Commercial Electrician License   Radio Technician License
HAM Radio Operator License   General Contractor License

PROFESSIONAL MEMBERSHIPS:

BOARD MEMBER	AMERICAN MANUFACTURING ASSOCIATION
BOARD MEMBER	GENERAL MOTORS EXECUTIVE COMMITTEE
BOARD MEMBER	CITIBANK OUTREACH COMMITTEE
MEMBER	AMERICAN TEXTILES ASSOCIATION

COMMUNITY MEMBERSHIPS:

Habitat for Humanity
United Way
Elmbrook School Parent-Teacher Association
Chattanooga County Parent-Teacher Association

VOLUNTEER EXPERIENCE

Volunteer Fundraiser, American Cancer Society, 2002 to Present
Corporate Giving Committee, United Way of Maryland, 2000 to 2002
Community Education Committee, BelAir Alliance, 1999 to 2002
Volunteer Fundraiser, BelAir Humane Society, 1998 to 2004

PERSONAL INFORMATION:

Born August 19, 1974 in Accra, Ghana. U.S. Citizen since 1998.
Extensive travel throughout Africa, Europe, and South America.
Conversational in French, Spanish, and several African languages.

PUBLICATIONS:

Co-Author	*Research Methods in Biopsychology* American Psychiatric Association 23(1), 2006
Lead Author	*Emerging Research Methodologies* American Psychiatric Association 14(3), 2004
Co-Author	*Psychotropic Drug Administration* American Pharmaceutical Association 22(4), 2003

PUBLIC SPEAKING

Presenter, Integrated Networking Technologies, IBM Advisory Council, Chicago, IL, 2006

Presenter, Next-Generation Networking Protocols, American Institute of Electrical Engineers, Detroit, MI, 2005

Panel Member, American Computing Society Annual Conference, San Diego, CA, 2003

FOREIGN LANGUAGES:

> Fluent in Mandarin Chinese and Cantonese Chinese.
> Conversational in Japanese.

Age *Does* Matter

If you're under the age of 50, you may want to skip this section. The following information is only pertinent to job seekers who are 50-plus years of age and *may* be faced with some form of age discrimination in their job search (or at least perceive that they are encountering age discrimination). It would be naïve to say that ageism doesn't exist, but trends are changing and the labor outlook may be brighter than you think.

Let's begin with a discussion about how the employment market has changed over the past decade. In generations past, people tended to stay with one or two employers throughout their entire careers. Many of us have fathers or grandfathers who put in their 30 years at the local mill or assembly plant and then retired. Even now, there are still some workers out there who went right from high school or college to their first job and are still working for that same company today.

The decade of the 1990s changed that for the majority of the workforce. With the advent of downsizing, rightsizing, corporate mergers, and massive layoffs, today's workers are on the move—from one job to another, from one career track to another, from one industry to another. The old model of employment longevity is long gone. Today, change and volatility in the employment market are the status quo. Likewise, workers are more mobile themselves. Recognizing that employers are more likely to lay people off during a business down-turn, they are much more willing to shop their skills and talents, test the market to see what they're worth, and *jump ship* when a better offer comes along.

As a result, companies have changed how they hire, realizing that they are not hiring for life. Rather, they are hiring employees they need *today* with the knowledge and understanding that in years to come, they may no longer need them. In this environment, older employees actually offer certain advantages. They often bring substantial experience and a unique expertise that can solve problems, reduce expenses, generate revenue, and even start up new companies. To the astute hiring manager, an older worker represents someone who's not necessarily looking for a long-term position but, rather, may be happy to work for a company for three to five years as a bridge to retirement.

In the context of writing your resume, it's appropriate to consider some of the traditional stereotypes of the older worker if only to better understand and dispel them. A few of the common ones include:

▶ Older workers are near the top of their pay scale and would be dissatisfied in lower-paying positions.

▶ Workers older than 50 have outdated skills compared to more recent graduates.

▶ Older workers aren't motivated to acquire new skills or knowledge.

▶ Older workers are unfamiliar or uncomfortable with technology, and therefore unable to function effectively in the electronic age.

▶ Workers older than 50 are inflexible and set in their ways.

By creating a resume that demonstrates your flexibility, eagerness to learn new skills and accept new challenges, and familiarity with technology as it relates to your particular career path, you can overcome most of these stereotypes and present yourself as a vibrant, engaged, and valuable candidate.

We strongly recommend that you focus on your most recent experiences and be judicious in how you display dates on your resume. Concentrate on your last 10–15 years of employment experience and summarize highlights from your earlier positions without necessarily including the exact dates. And, if you are older than 50 and earned your college degree in your early 20s, we suggest that you do *not* include your date of graduation. Not all employers discriminate, but why give an employer a reason to possibly exclude you from consideration? Of course, if you completed your degree within the past 10 years, then include the date and let potential employers draw their own conclusions.

It's not unethical or dishonest to prepare your resume in a way that best portrays your true capabilities. It is perfectly acceptable to leave out information that's a tip-off to your age. Remember, a resume is not an autobiography. Rather, it's a document designed to *sell* you into your next position. Use your resume wisely to get interviews. Then, once you're in the door, you will have the opportunity to sell prospective employers on just how dynamic, knowledgeable, and adaptable you can be in contributing to their success.

Streamlining Your Writing Process

Just as with any other activity, resume writing gets easier and faster the more often you do it. We recognize that it's not something that most job seekers do on a regular basis, so here are a few *tricks of the trade* that should make writing your resume easier and faster.

1. **Write when you're fresh.** Professional resume writers know they have a certain time each day when they're freshest and do their best work. For one of us, it's first thing in the morning. For the other, it's late at night. Determine when your *prime time* is and be sure to write your resume then.

2. **Write alone.** You'll find it will be much easier to work on your resume if you do it when it's quiet and you have no distractions. Bottom line: you're going to need to think—and think hard—about what information to include, how to include it, and where to include it. The less noise around you, the better. Ignore the phone, ignore your e-mail, and focus 100 percent of your energies on writing.

3. **Write the *easier stuff* first.** There are certain sections in your resume—contact information, education, professional memberships, community memberships, publications, and public speaking, for example—that are generally straightforward and factual. These sections usually include simple listings of information. As such, it should be easy to complete these sections of your resume first and use them as the foundation on which to build.

4. **Write piece by piece.** Writing your job descriptions can seem to be a daunting task, but it doesn't have to be. The easiest thing to do is first type in your job titles, employers' names, and dates of employment for each position. Next, fill in the essential duties and responsibilities of each job, along with any factual information about the company (for example, revenues, locations, line of business). Then, go back and write your key accomplishments, project highlights, and contributions for each position. Now all that's left to do is to consolidate the information that you've *already* written and integrate appropriate action verbs and keywords to *boost* the resume.

5. **Write it *while* you're writing.** The easiest way to write your career summary is to begin writing it as you're writing the rest of your resume. Whether you're writing job descriptions, listing educational credentials, or completing any of the *extra* resume sections, as you encounter thoughts, ideas, words, and concepts that will be important to include in your career summary, write them into that section. Then, once you're finished writing the rest of the resume, you'll see that your career summary is already half written! A few more minutes of work, and then you're all finished and ready to launch your search.

Refer to Appendix A for resume worksheets you can use to collect all the information you will need as the foundation to write your resume. Feel free to make copies if you need more forms than we've provided.

Chapter 4

▶ Simple Truths About

Electronic Resumes

By now, you've probably spent a great deal of time writing and designing your resume. In Chapter 1, you more clearly *defined who you are* professionally by identifying the core skills and competencies you offer to a new employer. In Chapter 2, you explored different strategies, designs, and formats to find just the *right* approach to *present your unique skills* in a compelling way. And, finally, in Chapter 3, you wrote your resume, step-by-step, carefully *organizing the details* of your career summary, professional experience, education, and other sections into a document that represents you well and *sells* you to a prospective employer.

What you have created through this process is a "conventional" printed resume, which is what you most likely imagine when you think about resumes. Even though it probably exists as an electronic, word-processed document, this is the version you will mail or fax to prospective employers and recruiters, take with you to job interviews, and use as an introductory and networking tool. In fact, we like to call it the *human-eye* version because the style, overall format, presentation, and paper choice are all designed to appeal to readers as they hold the document in their hands, making that all-important, attention-grabbing, first impression.

Although your printed resume is essential, there are other versions of your resume that you'll most likely need during the course of your job search. In today's job market, employers and recruiters are relying more and more on e-mail and other online methods of transmitting and tracking information about you, the job candidate. It's vital for the soon-to-be successful job seeker (*you*) to have the proper electronic versions of your resume—in addition to that attention-grabbing printed resume—to cover all your bases.

Electronic Resumes

The importance of the electronic resume is really twofold. First, using the latest technology allows you to get your job-search documents into the hands of the appropriate hiring authority quickly and efficiently. There's no need to wait for "snail mail" when you can immediately transmit your resume electronically and have it in the hiring authority's hands within minutes. What's more, that individual can then share your resume with others throughout the organization. For example, a human resources manager can quickly and effortlessly forward your resume to the manager who will ultimately be making the hiring decision. E-resumes have streamlined the process of resume distribution and provided all of us with the ability to job search in *real time*.

Beyond the *convenience factor* that e-resumes allow, employers often use the electronic submission process as a subtle way of testing your comfort level with technology. As an executive recruiter once told us, "If a candidate isn't savvy enough to quickly e-mail me his resume [without any glitches], then he's probably not someone we really want to talk to." That doesn't mean you have to be a technological whiz, but it does mean you need to have a reasonable familiarity with the basics of electronic resume design and distribution. Therefore, it's key to understand how to create the four different electronic versions of your resume, integrate them into your job search, and efficiently transmit them to potential employers or recruiters. These four versions are:

▶ **E-mail attachments**
▶ **ASCII text files**
▶ **Scannable resumes**
▶ **Web resumes**

E-mail Attachments

Chances are, whatever your profession or your industry, you'll be e-mailing resumes to prospective employers and recruiters on a routine basis. In fact, you'll find that e-mailing is probably your most frequently used method of resume distribution.

The e-mail attachment you send should be the word-processed, print version of your resume. We strongly recommend that you prepare your resume in Microsoft Word because it is the most commonly used word-processing software, and you can be relatively certain your resume will download at the other end in the same format and presentation style as the original document you prepared. If you do *not* use Word as your word-processing software, chances are your resume will not transmit well and will lose much of its presentation value. Even worse, it can arrive in an unreadable format. As such, we suggest you either purchase a copy of Microsoft Word, use a friend's computer with an up-to-date version of Word loaded on it, or consider sending your resume in a

Rich Text Format, Portable Document Format (PDF), or as an ASCII text file. (More information follows about each one of these options.)

To prepare your resume for e-mail transmission, there are several precautions you'll want to take to ensure that it arrives in an attractive and readable format. In light of the wide variety of software and operating systems currently in use (including multiple versions of Word), your attractively formatted resume document may appear quite differently when viewed and printed by the intended recipient. This potential problem is compounded by the vast array of printers on the market, each with its own printer driver. For example, a tightly formatted two-page resume can wind up on four pages because of different default margins on the printer at the other end, or because of the use of an unusual type font. It's difficult to totally eliminate these potential problems, but here are some guidelines for minimizing such complications:

▸ Use .75-inch margins on all four sides of the page.

▸ Choose a common font. Times New Roman and **Arial** are virtually universal to most versions of Microsoft Word currently in use. That doesn't mean you can't use other typestyles for your *printed* resume, but for the best chance of compatibility with those reading your e-mailed resume, use the recommended fonts.

▸ If you use word-processing software other than Microsoft Word, consider saving the file in Rich Text Format (.rtf). In most word-processing applications, this is a choice from the "Save As" menu, and the .rtf suffix generally appears at the end of the file name when the document is saved. This is a more universally accepted file format by most software and overcomes many compatibility issues.

▸ Consider sending your resume attachment as a Portable Document Format (.pdf) if your resume has unique design elements (potentially corruptible by software compatibility issues) and if design skills are key to the position(s) you are pursuing. PDFs are viewed as graphics and are not editable. For this reason, they cannot generally be downloaded and stored in searchable databases. However, a PDF resume *can* be advantageous if your resume has unique design characteristics, because this format allows you to preserve your attractively designed resume the way you intended it to appear.

▸ Send the e-mail attachment to yourself and to several friends who are aware of your job search. This way, you have the opportunity to see how your resume looks when downloaded and opened, and enables you to make any adjustments and correct any problems prior to sending your resume to an employer or recruiter.

Once your resume has been prepared for electronic transmission, you can send it just as you would any other attachment. Simply open your e-mail program, create a message, attach your resume, and send the e-mail message with the document attached. It's that easy and only takes a minute. You do, however, want to pay special attention to what you include in the subject line and the body of the e-mail message.

A quick rule of thumb for the subject line is to include the title of the position for which you are applying (and the job/vacancy announcement number, if applicable). In addition, we recommend that you include the words "Resume of" followed by your name. This format immediately alerts the recipient that you're responding to a specific job announcement and have forwarded your resume. Here's an example:

VP of Manufacturing (#45893) – Resume of Jonathan Johnson

If you're not responding to a specific job announcement and are simply e-mailing your resume to a prospective employer or recruiter in anticipation that they may have an opening for a candidate with your qualifications, use a *headline* similar to what you may have used in the summary section of your resume. This clearly identifies *who* you are and the type of position you are seeking. For example:

Vice President of Sales / Director of Business Development

When writing the body of your e-mail message, you can do one of two things:

1. You can include a text version of your cover letter as your e-mail message, referencing that your resume is attached as a Word file.

2. You can include a brief statement in the body of your e-mail that states, "Please see the attached resume and cover letter in response to your recent job announcement for a *(position title)*."

Either option is perfectly acceptable. You make the decision based on the length and visual presentation of your cover letter. If your letter is short and succinct, we recommend you include it in the actual e-mail message. If your letter is a bit longer, has more information, and/or has certain design characteristics, you'll want to include it as an attachment.

An example of a Word resume ready for electronic submission is shown on page 64.

ASCII Text Files

Some recruiters and employers may insist on receiving an ASCII text version of your resume. There are certain advantages for the recipient, most notably the fact that Internet viruses and worms can't hide in an ASCII text file. As a matter of policy, some businesses simply do not accept any e-mails with attachments. If this is the case, pasting your ASCII text resume into an e-mail message is the only way to send it electronically to those organizations.

ASCII text files are also useful when you are required to paste your resume into an online job application. By having the text version of your resume open on your computer at the same time you are viewing the online job application, you can click back and forth between the two documents to copy and paste sections of your resume into the application. This is a huge time-saver and makes an ASCII text version a valuable tool for *every* job seeker.

You may also rest assured that an ASCII text file will, by its very nature, be a scannable resume, and can serve *double duty* in that regard. We'll further explore the value of scannable resumes later in this chapter, but be certain that if someone asks for a scannable version of your resume *and* they do not open attachments, an ASCII text version of your resume is the document to submit.

To ensure that you create an ASCII text resume that is readable and correctly formatted, follow these simple steps (for Microsoft Word and similar word-processing programs):

▶ With your resume document open on the screen, choose "Save As" from the File menu.

▶ Select "text only," "ASCII," or "plain text" as your choice in the "Save As" option box. You may want to give the file a slightly different name to differentiate it from your word-processed version. When you click "Save," you will get a message warning you about losing content or formatting by saving the file in ASCII format. Ignore the message and click on "Yes" or "OK" (whichever your computer displays).

▶ Close the file and then reopen it. You will see that your resume has been stripped of all formatting and appears as left-justified text in the Courier font.

▶ Now set both the left and right side margins at two inches. This will center the text on the screen and optimize its readability when the file is reopened at some later time. This will also allow you to recognize any unusual line breaks that lead to awkward changes in format, which you can easily fix.

▶ Carefully proofread the resume for any "glitches" that may have occurred during the file conversion. You may wish to print the resume and proofread from a "hard copy"—many people find it easier to spot errors on the printed page. You may see that many characters, such as quotation marks, dashes, or apostrophes, now appear as question marks or some other character. Simply replace these by typing in the appropriate character from your keyboard.

▶ Make any other adjustments you feel improve the readability of your text resume (for example, adding line returns and creating horizontal dividers to separate sections).

▶ Be sure to save the corrected version of your resume document.

> ▶ Proofread again, preferably after some time has passed, to ensure that you haven't missed anything.

An example of an ASCII text resume is shown on pages 65–66.

Scannable Resumes

You could say that the scannable resume is the ultimate *no-nonsense* resume. All the fancy fonts, use of **bold** and *italics,* and any other graphics such as borders, underlining, or unique symbols, are stripped away to create a plain-Jane version of your resume. The goal is to make your resume able to be easily read and interpreted by scanning software that many employers and recruiters use to upload and file your resume in a database for later retrieval. To maximize the likelihood that this will happen smoothly, follow these guidelines to prepare a scannable version of your resume:

> ▶ Choose an easy-to-read font such as Times New Roman or **Arial**.

> ▶ Avoid using **bold,** *italic,* or <u>underlined</u> type.

> ▶ Stick to type sizes of 11 pt. or larger (12 pt. is probably optimal).

> ▶ Make sure that only your name appears on the top line of the first page, followed by your contact information.

> ▶ At the top of each subsequent page, type your name on the first line, your telephone number on the second line, and your e-mail address on the third line.

> ▶ All of the text should be left-justified with a "ragged-right" margin.

> ▶ Be careful about using abbreviations. Widely used acronyms, such as B.A. for Bachelor of Arts or OSHA (Occupational Safety & Health Administration), are fine to use, but if you have any doubts about the proper interpretation, you should spell it out in full.

> ▶ Eliminate borders or graphics, including horizontal or vertical lines, tables, and columns.

> ▶ Use common keyboard symbols (such as: *, -, >) in places where you would use a bullet in your printed resume.

> ▶ Instead of using characters such as % or &, spell out the words ("percent" or "and").

> ▶ If slashes (/) are used, make sure you leave a space before and after each slash to ensure the scanner won't see it as a letter and misinterpret the word or phrase.

> ▶ Use a laser printer and print your document on smooth, white paper, rather than paper with any kind of texture, color, or pattern. White photocopy paper that you can purchase at any office supply store is fine for this purpose.

▸ Always use a paper clip; never staple the pages together.

▸ Mail the resume flat in a 9 x 12 envelope, so it won't be folded.

Scannable resumes are becoming less and less necessary as technology continues to evolve, but they are still requested by some recruiters or employers, and should be an available tool in your job search toolbox. As previously mentioned, ASCII text resumes can also double as scannable resumes, but if you'd prefer to see your document in a typestyle other than Courier you may wish to create a separate scannable document using Times, **Arial**, or one of the other most common fonts available.

An example of a scannable resume is shown on pages 67–68.

Web Resumes

One of the newest innovations in electronic resumes is the Web resume. As the popularity of the Internet continues to grow, more and more job candidates are establishing their own Websites where employers can view their resumes online. To create a Web resume, you will want to have your own URL (Website address), which you can set up on your own or with professional assistance.

Web resumes vary tremendously in their presentation. Some candidates merely have an electronic representation of their printed resume, which the employer can access to download and print; others have a fully designed Website that functions as an online professional portfolio. You can include a link to your Web resume in any correspondence you send out electronically, allowing a prospective employer or recruiter to view your resume with just one click.

Technology professionals, and others who are techno-savvy, can use their online portfolio to highlight a broad range of skills and achievements that are not practical to include on a conventional resume because of page-length restrictions. Consider including a complete listing of your technology skills and competencies, a complete listing of your technical training and certifications, and/or a complete listing of all the technology projects on which you've worked. E-resumes and e-portfolios are also golden opportunities for these professionals to actually demonstrate their technical prowess by designing the Website themselves.

The electronic portfolio concept can also be a compelling option for non-technical job seekers. Perhaps you're a marketing executive who wants to include successful marketing plans or advertising storyboards as pages on your Website. Or, maybe you're a professional designer and want to include several pages of your designs as evidence that you are creative, innovative, and well-qualified. It's even possible to have a video clip introducing yourself and directing the viewer to other pages on the site. The opportunities you have to develop a powerful Web presentation are limited only by your imagination.

If you're adequately techno-savvy, creating an online portfolio can be both advantageous to your job search as well as great fun. For most of the rest of us, whose core skills do not include technology, consider hiring a professional to help you design your Website. You'll be surprised at how affordable this can be. To get a sense of what e-resumes and e-portfolios are all about, we suggest visiting these Websites:

www.blueskyportfolios.com

www.brandego.com

www.portfoliovault.com

Transmitting an e-mail message that references your Web-based resume is easy to do. Instead of attaching a Microsoft Word document to an e-mail message, you simply include the link that will take the reader to the Website where your resume may be viewed, enlarged, printed, and evaluated by prospective employers and recruiters. What's more, it's easy to make changes to your Web-based resume if you need to update it.

Electronic Resumes: Design Considerations

	Word-Processed Resumes	ASCII Text Resumes	Scannable Resumes	Web Resumes
Typestyle/ Font	Crisp, clean, distinctive (see recommendations in Chapter 2).	Courier.	Stick to the basics: Times New Roman, Arial.	Choose fonts that look attractive on screen and reproduce well when printed.
Typestyle Effects	Bold, italics, and underlining are all acceptable and recommended.	Capitalization is the only enhancement available.	Capitalization is the only enhancement that will scan reliably.	A full range of design elements are available, including color.
Type Size	11 pt. or 12 pt. for body of the document. Use larger sizes (14, 16, 18) for name and headings.	12 pt.	11 pt. or 12 pt. preferred.	11 pt. or 12 pt. for body of the document. Use larger sizes (14, 16, 18) for name and headings.
WhiteSpace	Use to optimize readability.	Separate sections to enhance readability.	Use liberally to maximize scannability.	Use to optimize readability.

Electronic Resumes: Production Considerations

	Word-Processed Resumes	ASCII Text Resumes	Scannable Resumes	Web Resumes
Text Format	Use centering, indents, etc. to create an appealing presentation.	Everything strictly flush-left.	Everything strictly flush-left.	Capitalize on the flexibility the Web offers to create an appealing presentation.
Preferred Length	Generally, one or two pages; three pages is acceptable for senior-level candidates.	Length doesn't matter. Converting the resume will undoubtedly make it longer than the printed version.	Length doesn't matter. Converting the resume will undoubtedly make it longer than the printed version.	Length is not critical, but be sure the site is well organized so that viewers can easily find what you want them to see.
Preferred Paper Color	White, ivory, or light gray are most preferred.	Not applicable	Bright white or cream (natural). No patterns or shading that might interfere with scanning.	Paper is a non-issue; choose background colors that allow for readability and reproduce well if printed.

Microsoft Word Resume

SYLVIE ST. PIERRE

212-949-7764 • sylvie@hotmail.com
259 West 76th Street, #4B • New York, NY 10024

HOSPITALITY INDUSTRY MANAGER

Hotel • Food & Beverage • Entertainment • Tourism

Advanced rapidly to GM role with respected hotel management company and delivered measurable improvements in multiple areas of performance: revenue, guest satisfaction, service, and safety. Built teams of talented professionals and motivated entire staff to work together to achieve stretch goals. Planned, managed, and executed large, complex functions to maximize revenue while maintaining exceptional customer satisfaction. Captured new business, restored corporate client relationships, and delivered creative, high-quality guest experiences.

EXPERTISE

- **Yield Management**
- **Quality Improvement**
- **Service Delivery**
- **Sales Relationships**
- **Event Management**
- **Creative Marketing**
- **HR Management**

EXPERIENCE AND ACHIEVEMENTS

MACOMBER & REYNOLDS   2001–Present

General Manager: Riverpark Luxor, Queens, NY, 2003–Present

156 guest rooms, full-service restaurant, meeting space

Reversed negative profit performance and stemmed decline of aging hotel in a competitive business/tourism market. Managed P&L and annual business plan to achieve performance objectives. Led a team of 9 operational supervisors and 3 sales managers.

- Quickly filled open managerial positions, replaced underperformers, and built a strong team.
- Delivered 11% RevPar increase in one year.
- Focused on quality improvement as a key driver of customer satisfaction. Took safety score from "unacceptable" to "excellent" and brought METS evaluations up to date and passed all components.
- Improved image and performance for key business and tourism events:
  - *Corporate event, part of the #1 piece of business annually in Queens:* Added activities, services, and menu variety. Grew revenue 50% and earned promise to return in 2005.
  - *New York Marathon:* Selected as one of host hotels for this major city-wide event. Emphasized F&B to drive guest satisfaction. Earned positive feedback from Convention & Visitors Bureau; sales manager named CVB "Hero of the Month" for exceptional efforts.

Assistant Manager: Iowa Conservatory Inn & Conference Center, Ames, IA, 2001–2003

139 guest rooms, upscale restaurant, convention space

Served as key liaison between the management company and university officials/board of directors for on-campus, highly profitable hotel property. Delivered monthly P&L reports to the board and interacted closely with members of tight-knit university community.

- Drove up revenues while delivering exceptional quality and service for the Inn's most challenging event—graduation-day dinners serving 1,500 people a white-tablecloth-quality meal in a seven-hour period in eight separate dining areas on three floors.

	2001	2002	2003
Revenue	$25K	$28K	$31K
Increase		*+12%*	*+10%*

EDUCATION: **B.A., Business Management,** University of Michigan, 2000

ASCII Text Resume

```
Sylvie St. Pierre
259 West 76th Street, #4B
New York, NY 10024
212-949-7764
sylvie@hotmail.com


+++++++++++++++++++++++++++++++++++++++++++++++++++++

Hospitality Industry Manager
Hotel * Food & Beverage * Entertainment * Tourism

Advanced rapidly to GM role with respected hotel management
company and delivered measurable improvements in multiple
areas of performance: revenue, guest satisfaction, service,
and safety. Built teams of talented professionals and
motivated entire staff to work together to achieve stretch
goals. Planned, managed, and executed large, complex
functions to maximize revenue while maintaining exceptional
customer satisfaction. Captured new business, restored
corporate client relationships, and delivered creative,
high-quality guest experiences.

Expertise
* Yield Management
* Quality Improvement
* Service Delivery
* Sales Relationships
* Event Management
* Creative Marketing
* HR Management


+++++++++++++++++++++++++++++++++++++++++++++++++++++

Experience and Achievements
Macomber & Reynolds     2001-Present

General Manager: Riverpark Luxor, Queens, NY,
2003-Present

156 guest rooms, full-service restaurant, meeting space

Reversed negative profit performance and stemmed decline of
aging hotel in a competitive business / tourism market.
Managed P&L and annual business plan to achieve performance
objectives. Led a team of 9 operational supervisors and 3
sales managers.
```

* Quickly filled open managerial positions, replaced underperformers, and built a strong team.
* Delivered 11% RevPar increase in one year.
* Focused on quality improvement as a key driver of customer satisfaction. Took Safety score from "unacceptable" to "excellent" and brought METS evaluations up to date and passing all components.
* Improved image and performance for key business and tourism events:
>Corporate event, part of the #1 piece of business annually in Queens: Added activities, services, and menu variety. Grew revenue 50% and earned promise to return in 2005.
>New York Marathon: Selected as one of host hotels for this major city-wide event. Emphasized F&B to drive guest satisfaction. Earned positive feedback from Convention & Visitors Bureau; sales manager named CVB "Hero of the Month" for exceptional efforts.

Assistant Manager:

Iowa Conservatory Inn & Conference Center, Ames, IA, 2001-2003

139 guest rooms, upscale restaurant, convention space
Served as key liaison between the management company and university officials/board of directors for on-campus, highly profitable hotel property. Delivered monthly P&L reports to the board and interacted closely with members of tight-knit university community.
*Drove up revenues while delivering exceptional quality and service for the Inn's most challenging event: graduation-day dinners serving 1,500 people a white-tablecloth-quality meal in a seven-hour period in eight separate dining areas on three floors.

Year	2001	2002	2003
Revenue	$25K	$28K	$31K
Increase		+12%	+10%

++

Education: B.A., Business Management
University of Michigan, 2000

Scannable Resume

Sylvie St. Pierre
259 West 76th Street, #4B
New York, NY 10024
212-949-7764
sylvie@hotmail.com

Hospitality Industry Manager
Hotel * Food & Beverage * Entertainment * Tourism

Advanced rapidly to GM role with respected hotel management company and delivered measurable improvements in multiple areas of performance: revenue, guest satisfaction, service, and safety. Built teams of talented professionals and motivated entire staff to work together to achieve stretch goals. Planned, managed, and executed large, complex functions to maximize revenue while maintaining exceptional customer satisfaction. Captured new business, restored corporate client relationships, and delivered creative, high-quality guest experiences.

Expertise

* Yield Management
* Quality Improvement
* Service Delivery
* Sales Relationships
* Event Management
* Creative Marketing
* HR Management

Experience and Achievements

Macomber & Reynolds   2001–Present

General Manager: Riverpark Luxor, Queens, NY, 2003–Present

156 guest rooms, full-service restaurant, meeting space

Reversed negative profit performance and stemmed decline of aging hotel in a competitive business / tourism market. Managed P&L and annual business plan to achieve performance objectives. Led a team of 9 operational supervisors and 3 sales managers.

* Quickly filled open managerial positions, replaced underperformers, and built a strong team.
* Delivered 11% RevPar increase in one year.
* Focused on quality improvement as a key driver of customer satisfaction. Took Safety score from "unacceptable" to "excellent" and brought METS evaluations up to date and passed all components.
* Improved image and performance for key business and tourism events:
  > Corporate event, part of the #1 piece of business annually in Queens: Added activities, services, and menu variety. Grew revenue 50% and earned promise to return in 2005.
  > New York Marathon: Selected as one of host hotels for this major city-wide event. Emphasized F&B to drive guest satisfaction. Earned positive feedback from Convention & Visitors Bureau; sales manager named CVB "Hero of the Month" for exceptional efforts.

Sylvie St. Pierre
212-949-7764
sylvie@hotmail.com
Page Two

Assistant Manager: Iowa Conservatory Inn & Conference Center, Ames, IA, 2001–2003

139 guest rooms, upscale restaurant, convention space

Served as key liaison between the management company and university officials / board of directors for on-campus, highly profitable hotel property. Delivered monthly P&L reports to the board and interacted closely with members of tight-knit university community.

* Drove up revenues while delivering exceptional quality and service for the Inn's most challenging event—graduation-day dinners serving 1500 people a white-tablecloth-quality meal in a seven-hour period in eight separate dining areas on three floors.

Year	2001	2002	2003
Revenue	$25K	$28K	$31K
Increase		+12%	+10%

Education: B.A., Business Management, University of Michigan, 2000

Chapter 5

▶ Resumes for

Accounting, Banking, and Finance Careers

Each and every industry and profession presents unique resume writing and design challenges. If you are interested in pursuing an accounting, banking, or finance career, be certain to incorporate these important success factors:

Success Factor #1

Be as "quantitative" as possible when listing your accomplishments. Accounting and financial professionals respect numbers and are accustomed to them. So, to the extent possible, use statistics that support your achievements.

Success Factor #2

Show your versatility: Highlight the different types of clients with whom you have worked. Different business sectors have distinctive accounting and financial management needs, so illustrate the diversity of your background by mentioning the different categories of businesses with which you have experience.

Success Factor #3

Demonstrate your value by emphasizing your diverse skills. Include any specific accounting procedures or financial analysis functions that you perform routinely. Documenting these capabilities will illustrate the breadth and depth of your experience.

Success Factor #4

Showcase your technical skills and qualifications. What accounting, financial analysis, mortgage processing, or budgeting software do you use? This expertise is essential in today's electronic information age and also shows your ability to adapt and learn new things.

Keywords and Keyword Phrases

Keywords and keyword phrases are a critical component of every successful job seeker's resume. By using just one or two words, you're able to communicate a wealth of information about your skills, qualifications, and experience. What's more, keywords are the basis for resume-scanning technology and are therefore critical to any job seeker's campaign in today's electronic-based job search market. For more information on keywords, refer back to pages 17–19 in Chapter 1.

Following are the top 20 accounting, banking, and finance keywords, some of which may reflect your skills and some of which may not be appropriate for you at this time. Use these words as the foundation for developing your own list of keywords on the Professional Keyword List form in Appendix B.

Top 20 Keywords

Accounts Payable and Receivable

Financial Analysis and Reporting

Asset Management

Foreign Exchange

Auditing

Internal Accounting Controls

Budget Control and Administration

Investment Analysis and Management

Cash Management

Lending and Loan Administration

Consumer and Commercial Lending

Mergers and Acquisitions

Corporate Treasury

Profit and Loss Analysis

Cost Accounting

Project Accounting

Cost/Benefit Analysis

Risk Management

Credit and Collections

ROI and ROE Analysis

Following are some excellent examples of resumes in the fields of accounting, banking, and finance.

DOMINIQUE ROULET

P.O. Box 1204, Philadelphia, PA 19143	215-876-2203 ♦ 267-808-6523	Email: droulet@hotmail.com

Accounting Professional

Articulate, ambitious professional experienced in financial industry. Proven ability to perform accounting and collections activities. Possess talent for quickly identifying and addressing needs of customers. Detail-oriented, with demonstrated problem-solving abilities. Excellent organizational and follow-up skills. Extremely dependable in completing projects accurately and on time. Competent with computer applications for word processing and accounting. Committed to professional growth and development.

Computer Skills

- Word
- Excel
- Peachtree
- WordPerfect
- Access
- PowerPoint

Professional Experience

Accounting

- Checked figures, postings, and documents for correct entry, mathematical accuracy, and proper codes.
- Complied with federal, state, and company policies, procedures, and regulations.
- Debited, credited, and totaled accounts on computer spreadsheets and databases, using specialized accounting software.
- Classified, recorded, and summarized numerical and financial data to maintain accounting records.
- Calculated, prepared, and issued bills, invoices, statements, and other financial documents according to established procedures.
- Compiled statistical, financial, accounting, and auditing reports and tables for cash receipts and expenditures.
- Accessed computerized financial information to answer general questions as well as those related to specific accounts.

Collections

- Received payments and posted amounts paid to customer accounts.
- Located and monitored overdue accounts, using computers and a variety of automated systems.
- Recorded information about financial status of customers and status of collection efforts.
- Traced and contacted customers about delinquent accounts by mail, telephone, or personal visits in order to solicit payment.
- Conferred with customers to determine reasons for past due payments and to review the credit terms.
- Advised customers of necessary actions and strategies for debt repayment.
- Persuaded customers to pay amounts due on credit accounts, damage claims, or nonpayable checks, or to return merchandise.
- Arranged for debt repayment or established repayment schedules based on customers' financial situations.

Customer Service/Sales

- Maintained records of customer transactions, recording details of inquiries, complaints, and comments, as well as actions taken.
- Resolved customers' service or billing complaints by exchanging merchandise, refunding money, and adjusting bills.
- Checked to ensure that appropriate changes were made to resolve customers' problems.
- Contacted customers to respond to inquiries or to notify them of claim investigation results and any planned adjustments.
- Referred unresolved customer grievances to designated departments for further investigation.
- Determined charges for services requested, collected deposits or payments, and/or arranged for billing.
- Completed contract forms, prepared change of address records, and issued service discontinuance orders.
- Obtained and examined all relevant information in order to assess validity of complaints and to determine possible causes, such as extreme weather conditions that could increase utility bills.

Employment History

2005 - Present	Collections Clerk	Alliance One	Trevose, PA
2003 – 2005	Collections Clerk	Academy Collection Service	Philadelphia, PA
1999 – 2002	Collections Clerk	Oxford Management Services	Farmingdale, NY
1998 – 1999	Collections Clerk	Credit Card Management Services	Plainview, NY
1997	New Accounts Representative	Bed Bath and Beyond	Farmingdale, NY

Education/Training

General Studies Courses	Farmingdale University	Farmingdale, NY
Computerized Accounting	Hunter Business School	Levittown, NY

Written By: Johnetta Frazier
Font: Garamond

Katrina Hartley

85 Stevens Crescent, Barrie, Ontario L9C 4V8
Phone: 705.595.7891   Email: khartley@hotmail.com

PAYROLL MANAGEMENT

Professional and highly skilled financial manager with over seven years of experience in large-scale, complex payroll practice management. Demonstrated strengths in managing weekly deposits of $5M and advanced abilities in managing multiple provincial payroll processing operations. Full understanding of all payroll processes from initiation to employee records management, government statements and remittances, and overall department management. Proven experience in leading and team building that has resulted in the development of efficient payroll departments. Core expertise includes:

Multi-Provincial Payroll Processing	Employee Records Management
Accounting Software Expertise (Peoplesoft 8.0, ACCPAC, Simply Accounting)	Payroll Compliance & Remittance Management (WCB, CCRA, Provincial Healthcare Plans, etc.)
Time Entry & Verification Management	Payroll Auditing and Process Improvement

Professional Experience

Arlington International Incorporated, Toronto, Ontario   2001 – Present

Payroll Manager   2006
Promoted to manage team of 8 people ensuring that weekly time entry, verification, and records management are completed in an efficient and correct manner. Selected achievements include:
- Implemented a new training program to ensure all existing staff and new hires understood the payroll system, time entry requirements, and the verification process. Resulted in a dramatic decrease in errors and increased overall job satisfaction.

Payroll Team Lead   2004 - 2005
Managed 3 weekly payroll systems for over 2,500 hourly consultants across Canada on a timely and accurate basis. Selected achievements include:
- Parachuted in to complete an audit of all banking and security controls to detect areas of potential fraud. Made extensive recommendations on process improvements that have been implemented across North America.
- Created a full review process of all incoming consultant files ensuring a high level of accuracy and minimizing overall errors.
- Interacted with diverse business groups within the organization to synergize the payroll process including walking staff through the various stages required to successfully hire a new consultant.
- Documented and facilitated the new hire training package to ensure consistency in understanding and usage of the time entry system and department policies and procedures.
- Ensured accuracy in all general ledger and year-end financial reporting requirements.

Payroll Specialist   1999 - 2004
- Reviewed and corrected $1M weekly payroll reports to ensure accuracy prior to deposit.
- Managed all aspects of employee records management for all consultants across Canada.
- Led year-end accounting procedures to ensure all legislative requirements were met.

Education

CANADIAN PAYROLL ASSOCIATION – Level II   2005
DIPLOMA – ACCOUNTING, Humber College   1998
- Graduated with honors
- Received top award in accounting for a graduating student

Written By: Denyse Cowling
Font: Tahoma

Susan Danville

906 Riverview Road • San Ramon, CA 97786 • 974.588.9900
SDanville@cox.net

Professional Summary

Accounting/Finance Professional with expertise in general accounting, financial analysis and reporting, financial systems, budget preparation and cash management. **Currently pursuing MBA in Finance.**

- Well versed in accounting principles, practices and systems as well as business operations.
- Team player who performs at high levels of productivity in fast-paced environments without missing a single deadline.
- Effective communicator, building positive relationships with management, customers, staff and financial institutions.
- Recognized for leadership and problem-solving strengths, as well as thoroughness and accuracy.

Experience

THE LYDEN COMPANY, San Francisco, CA   1983 to 2006
  Senior Accountant (2000 to 2006)
  Accountant (1991 to 2000)
  Accounting Technician (1983 to 1991)

Promoted through progressively responsible positions in Accounting Department in recognition of consistent performance results. Accomplishments:

Accounting/Auditing
- Managed accounts payable disbursements totaling more than $1.7 million annually, accounts receivable processing and over $1 million in capital assets.
- Verified and maintained GL system. Developed and implemented accounting policies/procedures.
- Instituted internal control procedures including suspense account reconciliations for premium collections, reducing write-offs by $75,000 annually.
- Coordinated audits with internal/external auditors and regulatory agencies. Compiled financial data for auditors. Prepared internal audit reports.

Financial Analysis & Reporting
- Coordinated and prepared NAIC financial statements in accordance with SAP and premium tax return filings for more than $1.8 million in 48 states.
- Prepared financial statements in accordance with GAAP for the Board of Directors and shareholders and semiannual SEC filings for 6 portfolios totaling $1+ billion in net assets.
- Analyzed and prepared variance reports for all management levels throughout business unit.

Cash Management/Budgeting
- Performed cash management functions to meet investment objectives and prepared timely corporate cash-flow forecasts.
- Developed and implemented banking policies for accounting, premiums, commissions and benefits.
- Coordinated $35 million budget preparation process for all departments within business unit.

Education

M.B.A. Candidate in Finance • Anticipated May 2007
Stanford University • Berkeley, CA

B.S., Accounting • May 1991
California State University • Sacramento, CA

Written By: Louise Garver
Font: Times New Roman

JULIA GRANT

123 State Street
Pittsburgh, Pennsylvania 15271

Phone / Fax: (724) 525-4872
JGrant@grafixservices.com

PROFILE

Corporate accountant with 16 years' experience in maximizing fiscal results and recovering millions of dollars through intensive research, analysis, and formulation of standardized systems to enhance efficiency, accuracy, and generation of effective performance metrics.

EXPERTISE

- Management of Multimillion-Dollar Accounting Operations
- Internal Auditing: Tracking and Evaluation of Financial Procedures
- Due Diligence: Best Practices Monitoring and Adherence
- Design and Implementation of Process Improvements, Increasing Bottom-Line Profitability
- Development and Enforcement of Corporate Policies
- Compliance with Multi-State and Federal Laws for Financial Reporting
- Participation in Internal, External, and Governmental Audits
- Strong Working Knowledge of Full Range of Standard Accounting Practices: General Ledger, Financial Statements, Accounts Payable, Accounts Receivable, Forecasting, and Year-End Closings

PROFESSIONAL EXPERIENCE

B. D. Alton, LLC, Pittsburgh, Pennsylvania   2004–Present
CONTRACT ACCOUNTANT
Global Transportation Corporation
- Managed large-scale project, finalizing fiscal data for $1.2 billion company restructuring mandate.
- Attained cash recovery of $10 million through resolution and elimination of unsettled claims.

Natural Power Services, Erie, Pennsylvania   1997–2004
CORPORATE ACCOUNTANT / ASSISTANT TO DIRECTOR OF ACCOUNTING
Regional Utility Company
- Managed accounting and auditing for 6 subsidiary companies with $163 million in annual revenues.
- Recovered $2.4 million in receipts not posted and saved $460,000 by eliminating duplicate payments.

Wellness and Fitness Systems Incorporated, Philadelphia, Pennsylvania   1990–1997
CORPORATE ACCOUNTANT / CASH MANAGER
International Retail Corporation
- Managed multimillion-dollar cash operations for 1,200 stores nationwide.
- Consolidated bank accounts, decreasing fees 50%. Initiated centralized purchasing, saving $100,000.

EDUCATION

Bachelor of Science Degree, Accounting (GPA: 3.5), *Duquesne University*, Pittsburgh, Pennsylvania 1990

Written By: Lee Anne Grundish
Font: Palatino Linotype

ANTHONY GAINES

154 Cincinnati Avenue
Valley Stream, New York 11580
516-751-2210 (Home); 516-435-8140 (Cell)
E-Mail: againes@aol.com

SUMMARY

Controller with broad and progressive experience. Demonstrated capabilities include financial analysis, budgeting, forecasting/modeling and monitoring cash flow. Additional strengths in financial statements, staff training and supervision. A highly motivated, hands-on, detail- and deadline-oriented self-starter who handles pressure well and possesses excellent problem-solving and communication abilities. Excels in performance through both individual and group efforts.

Computer proficiency includes: MS Excel, Word, PowerPoint, Access, Outlook; Quickbooks Pro, Peachtree, ADP Payroll, Lotus Suite, TurboTax Pro, Financial Navigator, Real World and Local Area Network (LAN) administration.

PROFESSIONAL EXPERIENCE

MEDICAL ASSOCIATES OF BROOKLYN, P.C., Brooklyn, NY 1988 - 2006
A multi-site medical group with 800 employees and revenues totaling $72 million

Began as a **Staff Accountant** and advanced to **Assistant Controller** to **Assistant Controller/MIS Manager** to **Controller.**

Controller

- Directed and coordinated daily accounting operations encompassing the areas of general ledger, ADP payroll, taxes, cash flow, cash reconciliations, grants, disbursements and receivables. Successfully met internal and external audits requirements.
- Trained and supervised a staff of five with minimal turnover.
- Prepared, monitored and controlled compliance to monthly and annual budgets involving 15 departments.
- Performed in a liaison capacity for all external financial, tax and pension audits in achieving compliance with audit requirements.
- Prepared all financial modeling/budgets for contract and union negotiations. Attained corporate recognition for effort.
- Supervised and participated in tax-deferred annuity plan valued at $62 million in net assets, pension plan valued at $45 million and all tax filings.
- Prepared and monitored reporting and reconciliation for productivity-based contract. Recommendations accepted by senior management.

Assistant Controller/MIS Manager

- Additional responsibility for maintaining computer network with a peak of 80 workstations.
- Researched, planned and implemented all software and computer purchases leading to enhanced operational efficiency and increased data security.

ANTHONY GAINES　　　　　　516-435-8140 (Cell)　　　　　　Page 2

Assistant Controller/MIS Manager (Continued):

- Acted in a liaison role with computer, network and software development consultants, which led to minimal downtime of systems.
- Troubleshot all computer software and hardware problems resulting in minimal disruption to daily activities.
- Designed and prepared financial analyses and made presentations covering the profit and loss, cash flow, variance analysis, statistical productivity and cost performance to senior management and Board of Directors.
- Prepared reports and monitored compliance for grants totaling $2 million.
- Created and reconciled all payroll tax filings to meet all deadlines.
- Selected and implemented a computerized accounting system, reducing turnaround time of accounting activities from two weeks to one day.
- Developed and implemented reporting systems covering budget, payroll and overtime compliance which enhanced communication of financial data to senior management.

Staff Accountant

- Prepared, monitored and maintained general ledger, bank reconciliations, cash disbursements and external monthly expense/staffing reports to continually meet all deadlines.

ADDITIONAL PROFESSIONAL EXPERIENCE

JDL ACCOUNTING ASSOCIATES, Long Beach, NY 1986 – Present
Part-time Tax Preparer/Accountant

- Prepare personal and corporate income taxes with a peak of 60 clients.

NAUTICAL GLOBAL, Monroe Township, NJ 1988 – 2003
A nautical equipment importing firm with sales of $1 million.
Part-time Accountant

- Handled sales, payroll taxes, general ledger, financial statements and audits.

EDUCATION

Brooklyn College, Brooklyn, NY
M.B.A. Degree "with Distinction"
Concentration: Accounting/CPA Preparation

Pace University, New York, NY
B.B.A. Degree, Cum Laude
Concentration: Business Management

Written By: Bob Simmons
Font: Arial

CHRISTOPHER J. MILLER
cjmiller@comcast.net

15 Pawling Street
Jersey City, NJ 07302

Home: 201-343-1071
Cell: 201-666-5998

FINANCIAL SERVICES OPERATIONS PROFESSIONAL

Turnarounds ▪ Start-Ups ▪ High Growth ▪ De Novo Operations ▪ Rightsizing ▪ Mergers ▪ Exit Strategies ▪ Risk Assessment & Compliance

- Over 15 years' experience managing diverse trust and fiduciary operations in U.S. and abroad.
- Entrepreneurial General Manager with exceptional success launching and managing numerous international multi-billion dollar businesses for emerging products and services.
- Catalyst for driving strategic and tactical process improvements and creating business infrastructures that deliver multi-million dollar ROI and build customer confidence.
- Visionary leader with passion for excellence, exceptional integrity, and knack for building and mentoring successful teams.

CORE COMPETENCIES & CAPABILITIES

Management

Organizational Redesign and Restructuring ▪ Information Systems and Technologies ▪ Cost Reduction and Avoidance ▪ Market and Operations Risk Assessment ▪ Client Relationship Management ▪ RFP Development ▪ Recruitment and Retention ▪ Training and Development

Operations

Global and Domestic Custody ▪ Clearance ▪ Mortgage-Backed Securities (MBS) ▪ Securities Lending Offshore Fund Administration ▪ Corporate Trust ▪ Transfer Agent ▪ Risk Management Cash Management ▪ Funds Transfer ▪ Money Markets ▪ Letters of Credit ▪ Loans

Compliance

AML ▪ BSA ▪ OFAC ▪ SAR ▪ FINCEN ▪ USA Patriot Act ▪ SOX ▪ Graham-Leach-Bliley ▪ SEC Rule 17 W-1099 and W-1042 Reporting ▪ Double Taxation Treaties ▪ Balance Sheet & P/L Reporting

PROFESSIONAL EXPERIENCE

THE BANK OF NEW YORK, New York, NY   1996 to Present
Vice President and Manager-Trust Operations: Managed global custody product with $85B in assets. Oversaw transactions for close to 500 accounts and led teams of up to 65 employees. Maximized client servicing by developing and integrating operational tools, analyzing workflow and technology capabilities, and training and developing staff.

Client Servicing and Business Development

- **Reversed strained relationship with $28B global client;** renewed five-year contract despite expectations that account was unsalvageable and secured an additional $4.8B in business.
- **Optimized client-custodian relations and account retention** by introducing an online trade initiation and reporting capability, developing standardized protocols for account administration, and auditing all customer correspondence.
- **Eliminated multi-billion dollar trade processing problems** and rejuvenated eroded client confidence by replacing antiquated system with cutting-edge browser system.
- **Spearheaded and developed operational capacity to support new offshore investment funds.**

Business Reengineering and Process Improvement

- **Trimmed operating costs $1.9M annually** by improving efficiencies, eliminating redundancies, promoting high-performing junior staff, and cutting 65-person staff in half.
- **Significantly improved account management capabilities** by introducing department's first formalized reporting systems including real-time reports for Asian markets and online reporting.

CHRISTOPHER J. MILLER   Page Two

- **Slashed back-log of paid bank bonds/unreconciled cash accounts from three million to 22,000** in 15 months and found virtually no occurrences of improprieties.
- **Consistently garnered exemplary audit ratings** throughout tenure with bank.

CITIBANK, New York, NY   1986 to 1996
Distinguished operations and business management performance securing promotions through series of increasingly responsible branch manager positions. Managed up to $450B in assets and staff of 100.

Vice President, Global Investor Services, Zurich Branch (1990 to 1996)
Selected by General Manager of bank's London branch to launch novel global securities lending product and merge corporate trust operation.

Global Securities Lending Product Launch
Tasked with researching and establishing industry contacts on buy-side, creating business plan, designing product profile, spearheading internal product review and approval, obtaining regulatory approval, preparing legal agreements, assessing potential tax consequences under various tax treaties, securing credit lines for borrowers, selecting staff of eight, writing procedures, and choosing system vendor and managing installation.

- **Accelerated loan portfolio from $1B to $22B in less than two years** with product revenues exceeding $5M per annum.
- **Evaluated market and operations risk for 30 countries.**
- **Designed and installed securities lending technology.**
- **Recognized as pioneer in securities lending field** and invited to speak at trade conferences and contribute content to trade publications.

Corporate Trust Operations Merger
Appointed to consolidate two corporate trust operations servicing the corporate issuers of Eurobonds.

- **Cut operating expenses by 20%** by auditing staff, systems, and documentation, defining intra-day credit risks, and instituting establishment of credit lines.
- **Recommended revisions in fee structure** that improved efficiencies and standardized practices.

Managing Director, Geneva Subsidiary (1988 to 1990)

- **Orchestrated a politically sensitive downsizing and consolidation** of the corporate trust and depository operation; closed foreign exchange, money market, and private banking operations.
- **Reduced balance sheet by two-thirds and staff by 50%** from 20 to 10.
- **Uncovered/remedied operating irregularities and improprieties** prior to sale of business.
- **Relocated office and outfitted new premises** within designated time frames and budget.
- **Sold business for close to $5M.**

Assistant Vice President and Operations Manager, Manila Branch (1986 to 1988)

- Managed loans, money market, FX, and L/C back-office operations.
- Supervised installation of mainframe computer and back-office automation.
- Enhanced operating revenues by 20% by developing and implementing L/C export bill service.

EDUCATION

B.A., Economics, St. John's University, Jamaica, NY

TECHNOLOGY

MS Excel and Word, HTML, SWIFT, DTC

LANGUAGES

Working knowledge of German

Written By: Barbara Safani
Font: Book Antiqua

CANDACE FOSTER

357 Lake Street ◆ Hoboken, NJ 07030 ◆ (201) 795-2500 ◆ cfoster@aol.com

Well-regarded bond trader with a wealth of product knowledge, a talent for maintaining long-term business relationships, and a commitment to maximizing bottom-line profitability.

SUMMARY OF QUALIFICATIONS

Licensed securities trader with a proven record of accomplishment as a brokers' broker for municipal bonds. Respected, credible business partner with ground-up knowledge of bond trading and extensive knowledge of the mid-Atlantic bond market. Known for open, forthright communication style. Highly successful in building confidence and trust while retaining long-term client relationships. Strong operations knowledge. Familiar with Bloomberg software system and all electronic trading platforms.

SELECT ACCOMPLISHMENTS

- Established record of success as municipal bond brokers' broker, generating revenues that averaged more than $750,000 per year over a 15-year period. Successfully executed trades, both large and small, with equal aplomb, including one worth $25 million.

- Joining regional trading desk at Clarkson-Mason, built and expanded mid-Atlantic portfolio, turning related bond trading activities into $1 million per year contribution.

- Earned confidence and respect of clients, successfully retaining accounts long-term. For example, maintained strong relationship with Wells-Fargo Bank that has generated as much as $4 million over span of 15 years.

- Built strong network of loyal clients through honest, straightforward approach and consistency in providing knowledgeable service and sound recommendations that meet client objectives.

- Tapped to oversee back-office operations while brokering trades, uncovered and rectified accounting errors, saving company from substantial penalties from the MSRB.

EMPLOYMENT HISTORY

DONALDSON & JONES, New York, NY   1994 to present
Municipal Bond Broker's Broker
Specializing in mid-Atlantic municipalities, buy and sell bonds to broker-dealers. Oversee back-office operations, addressing issues and problems. Manage payroll for entire desk. Serve as liaison to senior management.

CLARKSON-MASON, New York, NY   1989 to 1994
Municipal Bond Brokers' Broker
Bought and sold bonds for regional trading desk, expanding mid-Atlantic business.

MARSHFIELD SECURITIES, New York, NY   1981 to 1989
Retail Trader, Mid-Atlantic Region (1986 to 1989)
Hired as desk assistant, rose through ranks to retail trader position while building expertise in municipal bond business and back-office operations.

PROFESSIONAL LICENSES & AFFILIATIONS

Series 7 and Series 63 licenses
Member, Municipal Bond Club of New York and Women's Bond Club of New York

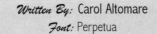
Written By: Carol Altomare
Font: Perpetua

JAMES MADISON
Investment Management & Trading

EXECUTIVE SUMMARY

Visionary and forward-thinking Investment & Portfolio Manager with a 16+ year career in financial markets highlighted by recruitment, promotion and retention by leading investment banks. Experienced both on the sell side and buy side in international and emerging markets. Able to balance the needs and requirements of customers while remaining focused on managing investments and proprietary positions. Provide exceptional results with vigor and tenacity utilizing the ability to identify strategic opportunities in all market cycles. Additional highlights include:

- Capital Markets Management
- Hedge Fund & Equities
- Short & Long Trades
- Fixed Incomes

- Portfolio Analysis
- Investment Management
- Global Currency Analysis
- Municipal Bonds

- Emerging & International Markets
- Consultative & Relationship Sales
- Asset Allocations & Management
- Fundamental Securities Analysis

ACHIEVEMENTS IN DEPTH

As **Portfolio Manager**, took over investment portfolios for Trust and Personal Investment Management accounts. Set up asset allocations for portfolios based on investors' stated objectives, risk tolerances and time horizons.

- Distinguished as the youngest analyst to be promoted to Portfolio Manager at the firm.
- Selected individual securities, both equities and fixed income, for inclusion into portfolios.
- Hand-picked to be the Junior Portfolio Manager on two separate Municipal Fixed Income Mutual Funds, each with assets well over $100 million USD.

As **Managing Director: Equities Trading**, brought onboard to manage international equity traders and trading books that have contributed between $2 million and $4 million in annual trading profits for the global books.

- Initiated both long and short trades in International Equities including Europe, Asia, Eastern Europe, South Africa and Latin America.
- Successfully repurchased shares for two major NYSE-listed company's buyback program and for one major NASDAQ listed company's program. Govern agency orders on NYSE and NASDAQ to ensure quality of trades.
- Hedge global equity positions with index futures or with actively traded ETF's (SPY and QQQ).

As **Director: Equity Trading**, managed UK European ADR arbitrage book, taking advantage of price differences between share prices in local exchanges and corresponding ADR's traded on NYSE and NASDAQ. Managed Latam and emerging markets ADR trading that produced trading profits of $8 million in the first 9 months of 1997 on capital limits of $35 million; later managing Latin America, Asia and emerging markets trading team in NY from 1997 to 2000. Implemented long volatility option strategies.

- Supervised trading teams in local offices throughout Latin America, resulting in trading profits in excess of $11 million within 9 months.
- Key player in establishing a new firm in Argentina that became one of the premier local brokers, achieving a consistent "Top 10" rating in volume on local exchange.
- Managed several portfolios for individuals with high net worth investing in Latin American Bonds and Equities.
- Traded ADR's on NYSE, NASDAQ and Pink Sheets.
- Actively monitored and hedged firm's global currency policy.

JAMES MADISON

As **Vice President,** established local broker network throughout the region. Executed institutional agency orders in local shares in South American region. Made markets on NASDAQ and institutional clients in ADR's.

- Drove profit of $500,000 on trading limits of $5 million after trading South American ADR's and local shares.
- Captured over $3 million in trading profits with capital limits of $2 million through trading Argentina, Brazil and Peru books.

CAREER CHRONOLOGY

Rapid advancement and recruitment based on consistent successes and performance-based promotions, excelling in every position. Selected to plan and execute mission-critical business initiatives. Formal recognition for personal contributions that drive corporate growth, improve operational performance and enhance profitability.

VVVC SECURITIES (USA) INC., New York, NY **Managing Director: Equities Trading**	2002 to Present
KENNEDY CORP., NY & London **Director: Equity Trading**	1997 to 2002
FOSTER FERRELL & GREEN, New York, NY **Director: Equity Trading**	1996 to 1997
MAXWELL SECURITIES, INC., New York, NY **Vice President**	1995 to 1996
BROOKS, BORSHT, & JONES SECURITIES, New York, NY **Vice President: Trader**	1993 to 1995
USA BANK, Buenos Aires, Argentina **Director**	1992 to 1993
CHATTANOOGA BANK & TRUST CO., Chattanooga, TN **Portfolio Manager**	1989 to 1992

EDUCATION & LICENSES

CASE WESTERN RESERVE UNIVERSITY, Cleveland, OH—1989
BA, Economics

> *CFA Level II Candidate*

> **Series 7, 8, 9 & 24 Licenses**

> *Language proficiency in* **English, Spanish and Portuguese**

Written By: Erin Kennedy
Font: Times New Roman

Chapter 6

▶ Resumes for

Administrative and Clerical Careers

Each and every industry and profession presents unique resume writing and design challenges. If you are interested in pursuing an administrative or clerical career, be certain to incorporate these important success factors:

Success Factor #1

Focus on the contributions you have made to the overall success of your employers, for example, increasing revenues, reducing costs, upgrading technologies, managing key projects, and improving productivity and efficiency.

Success Factor #2

Highlight the vast array of skills, qualifications, competencies, and talents that you offer, which, for most administrative professionals, is quite extensive due to the varied nature of the work you perform.

Success Factor #3

Demonstrate your value by emphasizing the number and types of people and organizations you have supported in each of your positions to give further "depth" to your experience. Don't forget your "customer service" skills, even if your "customers" are internal.

Success Factor #4

Showcase all your technical skills and qualifications. Be sure to include coursework or training sessions, even if they were "in-house" programs presented by your employer. Word processing, spreadsheets, accounting software, and customer databases can all be important. They are essential in today's electronic world of work!

Keywords and Keyword Phrases

Keywords and keyword phrases are a critical component of every successful job seeker's resume. By using just one or two words, you're able to communicate a wealth of information about your skills, qualifications, and experience. What's more, keywords are the basis for resume-scanning technology and are therefore critical to any job seeker's campaign in today's electronic-based job search market. For more information on keywords, refer back to pages 17–19 in Chapter 1.

Following are the top 20 administrative and clerical keywords, some of which may reflect your skills and some of which may not be appropriate for you at this time. Use these words as the foundation for developing your own list of keywords on the Professional Keyword List form in Appendix B.

Top 20 Keywords

Budget Administration	Meeting Planning
Business Administration	Office Management
Clerical Support	Policy and Procedure
Client Communications	Productivity Improvement
Confidential Correspondence	Project Management
Contract Administration	Records Management
Corporate Recordkeeping	Regulatory Reporting
Document Management	Resource Management
Efficiency Improvement	Time Management
Liaison Affairs	Workflow Planning/Prioritization

Following are some excellent examples of resumes for administrative and clerical careers.

Sierra Cantrell

1334 Red Bank Lane, Apt. D   Chapel Hill, NC 27514   314-431-5675

Objective: A challenging position as an Administrative Assistant.

Strengths: * Detail oriented
                      * Highly organized
                      * Prioritize accurately
                      * Work well under pressure
                      * Take initiative
                      * Excellent interpersonal skills

Experience: Great Heights Tree Service   Chapel Hill, NC
                      Administrative Clerk   2004 to Present
                      Proficient in MS Word, Windows, and Excel.
                      Prepared records, maintained files, and designed forms.
                      Answered 12 incoming phone lines.
                      Trained employees on software programs.

                      Oakdale Title Company   Chapel Hill, NC
                      Receptionist/Escrow Secretary   2002 to 2004
                      Provided excellent customer service.
                      Processed Loan Packages and daily deposits for escrow.
                      Dispersed checks to mortgage companies, real estate agents, and customers.

                      Stoneybrooks   Chapel Hill, NC
                      Customer Service/Cashier   1999 to 2001
                      Coordinated cash handling and customer service.
                      Managed inventory control and supply ordering.
                      Maintained credit files.

                      Sherrell Tax & Bookkeeping Services   Fayetteville, NC
                      Receptionist/Bookkeeper   1996 to 1998
                      Responsible for A/P, A/R, payroll, and bookkeeping.

Education: Fayetteville Community College   Fayetteville, NC
                      Business Communications, Human Relations on the Job

                      Fayetteville ROP   Fayetteville, NC
                      Administration, Office Management

                      Pine Forest High School   Fayetteville, NC
                      Diploma

References: Available upon request

Written By: Laura Barbeau
Font: Garamond

ADELE YOUNG – ACCOMPLISHED ADMINISTRATIVE ASSISTANT

123 Main Street
Laguna Hills, CA 92653

949.123.4567
ayoung@internetco.net

SUMMARY PROFILE

Talented, energetic and personable Administrator with proven experience in fact-paced private and public sector positions. Strong background in all aspects of administrative support and customer service. Exceptionally dependable, creative problem-solver with excellent computer skills and ability to achieve goals and meet deadlines while handling multiple priorities.

KEY COMPETENCIES

➢ Reputation for **organization, time management** and delivering **results that surpass company goals and objectives**.
➢ Preparation of routine to **Executive Reports** using Microsoft® Office applications.
➢ **Professional image** combined with **persuasive communication, presentation** and **interpersonal skills**.
➢ **Distinguished from others by intensity of commitment** to **exceeding performance expectations, reliability** and **integrity**.

EDUCATION AND TRAINING

Saddleback Valley College – Mission Viejo, CA
Associate in Arts – Major: Business Administration – 3.8 GPA   **1998**

Microsoft® Outlook and Word   "Take Charge Assistant"

CAREER BACKGROUND

City of Anaheim – Anaheim, CA   **2001 – Present**
Administrative Secretary
➢ Consistent record of outstanding performance earned a series of promotions.
➢ Completed correspondence, reports and diverse special projects.
➢ Maintained executive calendars, scheduled meetings, recorded minutes and planned numerous community events.

Premier Metals Manufacturing, Inc. – Tustin, CA   **1989 – 2000**
Office Manager
➢ Oversaw all aspects of office administration including accounting, inventories, purchasing and inside sales for this well-established manufacturing firm.

ADDITIONAL VOLUNTEER EXPERIENCE

Forest School – Mission Viejo, CA   **2002 – 2005**
Administrative Coordinator – Girls Soccer Team
➢ Planned activities related to home games, fund-raisers and special events including a season ending awards banquet attended by over 350 guests.
➢ Created Excel spreadsheets to calculate athlete statistics.

Valley Elementary School – Big Canyon, CA   **1999 – 2001**
Spirit Wear Coordinator
➢ Led project to design a school logo, purchase embossed merchandise and conduct monthly sales for fund-raising.

Written By: James A. Swanson
Font: Times New Roman

SARA J. WALTERS

8810 Forrest Drive, La Crosse, WI 54601
(608) 796-5555 Home ▪ sara_walters@comcast.net

SECRETARY / ADMINISTRATIVE ASSISTANT / COORDINATOR

Soon-to-be Bachelor's Degree graduate (BA Religion and Psychology) with secretarial, customer service, independent field research, SPSS analysis and program coordination experience. Proven multi-tasking, interpersonal and communications skills. Conscientious team player and self-starter. Adept in:

☑ Customer Relationship Management	☑ Administrative & Office Support	☑ Project Coordination
☑ Records / Database Management	☑ Academic Research Projects	☑ Office Technology

KEY SUPPORTING SKILLS

- **Administration:** Independent administrative and organizational experience includes office support for architectural firm, upscale café operations coordination, and teaching assistant program facilitation.

- **Technology Skills:** Windows XP, MS Office 2003 – Word, Excel, Access, Outlook, SPSS, Internet Explorer. Peripherals: printers, fax machines, scanners, copiers and digital cameras.

- **Communications:** Experienced in composing and editing letters, memos, email communications and reports using APA style guide. Familiar with conversational Spanish (reading, writing, speaking).

EDUCATION

BA, Religion and Psychology (GPAs 3.51, 3.49), Viterbo University, LaCrosse, WI – due May 2007
Study Abroad in China and Tibet (Asian Studies), University of Wisconsin-Madison, WI – May/June 2003

PROFESSIONAL EXPERIENCE

Teaching Assistant, Viterbo University, La Crosse, WI   September – December 2006
✓ Strategized with tenured professor on content, format, locations and scheduling of 200-level, seminar-style, weekly discussion groups for Psychology of Motivation. Reviewed and graded homework for 20 students per week (48-hour turnaround), and calculated final grades for 40 students within one week.

✓ Adapted class readings to discussion themes for two 20-person groups, facilitating dialogue through clarification, questioning, anecdotes, summarizing, encouragement and interactive exercises.

Secretary, Sandoski Architects, Madison, WI   Summers 2000 – 2005
✓ Provided secretarial support for well-respected architect firm with 4-8 staff. Handled up to 50 calls daily using multi-line phone system. Maintained Access database of 300 business clients and 70 vendors.

✓ Conducted Internet research for historical architectural projects and presented synopsis of research to owner. Wrote business correspondence and kept fastidious records on 5-10 current projects (each with 15-20 sub files), along with 30-40 additional active files, ensuring due diligence on liability aspects.

✓ Opened, sorted and distributed mail; processed outgoing mail with postage meter and arranged FedEx pick-ups. Ordered office supplies ($50-$100/month) and maintained accurate inventory control.

Café Assistant, Health Foods Pantry and Café, Madison, WI   September 2001 – May 2002
✓ Promoted from counter person to Café Assistant / Prep Chef with responsibility for opening, setting up and closing 20-seat/take-out café in largest natural food market in southern Wisconsin. Served up to 200 orders per day for diverse clientele in college town, with cash transactions up to $3000 daily.

Counter Person, Santori's Grill and Restaurant, Vero Beach, FL   Summers 1998 – 2000
✓ One of two counter persons at busy, 40-seat/take-out beach resort restaurant. Developed quick response time, combined with accuracy and creative problem solving, in demanding food-service position (200 orders per day). Handled $1000 - $6000 in daily register transactions.

Written By: Susan Guarmeri
Font: Arial

ANNA CLARK
(416) 654-3928
abc@canada.com

223 TERRY FOX BLVD
SCARBOROUGH, ONTARIO
M1B 2A3

ADMINISTRATIVE ASSISTANT WITH
WRITING & EVENTS PLANNING EXPERIENCE

WORK EXPERIENCE

ADMINISTRATIVE ASSISTANT / EVENTS PLANNER	Campbell Human Resource Consulting Executive Offices	2000 – 2006

- Organized events for 20 to 400 people.
- Arranged site and catering for all company events over 100 people.
- Served as Senior Management Assistant to 3 senior partners.
- Prepared agenda and took and transcribed minutes for all Board of Directors' meetings.
- Managed budget for all events over 50 people.

ADMINISTRATIVE ASSISTANT	New Phone Systems Inc. Communications Department	1997 – 2000

- Wrote and edited newsletter for line staff.
- Designed flyers for internal events.
- Managed website for line staff volunteers.
- Maintained all office equipment.
- Managed administrative support functions for department of 12.

SALES ASSISTANT	Working Ventures Entrepreneurs	1995 – 1997

- Assisted 6 salespeople in maintaining good customer relationships.
- Coordinated media relations.
- Bought and organized all office supplies.

RECEPTIONIST	Working Ventures Entrepreneurs	1993 – 1995

- Managed incoming/outgoing mail for staff of 30.
- Handled 6-line phone system, transferring calls to 30 extensions.

EDUCATION / PROFESSIONAL DEVELOPMENT

ACCPAC & SIMPLY ACCOUNTING (self-directed tutorials)	Office Workers Career Centre www.officeworker.org Toronto	2006
ONLINE WRITING LAB (business-writing program)	Purdue University www.purdueu.com	2005
MICROSOFT PROFESSIONAL PROFICIENCY CERTIFICATION	International Professional Business School Toronto	2001
INTRODUCTION TO THE MICROSOFT SUITE	New Phone Systems Inc. Training Centre Mississauga	1998
WORDPERFECT & LOTUS CERTIFICATE	Computer Skills International Toronto	1995

Written By: Anne Brunelle
Font: Times New Roman

Marilyn Grady

21-200 Drake Crescent * Toronto, ON * M4L 3S3
Home: 416.212.9661 * Cell: 416.300.1234
mgrady2424@msn.net

DENTAL OFFICE MANAGEMENT / HYGIENE PRACTICE MANAGEMENT

Professional and highly skilled Office Manager with over 10 years of experience in dental practice management. Demonstrated strengths in hygiene program coordination and advanced abilities in patient scheduling, receivables and insurance claims administration, and overall continuing care programs for patients. Proven experience in office management and team building that have resulted in the development of successful dental practices. Areas of expertise include:

- Office Management
- Bookkeeping (Accounts Receivables)
- Dental Nomenclature
- Computerized Health & Dental Software
- Insurance Claims Administration
- Continuing Care Program Coordination

SKILLS AND ACCOMPLISHMENTS

- Optimized day-to-day operations of the office through efficient management, scheduling, and training of a caring and motivated administrative and clinical staff.

- Applied knowledge of dental nomenclature, patient charting, dental office procedures, and insurance claims management processes to engineer productivity and profitability for the practice.

- Implemented a patient hygiene care program designed to improve attendance at appointments and increase the number of regular office visits. This was achieved through a series of follow-up calls to patients designed to remind them of upcoming appointments or to re-schedule missed appointments. This program has been instrumental in the growth of multiple dental practices.

- Assisted in the implementation of automated dental health care software that provides a common patient scheduling, chart management, accounts receivable, and insurance claims vehicle for all staff to utilize.

- Reduced outstanding receivables to less than 30 days by working in partnership with both patients and insurance companies to ensure all documentation and issues were resolved.

- Spearheaded a patient awareness telephone campaign, resulting in dramatic increases in the number of new and returning appointment bookings to the practice.

PROFESSIONAL EXPERIENCE

Office Manager and Hygiene Management Coordinator – Dr. Moffat	1999 to present
Receptionist and Dental Assistant - Dr. Samson and Dr. Mason	1996 to 1999
Receptionist and Treatment/Hygiene Coordinator - Dr. Matthews	1995 to 1996
Receptionist (co-op term) - Dr. Samson and Dr. Mason	1994 to 1995

EDUCATION

George Brown College, Toronto, Ontario **CERTIFICATE - Preventive Dental Assistant, Level II**	1997
George Brown College, Toronto, Ontario **CERTIFICATE - Certified Dental Assistant**	1995
George Brown College, Toronto, Ontario **CERTIFICATE - Dental Office Administration**	1994

Written By: Denyse Cowling
Font: Verdana

SHARON P. SINGER

27422 Mason Ave.   212-555-7465
New York, NY 22578   singers@aol.com

OFFICE MANAGEMENT PROFESSIONAL

High-Performance Administrator with over 15 years of experience supporting small- to medium-sized offices within various industries. Experienced in all aspects of payroll, accounts payable and receivable, documentation management, and database administration, while redesigning administrative processes to streamline functions, eliminate redundancy, and expedite workflow. Expert organizational, leadership, and communication skills. Recognized for professionalism, resourcefulness, and proficiency in managing affairs while supporting company goals. Highlights include:

Policy & Procedure Compliance	**Vendor & Customer Communications**
Special Events & Meeting Management	**Problem Solving & Decision Making**
Workload Planning & Prioritization	**Payroll, Accounting, & Bookkeeping**

PROFESSIONAL EXPERIENCE

SUPER DRIVE CORPORATION, New York, NY   1990 to Present
Office Manager (1990 to Present)

Maintain complete administrative operations for this leading manufacturer of disk-drive components. Advanced rapidly based on continuous successes with office operational performance. Manage staff and delegate assignments to office personnel. Demonstrate strong customer service/relations ability through sales order processing and problem resolution. Prepare and maintain all general correspondence. Knowledgeable of international shipping laws. Excellent typing skills. Data entry 350 accurate strokes per minute (numeric).

- Expertise with accounts payable, accounts receivable, and payroll.
- Designed, prepared, and formatted operations manual for company products.
- Authored and implemented all departmental policies and procedures.

Assistant to Controller (1995 to Present)

Promoted to concurrently fulfill accounting responsibilities including data entry of accounts payable/receivable, daily cash receipts, shipping, and receiving. Prepare and analyze budget requests and department expenditures. Process sales orders, purchase orders, and sales invoices. Aptitude for sales tax reports and sales tax audits.

- Perform month-end closing through journal entries; organize bank statements, weekly timesheets, labor reports, and online ADP/Intuit payroll processing.
- Coordinate employee benefits preparation and presentations through 401K programs.

GENOVA ASSOCIATION, Naperville, IL   1983 to 1990
Executive Secretary/Bookkeeper

Recruited as Executive Secretary to the General Manager to organize business records and filing systems, transcribe business correspondence, and maintain GM's daily schedule. Prepared agendas and reports for monthly meetings, including minutes. Performed time keeping, payroll, bank deposits, month-end closing of accounts, and preparation of monthly financial reports. Reconciled daily cash register receipts.

- Managed and maintained annual million-dollar budget, general accounts, and 50 club accounts.

TRAINING & COMPUTER SKILLS

Accounting Principles, ELM JUNIOR COLLEGE, Naperville, IL—1985
**Lotus 1-2-3, MS Office, WordPerfect, Simply Accounting, FoxPro Accounting, Quattro-Pro, and
Harvard Graphics**

Written By: Erin Kennedy
Font: Garamond

ERIC B. GRAY
7 Bermuda Court, Garden City, NY 11530
Home (516) 463-1343 • Cell (516) 235-0618
egray@aol.com

DECISIVE, ACCOMPLISHED, SENIOR-LEVEL OFFICE SERVICES PROFESSIONAL
Expertise in... Customer & Vendor Relations / Inventory Control / Deadline Management

---

PROFESSIONAL EXPERIENCE

Skatt & Mendelson LLP   New York, NY
(New York City-based real estate law firm with eight offices and more than 700 employees)
Mail Room Manager   June 1993–Present
Personnel Management
- Direct mailroom operations with 17 direct reports, including two coordinators and 15 staff employees.
- Hire, train and supervise all staff. Conduct annual performance and salary reviews.
- Define job responsibilities of staff and coordinate work-task scheduling.
- Draft and finalize departmental budget. Implement and follow through with cost-saving plans.
- Establish and maintain effective working relationships with employees, management, vendors and staff.
Inventory Control
- Serve as primary purchasing agent for office supplies, including firm letterhead, envelopes, business cards, paper, toner and general office supplies.
- Receive internal customer inquiries and facilitate placing approved orders.
- Acquire, distribute and store office supplies for New York headquarters location.
Shipping and Distribution
- Coordinate messenger staff for hand deliveries, including filing of court papers and patent documents.
- Coordinate shipment of documents and supplies to trial locations, including critical and time-sensitive daily courier service to trial teams.
- Supervise the swift collection and distribution of all outgoing postal mail and inter-office mail firm-wide.
- Ensure that courier deliveries, postal mail and inter-office mail from the firm's branches are correctly and efficiently processed and distributed.
- During deadline-intensive periods, assist staff in processing courier packages for shipment.
- Train evening staff to coordinate with late-night couriers for hand delivery of sensitive documents.

Accomplishments
- ➤ Instrumental in the smooth transition during a relocation of the entire department. (October 2000)
- ➤ Implemented e-mail system to order supplies for New York office with an improved turn-around delivery time of only two hours. New system saved money through improved inventory control. (October 2000)
- ➤ Implemented Pitney Bowes Arrival System which utilizes bar-code technology for greater efficiency in tracking incoming deliveries, including Federal Express, DHL, Airborne and UPS. (March 1998)
- ➤ Outlined cost-saving opportunities by eliminating overtime and varying shift start times. (2003-2004)
- ➤ Completed on-site training for Pitney Bowes CM900 mailing machine. (2002)

Track Record of Internal Promotions:
Manager of Mailroom & Inter-Office Mail	Promoted June 1993
Manager of Mailroom, Photocopy & Fax Departments	Promoted February 1989
Head Xerox Operator	Promoted September 1986
Xerox Operator	Promoted November 1985
Messenger	Hired June 1984

COMMUNITY SERVICE

Progressive Weona Civic Association–Current Member, President (1997–2000); Vice President (2001–2003)

Written By: Laura Berenson
Font: Tahoma

Cheryl G. Ross

12207 North Meridian, Norman, OK 73072
Residence: (405) 898-5645   c.g.ross@aol.com

OFFICE MANAGEMENT / BUSINESS ADMINISTRATION
Accounting, Project Coordination, and Performance Improvement

Highly motivated, well-organized, and hard-working professional with a record of accomplishment, improving business procedures that maximize productivity while reducing costs. Works well under pressure in support of company goals. Resourceful in troubleshooting problems and implementing innovative solutions. Communicates well with clients and co-workers at all levels. Excellent cash management skills.

Strengths include:
Computer Literacy / Office Administration / Cross-Functional Teamwork / Leadership
Client & Vendor Relations / Research & Analysis / Training / Data Management

SELECTED ACHIEVEMENTS

Accounting: Directed all accounting functions supporting $12 million project. Tracked all costs, purchases, cash flow, billings, and correspondence with owners on required project paperwork. Finished project on time and fully paid.

Leadership: Led creation of equipment tracking module to assist asset management decision process. Tracked labor, repair, and maintenance costs of old equipment to compare productivity and dollars spent. Helped management make future decisions to maintain old or purchase new equipment.

Process Improvement: Restructured job-cost tracking, allowing variance analysis in both costs and revenues. Results permitted timely changes in capturing lost revenues. Allowed estimators to more accurately bid performance of field and improve business revenues and profit margins.

Data Management: Developed method for allocation of administrative overhead to all construction project costs throughout the year. Taught other division heads how to utilize method. Created accurate picture of true project costs.

Vendor Relations: Avoided potential problems with subcontractors caused by slow payment. Maintained open lines of communication with subcontractors, informed them of problems, obtained required documentation to process payments, and notified them of anticipated payment dates. Built good vendor relations for future projects.

Training: Demonstrated exceptional ability to significantly raise the level of quality professionalism in accounting department. Taught employees how to cross check data on reports to verify accuracy and improve balancing subsidiary ledgers to the financial statements.

Computer Literacy: Assisted computer programmer to write cost-plus billing system. Coordinated input from five departments, consulted with Director of Finance, and worked with programmer to finish project ahead of schedule. Created new pricing tool that gave company a competitive edge in the marketplace.

Cheryl G. Ross – c.g.ross@aol.com   Page 2

PROFESSIONAL EXPERIENCE

Office Manager, **G.L. Stoner Contractors, Inc.**, Norman, OK, 1999 - 2006
- Managed all accounting functions including A/R, A/P, G/L, payroll, insurance, pension programs and cash receipts.
- Provided management with accurate and timely reports for decision making.
- Produced WIP schedules, improved collections, tracked job-costs, and monitored equipment usage.

Urig Paving Materials, Tulsa, OK, 1992 – 1999

Construction Administrator, 1993 - 1999
- Reconciled G/L for construction job costing and equipment to subsidiary ledgers.
- Developed new procedures and systems to improve accuracy and simplify reporting.

Job Cost Accountant, 1992 - 1993
- Tracked cash receipts for nine divisions.
- Calculated and recorded daily costs and revenues to individual projects.
- Maintained billings for customers, equipment usage, and subcontractor payments.
- Produced end-of-month aging and financial reports for corporate office.

Accounting Clerk, **Walsh Industries, Inc.**, Stillwater, OK, 1988 - 1992
- Prepared monthly billings, closings, cash receipts, spreadsheets, and job costs.
- Assisted programmer in development of cost-plus billings on CGC software.

Office Manager, **GM Mechanical, Inc.**, Langston, OK, 1986 - 1988
- Handled G/L, A/R, A/P, insurance, payroll, tax filings, pension, employee files, job costing records, computer operations, and cash receipts.

Pharmacy Technician
Mercy Hospital, Bartlesville, OK, 1984 - 1986
- Kept monthly records of supplies purchased throughout hospital.
- Charted and billed patients' daily medicine charges including the ER.
- Read doctor's orders, mixed IV's, filled drug cart, and delivered patients' medicine hourly to nurses.

EDUCATION and TRAINING

Bachelor of Science (BS), *Accounting*
OKLAHOMA STATE UNIVERSITY, Stillwater, OK

Associate of Science (AS), *Accounting*
NORTHERN OKLAHOMA COLLEGE, Stillwater, OK

Written By: Michael S. Davis
Font: Garamond

Chapter **7**

▶ **Resumes for**

Government Careers

Each and every industry and profession presents unique resume writing and design challenges. If you are interested in pursuing a career within the government, be certain to incorporate these important success factors:

ᛟ **Success Factor #1**

When writing your resume for a government position, carefully read the job posting to be sure that your resume explicitly answers all the requirements listed. Make sure you comply with the requirements for contact information, which will most likely be different and more detailed than on a private-sector resume.

ᛟ **Success Factor #2**

Be thorough and complete in documenting your education. In the private sector, it's not unusual to leave out dates of graduation and other details, but on resumes for government positions, the hiring agency will want to see a comprehensive list of degrees with graduation dates, plus any special training programs. Even if you didn't graduate, show college courses you completed.

ᛟ **Success Factor #3**

Make certain that your work history is listed in reverse chronological order, with complete details for the past 10 years. This may need to include employers' addresses and phone numbers, and the names of supervisors, if requested.

ᛟ **Success Factor #4**

If Key Skill Areas (KSAs) are part of the application, make sure to respond with narratives (stories) that clearly demonstrate the skills requested. Use the "CAR" format to describe the *Challenge* you faced, the *Actions* you took, and the measurable *Results* that demonstrate your mastery of the skill in question.

Keywords and Keyword Phrases

Keywords and keyword phrases are a critical component of every successful job seeker's resume. By using just one or two words, you're able to communicate a wealth of information about your skills, qualifications, and experience. What's more, keywords are the basis for resume-scanning technology and are therefore critical to any job seeker's campaign in today's electronic-based job search market. For more information on keywords, refer back to pages 17–19 in Chapter 1.

Following are the top 20 government keywords, some of which may reflect your skills and some of which may not be appropriate for you at this time. Use these words as the foundation for developing your own list of keywords on the Professional Keyword List form in Appendix B.

Top 20 Keywords

Briefings and Trainings

Budget Planning and Allocation

Congressional Affairs

Cross-Cultural Communications

Cultural Diversity

Foreign Government Relations

Governmental Affairs

Inter-Agency Relations

International Trade and Commerce

Legislative Affairs

Liaison Affairs

Lobbying

Press Relations and Media Affairs

Procurement and Acquisitions

Program Design and Management

Public Advocacy

Public Works

Regulatory Reporting

SEC Affairs

Zoning and Compliance

Following are some excellent examples of resumes for government careers.

Elizabeth M. Singh

| 1775 Grover Street | Home: 410-837-5555 |
| Baltimore, MD 21201 | lizsingh@verizon.net |

PUBLIC RELATIONS / PUBLIC INFORMATION OFFICER

- **Award-winning Public Health Information Officer with Bachelor's Degree in Journalism.** Track record of creating, editing and coordinating health information projects, website content, press releases, and press events, both independently and as team member for more than 20 years.

- **Web Content Manager.** Gained reputation as expert web content writer and editor after successfully collaborating on State Department website overhaul, as well as launch and rewrite of more than 25 sub-websites since 2004. Relied on by Webmaster to screen, organize, and write wide breadth of content.

- **Experienced communicator and public spokesperson.** Adept in clarifying and communicating complex topics in easy-to-understand written content and charts. Senior spokesperson for large state government department, with widespread media, intra-agency, and community relationships.

- **Consistently dedicated, meeting short deadlines while managing multiple projects.** Work well under pressure, formulating and/or editing written copy for high-level state government policymakers. Serve as communications liaison between State Commissioner, outside agencies and government officials, management and staff, community organizations, consumers, and media representatives.

AREAS OF EXCELLENCE

- Web Content Writing & Editing
- Copyediting & Proofreading
- Media & Community Relations
- Writing & Editing
- Press Releases
- Press Events
- Public Health Education
- Risk Communications
- Project Management

PROFESSIONAL EXPERIENCE

MARYLAND DEPT. OF HEALTH AND SENIOR SERVICES (MDDHSS), Baltimore, MD   1987 – present
Oversees public health and older-adult services statewide, including regulatory oversight of health care institutions. $5.4 billion agency with 3200 employees.

Public Information Officer / Senior Spokesperson & Web Content Manager
Cover diverse topics including public health and environmental services, senior services, health care policy and research, minority and multi-cultural health, and health-related aspects of terrorism. Subject matter expert for community cancer concerns, disease outbreaks, anthrax/bioterrorism and West Nile virus.

- **Web Project Management.** Co-led team that revamped DHSS website, in collaboration with Abernathy Consultants, to increase usability for consumers and showcase information, resources, and links. Created online survey to query website visitors on usage patterns, information requested, and needs.

- **Web Content and Web Policy Development.** Key contributor (organizing, writing, reviewing, and editing) to primary and secondary sub-sections of DHSS main website (at least 25 since 2004). Researched and developed new DHSS policy on web links. High-visibility projects included HealthLink, Bureau of Vital Statistics, Health-in-Schools, Community Health Centers, Education Campaign on Medicare Part D Drug Coverage, Patient Safety, Medical Milestones, and Cultural Competency.

- **Press Releases and Events.** Prepare press releases, briefings, confidential memos, and speeches, consulting with top policymakers, scientists, physicians, and Governor's Office. Organize press events that garner national, regional, and statewide coverage. Publicize wide-ranging public health issues including anti-tobacco initiatives and first major expansion of statewide Newborn Screening Program.

  Major press events for 2005: Hospital Performance Report, PAAD/Senior Gold Campaign, Minority Health Month, Cardiac Surgery Report, Discount Drug Program Expansion, and Bariatric Report.

Elizabeth M. Singh | Home: 410-837-5555 | lizsingh@verizon.net | **Page 2 of 2**

DHSS continued

- **Risk Communications.** Anticipate emerging media issues and advise Commissioner and key staff on response strategy. Collaborate with senior staff to prepare accurate responses, consistent with agency policy, to heavy volume of requests from state, national, and international organizations.

- **Health Information Project Management.** Given sole responsibility for high-visibility information projects, such as Cardiac Surgery Report Card, Managed Care Report Card, and web-based report on hospital fines. Collaborate with reporters on long-term, multi-part stories requiring special data runs and document requests. Associate Editor and Co-Author of Department Accomplishments Report.

MARYLAND DEPARTMENT OF EDUCATION, Baltimore, MD   1984 – 1987
Public Information Officer

- Spearheaded communications (press releases, press conferences/events) for Basic Skills Testing Program. Developed communications handbook adopted by school districts statewide. Authored Op-Ed articles and executive-level speeches, including annual budget testimony by Commissioner to Legislature.

NEWS REPORTER   1974 – 1984
Staff writer and reporter covering education, health, courts, and government affairs. Wrote for Gannett News Service, USA Today, The Press (Washington, DC) The News Enquirer (Norfolk, VA), The Associated Press (Cleveland, OH) and others. Received local news reporting awards.

EDUCATION & TRAINING

Bachelor of Arts, Journalism, University of Maryland, College Park, MD
Graduated Phi Beta Kappa with 3.88 GPA
Internship, Washington Bureau, Knight Newspapers (Bureau served The Free Press, The New York Inquirer, Chicago Herald, and others)

Ongoing Professional Development
Terrorism Incident Reporting Structure, FEMA, Washington, DC – 2006
TOBE 2005 (Top Officials Bioterrorism Exercise) – 2005
Maryland's Strategic National Stockpile Exercise – 2004
Risk Communications, Center for Risk Management, Washington, DC – 2003

Computer Skills: Windows XP, MS Office 2003 (Word, Excel, PowerPoint), Lotus Notes, Internet Research

PROFESSIONAL ASSOCIATIONS & AWARDS

Federal Web Content Managers Forum – Member; National Public Health Education Coalition – Member

☑ Team Award: 2005 Gold Award for Excellence in Public Health Communications
   National Public Health Education Coalition. Outsourced Information Campaigns for "Maryland's Rapid HIV-Testing Campaign." Key contributor to Rapid HIV-testing website.

☑ Team Award: 2005 Bronze Award for Excellence in Public Health Communications
   National Public Health Education Coalition. In-House, Thinking on Your Feet: Real-Time Risk Communications for "Small Pox – First Case in the U.S. in 15 Years."

Written By: Susan Guarneri
Font: Arial

CLARK JACOBS

432 Gillette Street • Southington, CT 09987 • (230) 634–5775 • cjacobs@aol.com

TOWN MANAGER

Offering 13 years of leadership experience in town government as an elected chief administrative and fiscal officer. Key contributor impacting operational, budgetary, staffing and resource needs throughout the municipality.

Extensive human resources and public speaking background. Effective communicator and team builder with planning, organizational and negotiation strengths as well as the ability to lead, reach consensus, establish goals and attain results. Additional business management experience in the private sector. Competencies include:

Management/Administration	Public/Private Sector Alliances
Fiscal Management/Budgeting	Economic Development
Project/Program Management	Staff Development/Empowerment

PROFESSIONAL QUALIFICATIONS

TOWN OF SOUTHINGTON, Southington, CT   1993 to Present

SELECTMAN

Administration/Management – Proactive executive providing strategic planning and leadership direction to diverse municipal departments as one of 3 elected board members governing the Town of Southington. As board member, direct town meetings, develop and oversee $10 million budget and administer various projects. Experience includes chairing Board of Selectmen for 3 years. Serve as Police Commissioner.

Human Resources – Authority for recruitment, promotion and supervision of town administrator, 10 department heads with up to 214 full- and part-time staff, as well as Department of Public Works and Police Department. Personnel functions also encompass recruitment, contract negotiations, benefits administration, employee relations and policy development/implementation.

Economic Development – Support strong public/private partnerships toward diversified growth and prosperity. Source and negotiate with businesses as well as secure agreements to retain and attract new businesses. Develop financial vehicles for public improvements.

Regulatory Affairs – Develop and manage relationships, as well as advocate for municipal affairs, with federal and state regulatory agencies, local business executives, congressional members and other legislators.

Public/Community Relations – Instrumental in enhancing Town's image and building consensus with all boards. Active participant in numerous annual community events; act as spokesperson with the media.

Contributions

- Turned around employee morale and productivity, instituted training and employee recognition programs and fostered interdepartmental cooperation, creating a positive work environment while restoring accountability and confidence in the administration. Municipality is recognized for having the "most-responsive and best-managed administrations statewide."

- Leader in the execution of several town revitalization projects, following failed attempts by prior boards:
  - $2.9 million renovations to Town Hall, Senior Center and Council on Aging
  - $5 million public safety complex
  - $1.3 million public library project with state library grant offsets of $200,000
  - $15 million sewer project with over $5 million secured in federal grant funding

- Personally negotiated Tax Incentive Financing (TIF) Agreements to retain and attract businesses.

- Effectively negotiated with the presidents of local companies to relocate their businesses back to Southington. Results led to construction of new manufacturing facility for 4 companies employing 550 people combined and an agreement to expand employee base.

- Spearheaded search for new providers and negotiated improved employee benefits program while avoiding any rate increase.

CLARK JACOBS - cjacobs@aol.com   Page 2

BUSINESS MANAGEMENT EXPERIENCE

MONROE & COMPANY, New York, NY   1992 to Present
(Global multibillion-dollar manufacturer)

DISTRICT MANAGER   1999 to Present
ACCOUNT MANAGER   1993 to 1999

Promoted to develop business plan and manage $23 million district that extends from the Northeast to Florida. Supervise 5 broker sales organizations.

Manage budgets, oversee and motivate the sales team, deliver sales presentations, and provide training on sales strategies, product knowledge, marketing programs and administrative policies/procedures.

Develop and implement sales and marketing programs. Interface with executives of multimillion-dollar corporations. Manage $3 million annual marketing/advertising budget, providing support to major customers.

Contributions

- Implemented successful sales/marketing programs that contributed to the district's growth and exceeded sales plan during last two trimesters in 2005 despite declining sales trend company-wide.
- Single-handedly transitioned the district from a direct sales force to a successful food broker network; efforts represent an entirely new direction for the company throughout territory.
- Elected to the Leadership Club in 1999 for consistently ranking among the top 10% in overall sales performance throughout company.
- Renegotiated marketing programs with major customers that increased sales and profits while achieving acceptable dollar spends.
- Succeeded in securing new authorizations, expanding existing accounts and opening key accounts generating substantial business volume.

EDUCATION / PROFESSIONAL DEVELOPMENT

BENTLEY COLLEGE, Bentley, VT
M.B.A., Finance, 1999
B.S., Business Administration, 1995

Continuing Education: Several seminars on municipal administration sponsored by Connecticut Municipal Association and Selectmen's Association

COMMUNITY AFFILIATIONS / LEADERSHIP

Selectmen's Association
Vice President, Southington Rotary Club
Chairman, Conservation Commission

Written By: Louise Garver
Font: Trebuchet MS

VANESSA D. BLACKSTONE
11400 Laurelwalk Drive
Laurel, MD 20708
Home (301) 953-7449 * Email vdb@cox.net

Social Security Number: 307-00-4233   Veterans' Preference: None   Citizenship: US
Federal Status: Budget Analyst, GS 12, June 2001–Present   Clearance: Secret (Active)

-----OBJECTIVE-----
Vacancy Announcement H-NWS-06110-MFW
National Oceanic and Atmospheric Administration, Program Analyst, GS-0343-13

-----PROFILE-----
Organized, energetic, and detail-oriented professional with over 9 years of progressive experience in the principles, methods, and systems of financial management programs and all areas of the budget cycle. Ability to multi-task and meet tight deadlines. Team player and skilled leader.

-----CORE COMPETENCIES-----
- **Budget Analysis:** Strong financial management skills and expertise in budget analysis. Extensive expertise in formulating and tracking annual operating budgets.
- **Planning and Management:** Expertise in working with senior financial managers to plan and implement budgets. Managed three employees over a 2-year period.
- **Regulatory Knowledge:** Comprehensive knowledge of the principles, concepts, laws, and regulations of performance budgeting for Office of Management and Budget (OMB), Department of Defense (DoD), and the Department of Treasury. Ability to review and interpret legislation that relates to Congressional budget actions.
- **Research/Data Analysis & Computer Expertise:** Adept at researching, compiling, analyzing, and tracking financial data. Highly proficient in developing, implementing, and maintaining Access databases. Proficient in MS Word, Excel, and PowerPoint.
- **Communication Skills:** A high degree of skill in the analysis and application of reasoning and conceptualization of financial/budgetary scenarios, resulting in the development of well-written documents and articulate presentations of strategies to address alternative solutions, justifications, and formulations.

-----PROFESSIONAL EXPERIENCE-----

Budget Analyst, GS-12
Tri-Care Management Activity, Falls Church, VA   June 2001–Present
Supervisor: Marge Jones, (703) 841-5533   40 hours per week
Ensure that program organizational goals and objectives are met through effective analysis, evaluation, and management of budgetary operations. Provide expertise in all areas of the budget cycle as follows:

Preparation
- Review and interpret legislation that affects the organization's budget.
- Ensure that Congressional budget actions comply with Congressional intent, Treasury Department guidelines, and DoD guidelines.
- Ensure that the Defense Finance Accounting Service official documentation is consistent to facilitate informed decisions by top-level management.

Formulation
- Conduct cost-benefit and trend analyses to determine if budget forecasting is accurate and reliable.
- Develop budget estimates and supporting documentation, including special exhibits.
- Analyze methodology for defining funding requirements.
- Identify potential problems and issues in proposed budget estimates.

- Review and edit narrative and statistical budgetary material for internal and external agency responses.
- Assessed and streamlined processes and procedures using various qualitative and quantitative tools for travel, supplies, facilities, telecommunications, contracting, and training programs resulting in $75,000 savings to the Government.
- Assisted in developing budget estimates and supporting documentation for the President's budget and budget estimate submissions, including special exhibits.

Justification
- Develop details and background documentation for use in presenting and justifying major budget estimates.
- Identify potential problems and issues in proposed budget estimates.
- Analyze estimates and make revisions to update program data for proposed obligations.
- Prepare background information for exhibits used in briefing key management officials appearing before Congressional committees.

Execution
- Compile monthly and quarterly reports to ensure consistency with Defense Finance and Accounting Service office reports and OMB Spend Plans.
- Maintain execution appropriation controls that reflect the status of budget/fund expenditures.
- Use the Program Budget Accounting System to manage and facilitate funds utilization controls. Determine effectiveness and make recommendations when necessary.
- Maintain and update reconciliation workbooks to facilitate the decision-making process for top-level management.
- Issue and reprogram funding authorization documents to numerous components with research and development, procurement, and operations and maintenance appropriations.
- Analyze prior year funds to explain current fund status.
- Provide current program analysis of the Management Activities Budget Accounting Group (BAG).
- Establish effective controls for funds utilization in accordance with organization and management operation requirements.

Budget Analyst, GS-11
Ballistic Missile Defense Organization, Arlington, VA   December 1998–June 2001
Supervisor: Jonathan Spriggs, (703) 841-4110   40 hours per week
Analyzed and evaluated budget operations for the Ballistic Missile Defense Organization to ensure that established organizational goals and objectives were met. Supervised three employees over a 2-year period. Provided expertise in all areas of the budget cycle.

Budget Assistant, GS-8
Ballistic Missile Defense Organization, Arlington, VA   May 1996–December 1998
Supervisor: Mildred Coates, (703) 882-3100   40 hours per week
Performed a variety of budgetary tasks relating to the execution and formulation of the overall budget program in association with the Defense Planning Programming and Budgeting Systems for the management operations of the Ballistic Missile Defense Organization. Analytical methods used for reasoning and conceptualization were a result of on-the-job training and formal education.
- Independently created, edited, updated, and maintained a myriad of spreadsheets, graphs, databases, and reports using general query languages to manipulate data from various applications such as Impromptu, Manpower, Personnel, and MS Office.
- Developed and provided recommendations and alternative solutions to determine funding needs.
- Determined if budget forecasts were accurate and reliable in accordance with DoD financial management policies, directives, instructions, and regulations and with DoD Federal Acquisition and Congressional budget processes.

Vanessa D. Blackstone
Vacancy Announcement H-NWS-06110-MFW

Page 3 of 3

Secretary, GS-7
Ballistic Missile Defense Organization, Washington, DC
Supervisor: Maury Matthews, (202) 399-8100

August 1995–May 1996
40 hours per week

Worked directly with the organization's Budget Analysts to gather, assemble, and analyze facts, draw preliminary conclusions, and devise solutions to various budgetary problems. Used acquired skills from both formal education and on-the-job training to develop and manage briefings and to prepare statistical, narrative, and other written communications.

- Independently created, edited, updated, and maintained a myriad of spreadsheets, graphs, databases, and reports using general query languages to manipulate data from various applications such as Impromptu, Manpower, Personnel, Harvard Graphics, and MS Office.
- Researched various DoD, non-DoD, and organizational resources for administrative requirements that affected the organization's budget.
- Consolidated budget estimates from internal program offices and adjusted budget amounts to reflect changes.
- Prepared recurring reports on account balances within the organization.

-----EDUCATION-----

B.A., December 2005
University of Phoenix, Phoenix, AZ
Major: Business Administration
Minor: Finance
Semester Credit Hours Earned: 120
Relevant Courses: Accounting, Statistics, Banking & Finance, Economics, Reasoning, International Economics, Marketing, and Management

High School Diploma, June 1987
Bowie High School, Bowie, MD

-----OTHER QUALIFICATIONS-----

Training Courses
Executive Leadership Program – USDA Graduate School, 2001
Certificate, Defense Planning, Programming, and Budgeting Systems (PPBS) – USDA Graduate School, 2000
Governmental Financial Management and Control – Management Concepts, Inc., 1997
Certificate, Budget Execution – USDA Graduate School, 1996

Skills
Microsoft Office Suite – MS Word, Excel, PowerPoint, and Access
Defense Planning Programming and Budgeting System (PPBS)
Program Budget Accounting System
Peachtree Accounting

Awards
Cash Awards for database resulting in Government savings – created tracking/reconciliation database for travel and training programs, resulting in $75,000 savings to the Government, 1999
Outstanding Performance – quality step increases and/or cash awards, 1993–2001
Letters of Appreciation, 1995–1999

Written By: Marcia A. Baker
Font: Garamond

CONFIDENTIAL   Ready to relocate
Vacancy Announcement 10-55

Katherine Shore

CMR 431 Box 672 APO AE 09175
✉katherine.shore@hq.3bde.army.mil – ☎011.49.5555.300000 (office) – 011.49.66666.500000 (home)

SSN: 555-55-5555   Highest Federal Civilian Grade Held: GS-5
Citizenship: United States of America   Current Security Clearance: TOP SECRET/ SCI
Veteran's Preference: 5 points

WHAT I OFFER UNITED STATES ARMY INTELLIGENCE AND SECURITY COMMAND AS YOUR NEWEST INTELLIGENCE SPECIALIST (OPERATIONS)

❏ The expertise to do intelligence analysis that users see as **critical to** their **counterintelligence operations and investigations,**

❏ The vision to help users **translate data into information** they can use, almost intuitively, to support their missions very well,

❏ The experience to move from **new concepts to proven "best practices"** in intelligence analysis and support,

❏ The skill to move quickly and seamlessly from providing intelligence analysis products at every level **from tactical to strategic,** and

❏ The confidence to go beyond just new capabilities to **train others to use them** as well as I can.

RECENT AND RELEVANT WORK HISTORY WITH EXAMPLES OF PROBLEMS SOLVED

❏ **Senior Counterintelligence Computer Forensic Analyst,** Crow Associates, 43rd Signal Analysis Activity and 39th Technical Support Element   Aug 2000 – Present
Crow Associates is a wholly owned subsidiary of Information and Infrastructure Technologies serving customers across North America, Europe, and Asia.

The administrative information you requested about this position

Salary: ~$88,000 per year   Hours per week: 45+
Employer's name and address: Supervisor's name and phone number:
Crow Associates, 4223 Morningside Dr. Ms. Janice Corinth, DSN 555.4444
Reston, VA 20100

What my responsibilities are:

I do extensive, **highly classified forensic analysis** for my primary customer: the US Army 39th Military Intelligence Group Technical Support Element. I also give them the **advanced technical guidance** they need every day to support their missions, including very **sensitive investigations and deployments.** My work spans every aspect of **software, hardware, and LAN security,** including updating and installing these components. In addition, I make contributions that help **US and allied law enforcement** and **intelligence agencies** reach their goals. I must also be completely current on any new forensic technology as well as the ever-changing regulations and laws that touch on my field. **Nearly all my work is** at or above **SECRET** because it helps **analyze** the **capabilities** and intentions **of foreign intelligence services and terrorist organizations.**

CONFIDENTIAL   *More indicators of potential ...*

Examples of contributions I've made (described within the tight restrictions that apply to classified information)**:**

Met a daunting challenge as soon as I arrived: we had one computer — and no standard operating procedures, no network, no methodology, no experienced staff, only a limited budget, and a rapidly growing backlog of critical projects. **Did it all**, from writing the required vendor requests for proposals to producing all our written procedures, to finding, recruiting, training, and retaining our staff. *Outcomes:* **Transformed a general concept into** a fully functioning, **critical mission capability. Turnaround** times to meet our customers' needs **dropped from months to** just a few **weeks.** Since customers no longer had to outsource this function, we **saved two man-years** of labor costs by the end of the first year.

Rationalized the varied and sometimes **incompatible formats** our customers used to document their requirements. By speaking with users, fashioned a compromise that serves them well and allows us to **build in speed, efficiency**, and **effectiveness.** *Outcomes:* Soon, we were translating raw data into information our customers could use almost intuitively. Our customers got **much better products much faster.** Thanks to my protocols, **users** now can **do trend analysis better** and **faster** than ever before.

Accelerated the flow of **critical information** and **hedged against liability** at the same time. Educated our staff and users about the benefits of a strong chain of evidence custody; then, designed, coordinated, and implemented the new system that got our work to headquarters. *Outcomes:* Users had **complete confidence** their hard-won evidence would **hold up in court.** My new system made it faster and safer to get evidence to those who needed it.

Relieved key planning concerns that computer forensics was "too hard to do." Once I analyzed what they needed, I persuaded the operations officer to grant me a training day. *Outcomes:* My briefings and demos showed what computer forensics is, how it works, and why it's valuable. As operational success rose, I used what customers found to **tailor my training even more closely to their needs.**

Took the initiative to draft a counterintelligence special operational concept (CISOC). That document tied priority intelligence requirements to immediate force protection measures. I **made it easy to use** by providing computer support. *Outcomes:* Even recognized experts saw the **value** of my work immediately.

☐ Internet Web Designer, Crowne Creations, Parke, Maryland   Aug 1999 – Jun 2000
This very small, independent company designed websites for small businesses.

The administrative information you requested about this position

Salary: Unpaid internship   Hours per week: 40
Employer's name and address: Supervisor's name and phone number:
vansantcreations.com   William Crowne, 410.555.5555

What my responsibilities were:

I updated websites using HTML and JavaScript programming.

Katherine Shore   **Intelligence Specialist (Operations)**   011.49.6666.500000

❏ **Assistant Security Manager** *with additional duties as* Administrative Assistant, Special
Operations Command Pacific, Camp H.M. Smith   1995 – 1998
*Our organization supported joint and combined operations in the Pacific area of responsibility, one of
the largest geographic regions assigned to any US command.*

The administrative information you requested about this position

Salary: approximately $25,000 per year (GS-5)   Hours per week: 40

Employer's name and address: Supervisor's name and phone number:
Operations Command, Pacific Director   Mack Sherman, 808.555.5555
of Operations, Camp Smith, Hawaii

What my responsibilities were:

I wrote, implemented, and maintained the administrative security instructions for our
Operations Directorate. My work included inspecting the physical security of our offices,
forwarding results of what I found in comprehensive written reports, and making
recommendations to ensure we maintained the best security practices.

Examples of contributions made:

I contributed in two major areas. First, at the staff level, I overhauled the administrative
security instructions for our directorate, found a way to track our incoming messages while
increasing security. Second, I trained and helped professionally develop staff.

TRAINING

❏ **Encase Forensic Software Training**, Martins Software, Inc., 224 hours   2001 – 2005
Advanced forensic methods including duplicating and processing evidence using forensically
sound methods, preparing evidence for court, and acquiring and analyzing evidence including
use of keyword searches, Windows NT registry signature and file analysis, verification of
evidence, deleted or encrypted email and chat retrieval, encryption, recovering NTFS file
system artifacts such as swap files, EFS files, registry values, file slack, and spooler files, deleted
files, and Internet history logs.

❏ **Defense Computer Investigations Training Program**, Department of Defense, Washington,
DC

2001, 2002, 2004

Introduction to Networking and Computer Hardware (80 hours): Configuring and
installing hardware and software components, network topologies, logical and physical
components to networks, and OS configuration in Windows and Linux environments.

Forensics Examiners Course (160 hours): Evidence handling, incident response, media
verification procedures and tools, data concealment (such as looking for hidden data in
alternate data streams, hidden entries in the registry, encryption, and cluster manipulation),
forensic utilities and detailed analysis, setup and maintenance of forensic workstations,
using correct terminology in an analysis report, techniques to explain evidence in a court of
law, chain of custody, and related legal issues.

C O N F I D E N T I A L   Vacancy Announcement number: 10-55

Katherine Shore   **Intelligence Specialist (Operations)**   011.49.6666.500000

EDUCATION

☐ BS, **Computer Information Technology,** Mountainside University, Boise, Idaho   Dec 2005
Graduated with Distinction

☐ **Computer Programming and Operations,** Maximum Technical Training Center, Baltimore, Maryland   2000

APPLICABLE CERTIFICATIONS

☐ EnCase Certified Examiner   2005
Scored a 96 on this 174-question examination.

☐ CompTia Network+   2002
Certifies me as network support and administration professional.

FORENSIC IT SKILLS

☐ **Expert in computer forensic analysis suites** including **networking and intrusion detection** software, DOS-based **data recovery tools,** utilities to include **Encase Forensic Edition V4 and V5,** and **Windows Forensic Toolkit Analyst Notebook.**

☐ Comfortable with HTML, JavaScript, Word, Excel, PowerPoint, Access, advanced Internet search protocols, **installing, configuring, and troubleshooting LANs.**

☐ Working knowledge of DOS, Windows 9x, 2000, NT, UNIX, Solaris operating systems.

PROFESSIONAL RECOGNITION (EXCLUDING END-OF-TOUR DECORATIONS)

☐ Joint Service Achievement Medal, Special Operations Command, Pacific   Dec 1998
For my work supporting three JCS Joint Deployments.

☐ Commendation, Special Operations Command, Pacific   Dec 1998
For building a program that increased message security.

☐ Army Commendation Medal (1 OLC), Walter Reed Army Hospital   Sep 1993
For my work in support of a major conference and my work as NCOIC.

☐ Army Commendation Medal, Walter Reed Army Hospital   Jan 1993
For my work in combat stress training in support of Desert Storm

PROFESSIONAL AFFILIATIONS

☐ Member, **High Technology Crime Investigation Association**   2002 – Present

PROFESSIONAL PUBLICATIONS

☐ Shore, Katherine, "Computer Forensics Forecast," Information Security Compilation, http://www.isccc.org/ccr/   2001

C O N F I D E N T I A L   Page 4 of 4

Written By: Don Orlando
Font: Book Antiqua

Chapter 8

▶ Resumes for

Healthcare and Social Service Careers

Each and every industry and profession presents unique resume writing and design challenges. If you are interested in pursuing a career in the healthcare or social services fields, be certain to incorporate these important success factors:

☕ Success Factor #1

Show your diverse experience by including the different types of patients/consumers you have treated or served. Including this information demonstrates your versatility and sensitivity to individuals with varying needs.

☕ Success Factor #2

Be sure to mention what procedures you can perform or equipment you can operate. Don't assume that your job title equates to the same job duties in a new organization. By documenting your skills, you ensure that your next employer will see what you can do and how you can add value to their company.

☕ Success Factor #3

List your credentials right at the top of the resume. Include either the appropriate initials after your name, or spell out your licenses or certifications and place them right after your contact information. Identifying the types of positions you're eligible for will make it much easier for HR to direct your resume to the correct hiring authority.

☕ Success Factor #4

Highlight your participation in any research projects or introduction of new procedures or techniques. Even though you may believe your role was relatively minor, your exposure to leading-edge treatments and protocols could be a point of interest for a new employer.

Keywords and Keyword Phrases

Keywords and keyword phrases are a critical component of every successful job seeker's resume. By using just one or two words, you're able to communicate a wealth of information about your skills, qualifications, and experience. What's more, keywords are the basis for resume-scanning technology and are therefore critical to any job seeker's campaign in today's electronic-based job search market. For more information on keywords, refer back to pages 17–19 in Chapter 1.

Following are the top 20 healthcare and social service keywords, some of which may reflect your skills and some of which may not be appropriate for you at this time. Use these words as the foundation for developing your own list of keywords on the Professional Keyword List form in Appendix B.

Top 20 Keywords

Ambulatory Care	Human Services
Behavior Modification	Inpatient and Outpatient Care
Case Management	Insurance Administration
Chronic Care	Integrated Service Delivery
Client Advocacy	Patient/Client Relations
Community Outreach	Practice Management
Crisis Intervention	Protective Services
Diagnostic Evaluation and Intervention	Regulatory Affairs and Reporting
Healthcare Administration	Risk Management
Healthcare Delivery	Vocational Rehabilitation

Following are some excellent examples of resumes for careers in the healthcare and social service fields.

HOLLY ZIMMERMAN, RN, MSN, FNP, CEN

714 Delaware Street   (419) 656-8248 (Home / Cell)
Oregon, Ohio 43616   HZimmer@grafixservices.com

PROFESSIONAL CREDENTIALS

- **Registered Nurse (RN) License:** State of Ohio, 1999–Present
- **Family Nurse Practitioner (FNP):** Board Certification, American Nurses Credentialing Center, 2004
- **Certified Emergency Nurse (CEN):** Through August 2006
- **Sexual Assault Nurse Examiner (SANE):** 2002–Present
- **Trauma Nursing Care Coordinator (TNCC):** Through December 2007
- **Advanced Cardiac Life Support (ACLS) Certification:** Through September 2007
- **Pediatric Advanced Life Support (PALS) Certification:** Through September 2008

PROFESSIONAL EXPERIENCE

St. Adelbert Health System, Toledo, Ohio
December 2003–Present
RN, EMERGENCY DEPARTMENT
- *Emergency patient care and treatment* in trauma setting with pediatrics commitment. Collaborate with physicians, nurses, trauma team, technicians, and therapists in meeting standards and goals.
- *Expertise:* Identify complex health problems, multi-system injuries, and massive complications.

College Hospital Health Alliance, Toledo, Ohio
October 2003–Present
RN/SANE, EMERGENCY DEPARTMENT
- *Comprehensive care* for sexual-assault survivors.
- *Forensics:* Conduct examinations, collect evidence, and provide expert testimony as needed.

Rivershore Hospital, Toledo, Ohio
June 1999–October 2003
STAFF RN, TRAUMA CENTER
- *Emergency care*, pediatrics to geriatrics, in Level-I trauma center.
- *Sexual-assault patient care:* Handled exams and evidence-collection; provided counseling / support.

EDUCATION

Master of Science Degree, Nursing (MSN), Nurse Practitioner, *The University of Toledo*, Toledo, Ohio
December 2003

Bachelor of Science Degree (BSN), Nursing, *The University of Michigan*, Ann Arbor, Michigan
June 1999

PROFESSIONAL ASSOCIATIONS

- **Emergency Nurses Association**
- **International Association of Forensic Nurses**

Written By: Lee Anne Grundish
Font: Book Antiqua

JANE MORRISON

1113 Garland Drive
Denton, Texas 36209
940/329-2979 / janemo@prodigy.net

Certified Registered Nurse Anesthetist

KEY STRENGTHS AND EXPERIENCE

- Clinically competent, with proven success in high-stress situations.
- Patient- and task-focused.
- Enjoy a spirit of cooperation with all care providers.

CRNA

- Over ten years' experience in leading facilities in Texas and Louisiana providing anesthesia to all classes of surgical patients.
- Extensive knowledge of ASA Class 3 and 4 patients involving invasive and TEE monitoring skills.
- Proficient in administering anesthesia for cardiac thoracic, vascular, neuro, renal transplants, GU, ophthalmic, orthopedic, and ENT cases.
- Experienced in regional anesthesia techniques including spinal and ankle blocks, fem-sciatic blocks, and management of cervical plexus blocks for carotids.
- Active participating member of code response team, frequently supervising CPR.
- Skilled in difficult airway techniques such as fiberoptic scope, intubating LMAs, Trachlight, and jet ventilation.

RN

- Two years in neonatal intensive care in a university setting.
- Circulating Core Leader and interim Head Nurse.
- Assisted in resuscitative procedures.
- Managed epidurals as labor and delivery nurse.
- As OR nurse, advanced staff awareness of procedures, scheduling, cost containment, productivity, and time management.
- Experience training new staff in policy and procedures.

PROFESSIONAL CERTIFICATIONS

Registered Nurse Anesthetist
Texas RN License
Louisiana RN License
Advanced Cardiac Life Support
Basic and Advanced Cardiac Life Support

PROFESSIONAL ASSOCIATIONS

Member AANA

EDUCATION

Southern Methodist University, Dallas, TX
Masters Nurse Anesthesia, 1995
B.S., Nursing, 1979

Delgado Community College, New Orleans
Associate Degree, Nursing, 1975

Continuing:　University of Dallas, Texas
Statistics Course, Summer 1992

Texas Woman's University, Denton
General Math/Science Courses, 1985-86

PROFESSIONAL EXPERIENCE

2003 – Present　**CRNA PRN**—Baylor University Medical Center, Dallas, TX

1996 – 2003　**CRNA**—Dallas VA Hospital, Dallas, TX

1995 – 1996　**CRNA**—Anesthesia Services, PC, Austin, TX

1984 – 1994　**Core Leader/Surgical Unit**—Denton Regional Medical Center, Denton, TX

1982 – 1984　**Staff Nurse/Neo-Natal Critical Care Unit**—Kindred Hospital, New Orleans, LA

1976 – 1982　**Staff Nurse/Surgical Unit**—Children's Orthopedic Hospital, New Orleans, LA

1975 – 1976　**Staff Nurse/Obstetric Unit**—Medical Center Southwest Louisiana, Lafayette, LA

Written By: Marilyn McAdams
Font: Bookman Old Style

SARAH O'RIELLY
131 Mill St. • Canton, OH 44718
330.305.1693 • sorielly@aol.com

PERIOPERATIVE NURSE MANAGER

Outstanding training, staffing and management of operating room nurses utilizing 20+ years of nursing and training experience in hospital, home health and primary care environments. Consistently successful in motivating and leading team members to top performance. Extensive qualifications in sales, marketing, and lecturing in the medical field. Excellent verbal and written skills.

PROFESSIONAL EXPERIENCE

St. Vincent's Charity Hospital, Cleveland, OH   2002 to Present
PERIOPERATIVE NURSE AND MANAGER
Manage two operating rooms and all aspects of pre-operative care through surgery, scrubbing and circulation. Follow-up in recovery for plastic, reconstructive, hand, orthopedic, ENT and general surgery. Conduct instrument processing and equipment repair as well as medication inventory and ordering. Perform chart audits for quarterly accreditation.
- Instituted dictation follow through of surgeons; setting up dictation templates for surgeons to aid in chart completion.
- Supervise clinical studies and conduct post-operative follow-ups for FDA study.

US Army and Army Reserves, Canton, OH   1972 to Present
LTC OFFICER
Accountable for Operating Room and Central Supply of support hospital. Manage schedule, staff, supply ordering and inventory for 150 combat personnel during war games. Analyze and troubleshoot problems in emergency setting. Train scrub technicians and assign personnel.
- Instituted new requirements for faster mobilization per global military plan of a new combat support hospital.
- Negotiated trades of services with other sections.
- Computerized support hospital's supply ordering and inventory system.

Akron General Medical Center, Akron, OH   2000 to 2002
OPERATING ROOM NURSE
Assisted as operating nurse in plastic, podiatry, orthopedic, urology and ophthalmology surgeries. Scheduled surgeries and aided in pre- and post-operative care and education to patients and their families. Negotiated in instrumentation conflict and acted as liaison for surgery center. Functioned as team nurse assessing needs of center and its ability to increase the flow of patient movement for on-time surgery.
- Appointed Head of Charts Audits within the unit for Joint Commission on Accreditation of Healthcare Organizations (JCAHO) inspections.
- Elected to assume Safety Officer role, primarily performing scheduled documentation maintenance checks.

SARAH O'RIELLY, Pg. 2
330.305.1693 • sorielly@aol.com

Summa Health System, Akron, OH   1999 to 2000
OPERATING ROOM STAFF NURSE
Brought on board as an operating room scrub nurse and circulated serving all areas of general surgery, plastic, vascular, orthopedic, urology and ophthalmology departments. Monitored and recorded all patient condition changes, treatments and concerns. Assisted physicians during simple and complex procedures, and provided pre- and post-operative patient care.

Happy Home Health Company Akron, OH   1996 to 1999
MARKETING MANAGER/ ACCOUNT REPRESENTATIVE
Hired to improve and increase customer service for home health and hospice care environments. Educated and pre-evaluated hospice patients and their families. Promoted to Marketing Manager through regularly delivering nursing care for ventilator-dependent and quadriplegic clients. Retained and developed new markets, working with hospitals, physical therapy establishments and several local retirement centers.
- Surpassed individual Account Representative annual marketing quota by 200%.

EARLY CAREER

Fast-tracked through college, early career and continued training while establishing strong and sustainable work ethics and gaining a reputation as an inspired and strong leader. Provided support as Army reservist and gained experience as a sales representative, nurse, consultant, editor and teacher in the medical field. Developed extensive computer and verbal skills.

EDUCATION AND TRAINING

OHIO STATE UNIVERSITY, Columbus, OH
BA, Nursing
Registered Nurse

Certifications

Perioperative Nursing School, Head Nurse Management, War College, Advanced Life Support, Emergency Trauma Life Support, Ballistic Trauma Support, Combat Casualty Care

Written By: Kris Plantrich
Font: Tahoma

Rebecca Boyd-Tillis, RN

282 Saint James Circle
Apartment #10 – C
Kingstown, SC 45882

rebtillis5@comcast.net

(445) 488–0402 (Work)
(447) 456–3937 (Cell)
(445) 488–2621 (Home)

OBJECTIVE

A position in utilization review / case management with particular interest in quality assurance.

QUALIFICATIONS

- RN with BSN degree and eight years of clinical nursing experience in acute care settings.
- Involved in all phases of health care delivery, admission assessments, initiation, and implementation of care plans, discharge planning, and home care.
- Well-established, stalwart professional background in medical, surgical, and cardiac nursing.
- Extensive knowledge and experience in utilization and case management.
- Excellent verbal and written communication skills; a proven, highly competent manager.

EXPERIENCE

Haverford Health Care of Newton County, Newton, NC
RN Case Manager, 2002 – present
- Assess patients and develop plans of care in accordance with benefit guidelines.
- Coordinate and monitor home care and other interventions to ensure quality and cost effectiveness.
- Identify and provide appropriate services to patients at risk with focus on frail elderly and catastrophically ill.
- Collaborate actively with physicians, providers, and members to develop, evaluate, and document care planning.
- Generate and file cost-benefit analyses to track effectiveness of services.

Wickfield Presbyterian Hospital, Wickfield, NC
Continuing Care Coordinator / Utilization Management, 2001 – 2002
- Charted review of Medicare patients for appropriateness of admission and proper utilization of hospital resources.
- Reviewed third-party payer admissions, determining medical necessity based upon payer guidelines.
- Utilized knowledge of medical guidelines and current state UR regulations.
- Responded to third party payer denials and initiated written appeals.
- Provided education to nursing staff and physicians regarding impact of third-party payer practices within hospital environment.
- Assisted in gathering data, compiling length of stay, and coordinating the discharge planning process.

Staff RN, Medical / Surgical / Telemetry Floor, 2000 – 2001
- Initiated, evaluated, and reviewed individual patient care plans.
- Competently managed nurse rotations and late substitutions.
- Coordinated patient care on 24-bed medical / surgical / telemetry floor.
- Disseminated patient information to appropriate personnel.
- Involved in performance improvement committee and development of standards of practice.
- Encompassed neurological, medical, surgical, and cardiac nursing in a critical-care setting.

Rebecca Boyd–Tillis, RN   ~~~~   Tel: (445) 488–2621   ~~~~   Page Two

OTHER RELATED EXPERIENCE

White Plains Hospital Medical Center, White Plains, NY
Volunteer to RN Staff, Telemetry Cardiac Step-Down Floor

Med-Pool Personnel, Syracuse, NY

City Hospital, Syracuse, NY
Temporary Staff, Medical Telemetry Floor

ALTA GROUP Life and Health Insurance, Dover, New Jersey
Group Claims Processor

EDUCATION

Long Island College of Nursing, Long Island, NY
Bachelor of Science in Nursing, 2000

<u>Professional Development:</u>

Althea Williams Hospital, Bristol, Long Island
Seminars: Case Management, Managed Care, Ethical Health Care Issues, 2003 – 2004

White Plains Hospital, White Plains, New York
EKG 1 & 2, 2002 – 2003

Wickfield County Hospital, Wickfield, NC
Preceptor Program, 2001

LICENSURE

Professional Nurse Licensure, New York State – RN 18872 – 06
Professional Nurse Licensure, North Carolina State – RN 9967 – 06

CERTIFICATION

Inter-Hospital Coronary Care for RN's, 2001 – Present
Interqual Certified Utilization Review Professional, 2000 – Present

AFFILIATIONS

National Registered Nurses Association
Adelphi Phoenix Women's Healthcare Alliance
Acute Care Group, Inc. – New York State
City Hospitals for Excellence in Care – Unified Presence, CHEC-UP
AllCity Healthcare Resource Association of Newton, NC

---

*Nurse Rebecca Boyd-Tillis has proven her professional and personal integrity in all that she has
accomplished at Haverford Health Care. We are fortunate to have her on our team!*

– Hester G. Schramm, VP, Human Resources/Administration

Written By: Edward Turilli
Font: Times New Roman

PAULINE L. HARRIS, CRC

32 Oak Drive
Buffalo, New York 14223
Phone (716) 555-6945 / plharris24@yahoo.com

OBJECTIVE

Position in the mental health and human services field, utilizing solid training and experience in rehabilitation counseling and case management.

CERTIFICATION

Certified Rehabilitation Counselor (CRC) / Qualified Health Professional (QHP)

EDUCATION

State University of New York at Buffalo
Master of Science in Rehabilitation Counseling, 1998
Bachelor of Science in Office Administration, 1994

Professional Development:
More than 125 CEU credits in the rehabilitation field. Recent training in Vocational Testing of the Learning Disabled Population and Grief Counseling.

QUALIFICATIONS

- Successfully manage large caseloads of dually-diagnosed populations, including MR/DD, MICA, physically disabled, and learning disabled.
- Develop and implement effective programs for individuals with chemical dependency, mental illness, or history of incarceration.
- Utilize knowledge of vocational and educational assessment instruments, including MESA, VALPAR & McCarron Dial, Strong, MBTI, PIAT, and WRAT.
- Use effective communication skills and familiarity with area agencies and community health systems to provide linkages and advocate for clients.

PROFESSIONAL EXPERIENCE

1998-Present

New Dawn Health Services, Buffalo and Tonawanda, New York
Senior Vocational Counselor/Testing Specialist (2003-Present)

Perform thorough situational assessments and test clients' problem-solving skills, clerical aptitude, and academic knowledge. Facilitate job search workshops, job readiness groups, and job clubs/support groups. Coordinate and monitor clients' progress and participation in rehabilitation services. Coordinate case conferences with VESID counselors.
★ Initiated and developed highly successful Niagara Falls vocational program.
★ Identified need and implemented work readiness groups for area sheltered workshops.

Senior Mental Health Counselor (1998-2003)

Provided comprehensive individual and group counseling to diverse disadvantaged populations, with emphasis on programs for chronically mentally ill and managed-care clients. Integrated services, including case management, daily living skills, socialization, medication management, and behavior modification.
★ Maintained 98% compliance rate in utilization review and documentation.
★ Received Special Achievement Awards for dealing with volatile and difficult cases.

1997-1998

Goodwill Industries, Rehabilitation Department, Buffalo, New York
Case Manager Internship

Provided support, direction, and evaluation to clients in work-adjustment training programs. Co-facilitated work readiness groups.

1995-1996

Erie County Medical Center, Rehabilitation Medicine, Buffalo, New York
Volunteer Assistant to VESID

Assisted clients with vocational testing. Participated in home visits for severely disabled clients to determine eligibility for State programs.

Written By: Freddie Cheek
Font: Garamond

SHARON GOLDSMITH

3 John Street ◆ Stewartsville, NJ 08886 ◆ 908-479-6200 ◆ sgoldsmith@aol.com

Credentialed therapist with demonstrated counseling expertise, solid foundations in various therapeutic techniques, and a keen passion for helping troubled individuals achieve higher levels of well-being.

SUMMARY OF QUALIFICATIONS

- Well-regarded therapist with master's degree in counseling, NCC certificate, and more than eight years of practical experience in the mental health field.
- Highly effective therapist with skill in individual, family, and group therapy. Known for solid understanding of various therapies and strong knowledge of when to apply them.
- Extensively trained in the use of dialectical behavioral therapy in treating patients with borderline personality disorders, substance abuse problems, and eating disorders. Certified in the application of Gestalt therapeutic methods.
- Proven record of success in working with broad range of populations, including tough, court-ordered, and prison system cases. Unflappable therapist who combines a compassionate approach with a pointed style to help patients achieve goals.
- Successful in establishing rapport with diverse groups of people while building confidence and respect. A trusted advocate who excels in crisis situations.

PROFESSIONAL EXPERIENCE

NEW BEGINNING, Phoenix, AZ   1996 to 2006
Counselor (1999 to 2006)
Provided out-patient behavioral counseling services to indigent and court-appointed clients in county mental health care system. Supervised three case managers while conducting assessments, developing treatment plans, and conducting short-term counseling and group sessions.

- Established record of success in assessing needs, developing plans, and managing the delivery of services to reach patient goals. Developed compassionate, but challenging, style that proved highly effective in gaining the attention of patients and mobilizing them to action.
- Effectively led case managers, building cohesive team that worked cooperatively to maximize effectiveness in delivering services.
- Gained training in dialectical behavioral therapy (DBT), a model that seeks to reduce costs for treating behavioral problems by focusing on mindfulness, interpersonal effectiveness, stress tolerance, and emotional regulation. Helped launch DBTR model in clinic, one of the pioneers in DBT therapy.
- Recognized for ability to defuse and de-escalate crisis situations; frequently called upon to intervene with suicidal and at-risk patients.
- Intervened to champion patients when no one else believed in them. For example, played instrumental role in the rehabilitation of an older patient whose likely next step was prison.
- Developed effective programs to equip family members with information and tools that enabled them to continue treatments and handle future crises on their own.

Social Worker (1996 to 1999)
Provided in-patient critical care services for 14-bed hospital.

- Successfully worked with difficult populations to meet their mental healthcare needs.

FAMILY CRISIS SERVICES, Tempe, AZ   1998 to 1999
Intern/Counselor
Conducted intake assessments on mentally ill patients and substance abusers referred from prison system.
- Hired as intern during completion of master's degree program; asked to stay on as counselor in recognition of effectiveness in working with difficult populations.
- Initiated and ran well-received counseling sessions for substance abusers.

WOMEN'S CRISIS CENTER, Edison, NJ   1992 to 1995
Shelter Advocate
Conducted intakes, ran groups, counseled residents, and provided crisis intervention support in shelter for victims of domestic violence and sexual assault.

EDUCATION

ARIZONA STATE UNIVERSITY, Tempe, AZ
Master's Degree in Counseling, 1999

RUTGERS UNIVERSITY, New Brunswick, NJ
Bachelor of Arts Degree in Psychology, 1992
Graduated magna cum laude.
Spoke at college graduation.

TRAINING & CERTIFICATION

National Certified Counselor, NBCC
Certified Gestalt Psychotherapist

Trained in Dialectical Behavioral Therapy (DBT)
Trained in Life Coaching

WORKSHOPS

Developed and delivered community presentations on handling stress and maintaining balance in life.

Conducted workshop on maintaining energy in therapeutic situations at a national meeting of the Association of Women in Psychology.

◆◆◆◆◆◆◆◆◆◆◆◆◆

Written By: Carol Altomare
Font: Perpetua

ANDREW G. COLVIN

3622 East Delaware Avenue, #2   (716) 555-2378
Buffalo, New York 14222   andrewcolvin@hotmail.com

CLINICAL PSYCHOLOGIST

**Highly effective, knowledgeable, and compassionate group facilitator and individual therapist.
Adept at shifting priorities and bringing flexibility and creativity to dynamic situations.
Proficient writer able to meticulously research, develop, and edit case studies.**

Education

Niagara University, Niagara Falls, New York
Master of Arts – Clinical Professional Psychology, 2006
➤ *GPA 3.82*
<u>Relevant courses</u>:

Psychopathology	Clinical Psychology	Multicultural Psychotherapy
Intermediate Statistics	Advanced Research Methods	Group Psychotherapy
Chemical Dependence	Marital and Family Therapy	Insight Psychotherapies
Human Development	Health Psychology	Professional Writing for Psychologists
Personality Assessment	Basic Clinical Skills	Professional, Legal, & Ethical Issues

Niagara University, Niagara Falls, New York
Certificate in Stress Management, 2005
<u>Includes training in</u>: Advanced ABC Relaxation Training and Active Coping Techniques

State University of New York at Stony Brook, Stony Brook, New York
Bachelor of Arts – Psychology, 2002
Bachelor of Arts – Sociology, 2002

Professional Experience

<u>Horizon Mental Health Services</u>, Buffalo, New York   2005-Present
Guidance Consultant / Resource Specialist
Provide consultation, referral, and support services to clients accessing the Employee Assistance Program offered by their employers. These services address childcare, eldercare, social, financial, legal, and work-life issues. Educate providers regarding Horizon services and procedures. Triage clients to appropriate services and programs, providing crisis intervention as necessary. Follow up with clients to ensure quality of service.
- Contributed significantly to team's efficiency and productivity goals.
- Received recognition for superior performance in completion and maintenance of case notes.
- Handled numerous "urgent cases" in a prompt, professional, and satisfactory manner.

<u>St. Anthony's Hospital</u>, Buffalo, New York   2004-2005
Clinical Psychology Intern / Psychiatric Case Manager
Performed psychosocial assessments, intake screenings, treatment and discharge planning, and case management for adult population with a variety of chronic mental and behavioral disorders. Provided individual and group therapy with treatment focusing on developing supportive, skill-building techniques in the areas of stress management, relaxation, anger management, assertiveness, self-esteem, relapse prevention, communication, and mental health. Served as patient and family advocate while upholding patients' right to privacy, dignity, and confidentiality.
- Facilitated and co-led general therapy, stress management, anger management, communication skills, mood and music, and prejudice education groups.
- Maintained a psycho-educational and referral list bulletin board which provided patients with pertinent health information and hotline numbers.
- Taught stress management in-service seminar to hospital employees.
- Achieved 97% accuracy rate in clinical diagnostic assessments while a student intern.

Andrew G. Colvin   Page Two

Research Experience

<u>State University of New York at Stony Brook</u>, Stony Brook, New York   Spring 2002
Research Assistant
"The Effects of Chronic Illness on Cognitive Task Performance"
Conducted literature review, interviewed participants, supervised data collection, assisted in research
design and methodology, and helped evaluate and interpret results.

<u>State University of New York at Stony Brook</u>, Stony Brook, New York   Fall 2001
Research Assistant
"Familial Demonstrations of Hostility"
Conducted literature review and supervised data collection.

<u>State University of New York at Stony Brook,</u> Stony Brook, New York   2000-2002
Head Undergraduate Librarian – Theodore Roosevelt Library
Performed a full range of library duties, including researching information, organizing materials, and
maintaining library records.

Research and Publications

Brown, A. C., & Colvin, A. Relaxation Dispositions and ABC Relaxation Theory. Published in *Psychology
Today*, December 2005.

Brown, A. C., Boyd, K., & Colvin, A. Stress Management Motivations and Symptoms in Adolescent Males.
Submitted to *Journal of Counseling Psychology*.

Brown, A. C., Boyd, K., Steele, D. & Colvin, A. Six Stress Management Skills: A Model for Assessment,
Instruction, and Clinical Intervention. Submitted to *Journal of Counseling Psychology*.

Affiliation

American Psychological Association

Technology

SPSS, Novell, Adobe, and Microsoft Word, Excel, PowerPoint, and Access

Chapter 9

▶ Resumes for

Hospitality and Food Service Careers

Each and every industry and profession presents unique resume writing and design challenges. If you are interested in pursuing a hospitality or food service career, be certain to incorporate these important success factors:

Success Factor #1

If you're in food service, mention the types of cuisine with which you have become familiar. Was the restaurant a four-star establishment? Likewise, what kind of guests does your hotel cater to, and what types of facilities do you have (for example, spa, golf course, tennis club)?

Success Factor #2

Do you plan, prepare food, or set up for banquets or large-scale receptions and parties? How many people attend these events? As you well know, a banquet for 500 people is much different logistically from day-to-day dinner or lunch in a medium-sized restaurant.

Success Factor #3

If you have studied or worked under a famous chef or at a renowned restaurant, hotel, or resort, be sure to mention it prominently, including documenting any particular training that was involved.

Success Factor #4

Include any administrative functions for which you have been responsible, such as purchasing, inventory control, and managing food costs. As a hotel manager, is there a sales component to your job such as calling on corporate accounts or networking with tourism industry professionals? Don't forget to include these important roles and the contribution they represent to your employer's success.

Keywords and Keyword Phrases

Keywords and keyword phrases are a critical component of every successful job seeker's resume. By using just one or two words, you're able to communicate a wealth of information about your skills, qualifications, and experience. What's more, keywords are the basis for resume-scanning technology and are therefore critical to any job seeker's campaign in today's electronic-based job search market. For more information on keywords, refer back to pages 17–19 in Chapter 1.

Following are the top 20 hospitality and food service keywords, some of which may reflect your skills and some of which may not be appropriate for you at this time. Use these words as the foundation for developing your own list of keywords on the Professional Keyword List form in Appendix B.

Top 20 Keywords

Back-of-the-House Operations

Catering Services

Conference and Meeting Planning

Corporate Dining Room Operations

Customer Service Management

Food & Beverage Operations

Front-of-the-House Operations

Guest Service and Satisfaction

Hospitality Management

Housekeeping Operations

Inventory Planning and Control

Labor Cost Controls

Menu Planning and Pricing

Multi-Unit Operations

Occupancy Management

Portion Control

Property Development

Resort Management

Revenue Planning and Reporting

Special Events Planning

Following are some excellent examples of resumes for hospitality and food service careers.

Henry Scoralick

PO Box 150
Yonkers, NY 11624

Home (914) 432-3850
Cell (914) 679-2950

SERVICE INDUSTRY PROFESSIONAL
*Experienced bartender with a professional reputation for the consistent execution of five-star service standards.
Offering exceptional people skills, a fine dining background and a passion for the hospitality profession.*

Professional Profile

- Skilled service trainer with efficient work habits and a solid grasp of best practices in customer service.

- Regarded as a loyal and competent employee with unquestionable honesty and a dedication to the company.

- Knowledgeable of the latest specialty drink trends as well as classic cocktail recipes and the standard favorites.

- Exposed to the most progressive and up-to-date techniques through work with celebrity chefs and hospitality experts.

Highlights of Qualifications

- Background includes cash management, costing/pricing, inventory control, purchasing and supplier relations.

- Proven ability to establish a loyal clientele of regulars that frequent the bar based on personal work schedule.

- Highly ethical individual who always recognizes the role as service provider and maintains the utmost professionalism.

- Well-developed understanding of the level of attention and responsiveness that an upscale clientele requires.

EMPLOYMENT EXPERIENCE

The Sagamore, *Lake Placid, NY*   **1983 to Present**
(America's oldest operating inn)

Senior Bartender (Sagamore Restaurant & Tap Room)   2/02 to Present
Senior Bartender (Sagamore Tavern)   7/91 to 10/98
Senior Bartender (Sagamore Hotel)   8/83 to 7/91

Oversee the bar operations for this independently owned, full-service restaurant and bar. Handle liquor ordering, pricing and inventory control. Strictly adhere to bar procedures, maintaining a working knowledge of the wines, spirits and liqueurs available on the market. Worked alongside several high-profile industry professionals and celebrity chefs. Acquired extensive experience in cost controls, VIP relations, supplier relations and special event support. Also involved with staff training, consumption reporting and inventory analysis.

Artist's Palette, *Lake Placid, NY*   **2004 to Present**
(A Zagat-rated restaurant that is consistently named "Best French Restaurant" by Culinary Magazine)

Bartender (part-time)

Serve as a substitute bartender for this French restaurant. Consistently requested to help with special events due to professional attitude, service excellence and high level of customer satisfaction.

JK Lumber, Inc., *Little Falls, NY*   **1999 to 2002**
Truck Driver / Delivery

Loaded truck and delivered product to job sites, operating a forklift and both boon and flat-bed trucks. Routed daily deliveries to maximize time; interacted extensively with customers to ensure prompt and accurate delivery as well as safety.

ADDITIONAL INFORMATION

Education
Herkimer Community College, Herkimer , NY
A.A.S. in Retail Business Management

Specialized Training / Certifications
- Air Brake Adjustment / In-Service Air Brake
- Forklift Operator / HAZMAT / Tank Vehicles
- Doubles & Triples / Tow Truck Operator

Additional Training
- Training for Intervention Procedures (TIPS)
- National Tractor Trailer School, Liverpool, NY

Other Information
- Mohawk Volunteer Fireman, four years
- Employee of the Month, two times (JK Lumber)

Written By: Kristin Coleman
Font: Times New Roman

Nancy Robbins

1245 Main Street ~ Anchorage, Alaska 99516

907.518.6170 ~ nrobbins@comcast.com

PROFILE

- Seasoned professional with an extensive background in food service and hospitality industries.
- Capably manages multiple priorities simultaneously in fast-paced environments.
- Outgoing, optimistic employee who is known for "going the extra mile."
- Skilled in short-order cooking, long-range meal planning and food preparation.
- Recognized for courteous, efficient service; consistently achieved a following of "regular" customers.
- Trained in dietary and nutritional requirements, and coordinating meal plans to fit diverse populations.

"Nancy, you always have a smile ready and such a steady diligence about your work. No matter how hectic things get, or
how difficult a customer can be, you just keep going with real professionalism."

Owner, Hunter's Cafe

EXPERIENCE

ANCHORAGE HOSPITAL, Anchorage, Alaska   2002 to Present
Nutritional and Dietary Aide

- Work with Certified Dietary Manager to ensure each patient's menu plan meets nutritional guidelines and
  diet restrictions.
- Collect patient meal choices daily and assist kitchen staff in preparation.
- Deliver food and beverages, and provide ancillary services such as helping patients with daily tasks.
- Attend ongoing educational in-services; completed CPR training and Nutrition for Diabetics course.

HUNTER'S CAFE, Anchorage, Alaska   1996 to 2002
Head Waitress

- Promoted to position after one year for consistently demonstrating ability to manage high customer volume
  successfully during peak periods – personally waited on up to 150 patrons during a six-hour shift.
- Supervised wait staff of 11 and planned weekly schedule to ensure appropriate coverage.
- Hired and trained new employees in restaurant operations; conducted quarterly performance appraisals.
- Ordered supplies and confirmed adequate inventories.
- Achieved overall accuracy rate of 98% in reconciliation of daily receipts.

ALLAGASH EXPERT GUIDE SERVICE, Allagash, Maine   1985 to 1996
Co-owner

- Co-founded and managed a successful hunting and fishing guide service for avid sportsmen.
- Gained recognition as a first-rate service for big-game hunters and fisherman nationally.
- Prepared, planned and provided meal and rooming accommodations.
- Led canoe transports to remote, hard-to-access locations and guided deer hunts.
- Helped to earn recognition from Outdoor Life in "New England's Best Guide Services" in 1995.

BEACHFRONT INN RESTAURANT, Lincolnville, Maine   1991 to 1996
Head Waitress

- Greeted customers; took food and beverage orders for seasonal clientele.
- Prepared tables and dining area for service; coordinated room arrangements for large parties.
- Provided prompt, friendly service and completed daily cash reconciliations.
- Updated menus with daily specials; advised kitchen staff on special dietary requests.

Written By: Jill Grindle
Font: Perpetua

MICHAEL J. CIPRIANO

1744 Seneca Lane
Mt. Prospect, IL 60056
847-458-4436
mjcip@msn.net

EXECUTIVE CHEF

Strong leadership and management qualifications combined with outstanding cross-cultural communications, interpersonal and team-building skills. Excellent qualifications in planning, budgeting, expense control, staffing, training and quality management. Fluent in English and Italian; conversant in Spanish.

AREAS OF STRENGTH

- Demonstrated mastery of food styles.
- Skilled in menu development and recipe creation.
- Staff training in culinary arts, image and concept.
- Start-up experience as a member of opening team for several units.
- Effective manager. Experience includes costing, sales and profit analysis.
- Skilled supplier negotiator.
- Extensive experience in the control of kitchen operations.
- Talented in the management of international kitchen.

PROFESSIONAL EMPLOYMENT:

EXECUTIVE CHEF
CARRIAGE HOUSE OF HIGHLAND PARK, Highland Park, IL, 2004 – Present
- Manage day-to-day operations including employee, training, and scheduling.
- Work closely with front-of-the-house management.
- Plan and create daily specials.
- Project budget costs and manage inventory control.
- Consistently achieve quarterly goals.

EXECUTIVE SOUS CHEF
CHIN'S CRAB HOUSE, Chicago, IL, 2004
- Managed day-to-day operations including new employee hiring, training, scheduling and evaluation.
- Handled inventory control.
- Planned and created daily food specials.

Michael J. Cipriano   847-458-4436
Résumé – Page 2

LINE COOK
MONTE DEL RE, Florence, Italy, 2003 – 2004
- Apprentice in culinary arts at a Five-Star Restaurant and Hotel. Developed skills in the preparation of pastas, sauces and pastries.
- Exposed to Italian language and culture; dual citizen of Italy and United States.

LINE COOK, SOUS CHEF
BUCCA'S, Chicago, IL, 2001 – 2003
- Ran day-to-day operations; assisted chef in all special events.
- Trained all new employees.
- Became proficient in pantry, pasta, sauté and grill stations; expanded knowledge and skill of butchery and pasta making.
- Costed-out entire menu and helped lower food costs from 32% to 28%.
- Restaurant went from two stars to three-and-a-half during my employment.

KITCHEN MANAGER
WEBER KETTLE OF HIGHLAND PARK, Highland Park, IL, 2001
- Checked-in and organized all deliveries.
- Assisted in developing new recipes for restaurant's opening.
- Trained new employees.

LINE COOK
ROTH'S STEAK HOUSE, Chicago, IL, 2000 – 2001
- Worked in Garde Manger station.
- Trained new employees.
- Assisted in developing new recipes for restaurant's opening.

FUNCTION DIRECTOR
CATERING BY ALGAUER'S, Morton Grove, IL, 1994 – 2003
- Managed and directed parties ranging from 100 to 8,000 people.
- Prepared and served food at events.
- Trained employees and developed their skills.

EDUCATION

KENDALL COLLEGE, Evanston IL, 2000 – 2002
Associate Degree in Culinary Arts

OHIO STATE UNIVERSITY, Columbus, OH, 1996 – 1999
Liberal Arts

Written By: Loretta Heck
Font: Arial

Antonio B. Videlio

Bringing seven years' creative and technical experience into the world-class hospitality arena. Detail oriented and dedicated to unsurpassed customer service with the capacity to handle sophisticated clientele.

Summary of Qualifications

Restaurant Management
- Launched and ran successful coffee shop with minimal investment.
- Sustained pristine environment and exceeded health department regulations for food handling and recordkeeping.
- Hired and supervised shift manager and crew of seven to staff new coffee shop/bistro.

Special Event Planning
- Developed positive working relationships with banquet halls, catering services, bakeries, limousines, hotel chains, and other entertainment companies.
- Planned conferences; lectures; weddings; bar mitzvahs, birthday and private parties, proms, homecomings, and a cappella groups.

Audio/Visual
- Ongoing self-education with special emphasis on audio and visual technological advancements.
- Expertise includes wireless microphones, large sound systems, projection equipment, video and laser production, intelligent lighting, and followspot.

Professional Experience

Major Music Entertainment LLC   1998–Present
Davenport, IN   **Manager/Operator**
- Recruit and manage team of contractors to meet changing business needs.
- Experience in lighting techniques and special effects for live productions, concerts, bands, film and video, and other events.
- Familiar with environments utilizing Delphi systems.

Central Perk Coffee Shop   2002
Lake City, IN   **General Manager**
- Increased profitability by introducing new food line and extending business hours.
- Optimized cash flow and decreased expenses with daily food ordering.
- Scheduled employees and maintained bookkeeping and tax records.

Trans Valley Community College   2000–2003
Novi, MI   **Instructional Staff**
- Set up major symposium events and provided on-site assistance to keynote speakers.
- Led appointment-based teaching for groups of 1-8 faculty members and 1-45 students.
- Assisted with recruiting by conducting guided tours for admissions department.

Education and Software

Bachelor of Arts Degree – Trans Valley Community College, Novi, MI
Economics and Management/Speech Communication

Microsoft Outlook, Word, Publisher, Access, Excel, PowerPoint, FrontPage; ACT!
Adobe Photoshop, Acrobat, Premiere, After Effects; Macromedia Dreamweaver, Flash
Pinnacle Commotion; DVRex; Handshake; Novell; GroupWise; multiple web browsers and OS's

Written By: Tammy J. Smith
Font: Bookman Old Style

RICHARD GILES

GENERAL MANAGER - FOOD SERVICE OPERATIONS

Seasoned restaurant manager whose accomplishments reflect excellent leadership abilities, strong management skills, a commitment to profitability improvement, and a passion for achievement.

CAREER PROFILE

Performance-driven general manager with a wealth of experience in the restaurant industry. Respected, hands-on leader known for open, upfront communications style and ability to motivate teams to achieve outstanding results. Strong fiscal management skills. Stellar record of accomplishment in:

- Maximizing profitability through effective leadership, budget management, and cost control.
- Building sales and reputation through effective promotions and community relations efforts.
- Launching new operations and establishing sound practices to position them for continued success.
- Orchestrating performance turnarounds in floundering stores.
- Recognizing and capitalizing on individual strengths to build strong management teams.
- Training and developing new talent.

PROFESSIONAL EXPERIENCE

CHILI'S   2000 to present

General Manager

Currently manage Bridgeton store in New Jersey, the company's third busiest location with $4.5 million in annual sales. Previously, managed Farmingdale and Parsippany locations.

Operations Excellence

- Excelling in company's training program, immediately took on general manager role in floundering Parsippany store. Turned around performance, assembling and mobilizing strong management team that stabilized operation while growing controllable profits to 33%.

- Slashed annual turnover from 200% to 80% by providing effective, hands-on leadership that fostered loyalty while motivating and empowering staff.

- Revamped store, upgrading facility to build a better customer experience. Financed renovations through effective budget management and cost controls.

- Orchestrated successful opening of new Farmingdale store, achieving $3.5 million in sales in first year.

- Won award for achieving the highest average customer satisfaction ratings in "mystery shopper" program within 50-unit regional franchise group that ranked first in the nation.

- Took over management of Bridgeton location, a training store with $4.5 million in sales but disappointing profitability. Implemented controls that brought down costs and revived profits in short time frame.

- Effectively addressed staff performance issue, implementing changes that got the right people in the right jobs while weeding out poor performers. Successfully increased productivity while reducing costs.

- Upgraded training programs to build highly competent, customer-focused team that shared in efforts to maintain top-notch store performance.

(Continued)

70 RIDGE ROAD ◆ WAYNE, NJ 07470
(973) 696-2000 HOME ◆ (973) 696-0888 CELL ◆ richgiles@msn.com

CHILI'S   Continued
General Manager

Promotional Successes & Community Leadership

- Introduced highly successful express lunch menu that capitalized on local environment, attracting customers from nearby businesses to substantially increase sales.
- Launched promotional deals with local minor-league baseball team that attracted new customers and were instrumental in achieving 13% increase in sales over previous year.
- Won chairman's award for taking initiative and donating catering services to support operators manning telephones during fund-raising event associated with September 11th terrorist attacks.
- Served as member of the area business association. Actively supported community programs such as the annual holiday parade, Toys for Tots, and the local food bank. Donated funds for the restoration of the USS New Jersey.

GARDENVIEW STORES   1992 to 1999
Managing Owner
Established and managed two European-style meat markets in New Jersey.
- Successfully launched business, achieving $1 million in sales.
- Attracted veteran butchers who brought a wealth of knowledge to production kitchen, to draw in upscale clientele with discerning tastes and position business to grow and prosper.
- Quickly built network of loyal clientele. Won many lucrative catering jobs, including several with local yacht club.

ADVANCE RESTAURANTS   1987 to 1992
Manager, Walt's Inn
Managed day-to-day operations for upscale, high-volume restaurant with $4 million in annual sales. Oversaw catering for private parties and banquets.
- Hired, trained, and developed strong staff, building knowledge and professionalism that complemented restaurant's fine food offerings.
- Oversaw ordering for restaurant and two bars. Implemented controls to maximize quality while holding costs down.

COPPER KETTLE   1980 to 1987
Assistant General Manager
Opened and managed franchise restaurants in Dallas, Fort Worth, and Arlington.
- Successfully launched new stores. Recruited, hired, and trained staff. Oversaw kitchen set-up.

EDUCATION

NEW YORK RESTAURANT SCHOOL, New York, NY
Restaurant Management Certificate, 1980

Completed 2 years of coursework towards Business Administration Degree at Rutgers University.

70 RIDGE ROAD ♦ WAYNE, NJ 07470
(973) 696-2000 HOME ♦ (973) 696-0888 CELL ♦ richgiles@msn.com

Written By: Carol Altomare
Font: Book Antiqua

Michael McAdams

4854 Pawnee Drive, Clive, Iowa 50325

Phone: (515) 781-3839   Cell: (515) 895-8863   McAdams@peoplepc.com

OPERATIONS MANAGEMENT

A management professional skilled in operations, utilizing proven abilities to launch new locations, turnaround under-performing sites, improve processes, and maximize profits through cost cutting and by building strong teams who deliver high-quality customer service.

QUALIFICATIONS

A resourceful, highly motivated professional with experience encompassing:

- Training and Motivating Teams
- Recruiting, Interviewing, Hiring
- Performance Metrics
- Revenue Forecasting

- Planning and Implementing Programs
- Troubleshooting, Crisis Management
- Presentation and Demonstration Skills
- Driving Customer Service Initiatives

SELECTED ACHIEVEMENTS

Operations Leadership: Recruited as fast-track GM for full-service, casual-dining steakhouse. Interviewed, hired, and trained staff, met all established timelines for operational set-up, and coordinated all new store opening activities. Achieved target revenue of $58,000/week at opening.

Team Builder & Coach: Implemented team approach to improve customer service rating for quick-service Bakery-Café. Led management and employees to focus on all aspects of customer service. Achieved 55% increase in customer service scores in less than three reporting periods.

Turnaround Operations: Promoted to AGM and transferred to under-performing, full-service casual-dining steakhouse. Re-organized and instilled a sense of leadership in staff to support cost-cutting changes and sales growth. Achieved an increase in store profitability of 7.4%.

Cost Savings: Restructured community operations facility due to reduction in funding. Streamlined management structure, reduced overhead costs, and invigorated revenue-generating opportunities. Achieved 35% reduction in operating costs.

Performance Improvements: Increased overall performance of family-entertainment restaurant. Re-organized staffing requirements and increased front-of-the-house presence. Achieved all target operational goals within six reporting periods.

Training Development: Led development of second training store for quick-service Bakery-Café. Assembled certified trainers from other stores to create optimal environment for management training. Achieved training status within four reporting periods while directing successful opening of another new location.

Michael McAdams

Phone: (515) 781-3839   Cell: (515) 895-8863   McAdams@peoplepc.com

PROFESSIONAL EXPERIENCE

Manager
Friendly's, Clive, Iowa, 2004 - Present
> Oversee all financial and organizational requirements; maintain P&L goals; train and supervise staff; manage food and beverage; and ensure guest satisfaction.

General Manager
Panera Breads, Clive, Iowa, 2001 - 2004
> Served dual-roles; GM for location and Training GM; managed opening of new location; recruited certified training staff for training operations.

Manager
Olive Garden Restaurant, Clive, Iowa, Feb 2001 – July 2001
> Directed all front-of-the-house activities; hired, trained, scheduled, and evaluated kitchen staff; supervised service staff.

General Manager
Lonestar Steakhouse & Saloon, Davenport, Iowa, Aug 2000 – Feb 2001
> Exercised stringent controls over P&L and operations, supply requests, inventories, and cost reductions; prepared work schedules and resolved all personnel problems; maintained high-performance staff.

Assistant GM
Longhorn Steakhouse/Rare Hospitality, Davenport, Iowa, 1998 - 2000
> Served in three roles; GM, Kitchen Manager, and location Manager eliminating extreme management turnover.

General Manager
Showbiz Pizza Co./Chuck E. Cheese, Denver, Colorado, 1996 - 1998
> Turned around under-performing location to receive "Most Improved Store Award."

EDUCATION and TRAINING

Master of Business Administration (MBA), Finance
UNIVERSITY OF COLORADO, Colorado Springs, Colorado

Bachelor of Arts (BA), Business Administration
MARQUETTE UNIVERSITY, Milwaukee, Wisconsin

Written By: Michael S. Davis
Font: Perpetua

John Roberts, CHA

662 Blossom Lane
Orange, CA 92856

Cell: 714/243-4602
johnroberts@hotmail.com

GENERAL MANAGEMENT: HOSPITALITY

Multi-faceted General Manager with extensive experience in operating, opening, and renovating large, full-service hotel properties. Proven leadership skills and decision-making abilities have produced profitable results. Increased sales and upgraded quality and efficiency through resourceful management, effective supervision of employees, and problem-solving skills. Capable of exceeding company objectives and substantially improving business operations. Devised and applied innovative sales and marketing plans that led to significant increases in market penetration, while ensuring optimum guest satisfaction. Excel in a fast-paced environment and apply strategies which result in optimal productivity. Recognized for providing excellent cross-functional leadership and team-building expertise.

AREAS OF EXPERTISE

Operations / General Management
Decision Making & Problem Solving
Leadership and Motivation
Food / Beverage Management
Recruiting, Training & Supervision
Administration & Organization
Guest Services & Satisfaction
Performance Evaluations / Goal Setting
Sales / Advertising / Marketing
Inventory Control / Purchasing

Grand Openings / New Hotel Construction
P&L Management
Financial Analysis, Budgets & Forecasts
Quality / Productivity Improvement
Staff Scheduling / Coordination
Communication (Bilingual: English/Spanish)
Strategic Planning
Team Development / Coaching
Negotiations / Problem Resolution
Partnerships & Alliances

PROFESSIONAL EXPERIENCE

INTERNATIONAL HOTELS & RESORTS   1991 – Present

Regal Hotel/Resort - Orange, CA
General Manager (2001 – Present)

- Opened this hotel which is the largest full-service "prototype" in the nation.

- Manage all aspects of daily operations; Formulate and administer organizational policies and procedures; Collaborate in determining cost effectiveness of operations; Develop and implement long-range goals and objectives.

- Hire and train six department heads who supervise 120 employees. Direct and coordinate activities of Food & Beverage, Sales & Marketing, Accounting, Engineering, Banquets & Catering, and Human Resource departments.

- Analyze activities, costs, operations, and forecasts to determine departments' progress toward achieving goals as well meeting objectives for capital and ROI projects.

- Work directly with owners and contractors during construction to ensure all building projects are completed on time, within budget, and according to quality standards.

- Oversee purchasing of all FF&E, soft goods, and case goods.

  Achievements:
  - Opened new Hotel and Resort with highest full-service quality score in the nation.
  - Opened hotel on opening date and decreased budgeted expense projections by $40K.
  - Attained the top service and quality scores in the Western Region and 2nd highest in company.
  - Achieved 103% MPI (Market Penetration) in the first six months.
  - Completed training at General Managers' Corporate Training Center.

John Roberts – johnroberts@hotmail.com   Resume – Page 2

PROFESSIONAL EXPERIENCE (Continued)_____

<u>Regal Inn Mountain View</u> (*Largest Regal Inn in New Mexico*) - Albuquerque, NM
General Manager (1999 – 2001)

   Achievements:
   ➢ Increased gross operating profit by 8% or $750K year over year.
   ➢ Increased total revenue by $1.2M.
   ➢ Attained the top account in the market (Southwest Airlines).
   ➢ Increased profitability and quality scores to ensure owner retained hotel and brand flag.
   ➢ Increased quality score by 27 points.
   ➢ Increased overall service score by 24 points.
   ➢ Received award for "Most Improved Service" in the Western Region.

<u>Regal Inn & Suites</u> - Odessa, TX
General Manager (1997 – 1999)

   Achievements:
   ➢ Increased GOP margin by 4%.
   ➢ Achieved service goals each quarter.
   ➢ Designed ROI project for a new SMERFE market "Party Room" which resulted in a positive
      return of $140K.
   ➢ Assisted in developing marketing and operating strategies for three managed properties.

<u>Regal Inn Select</u> - San Antonio, TX
Director of Operations (1991 – 1996)

   Achievements:
   ➢ Achieved budgeted operating profits each quarter.
   ➢ Attained largest government contract in San Antonio.
   ➢ Achieved service goals each semester.
   ➢ Directed multi-million dollar renovation.

EDUCATION_____

   ▪ **Certified General Manager**, International Hotels & Resorts (1996)
   ▪ **CHA, CRDE** Educational Institute of the AH&LA (1994)
   ▪ **Graduate**, Dale Carnegie (1992)
   ▪ **Associate of Applied Science in Hospitality Management**, Malibu University (1990)

COMMUNITY ACTIVITIES / MEMBERSHIPS_____

   ▪ Honoree, American Society of Distinguished Professionals
   ▪ Former Vice President of Albuquerque Innkeepers Association
   ▪ Former Executive Board Member of CVB and Tourism Council
   ▪ Member of the LA and Orange Chambers of Commerce

Written By: Pearl White
Font: Times New Roman

LOUISE RANDALL

350 W. Bay Harbor Drive
Bay Harbor, FL 33144
Home: 300.777.0000
Cell: 300.555.7772
LouiseRandall20@aol.com

TRAVEL PROFESSIONAL
Director of Land Services for Cruise Line / Travel Planning Executive

Thirteen-year career in the planning, promotion, and management of cruise itineraries, shore excursions, dive programs, and onboard entertainment for a small cruise line....**H**igh-energy business builder combining cross-functional expertise in Business Management, Marketing, Promotions, Event Management and Finance....**E**xcellent interpersonal skills.

Career Highlights:
> Advanced to senior management, making the challenging transition from ship to shore. Maintained position through various management shake-ups, downsizing, and outsourcing. Well-respected by peers.
> Transformed the Shore Excursion Program into a major revenue source, increasing net profits by 700% to date, with strategy in place to continue that growth.
> Designed, developed, and implemented new cruise itineraries in the ABCs, Belize & Bay Islands, Costa Rica, French Polynesia, Panama, Puerto Rico, and Venezuela.
> Centralized control over all port agent accounts, significantly reducing spending through implementation of more stringent accounting controls and analysis of port pricing structure.

PROFESSIONAL EXPERIENCE

ADVENTURE CRUISES, Miami Beach, FL   1992 - Present
Cruise line has five ships that operate in the Bahamas, the Caribbean, Central and South America, and French Polynesia
MANAGER, OPERATIONS & PASSENGER SERVICES (1996 – Present)

Promoted to position to manage the shore excursion program and assist in the development of new itineraries. Responsible for port and port agent contracts and accounts, as well as compliance with foreign and US Customs/Immigration regulations. The combined value of managed accounts was initially $1 million, and the current value is $4 million.

- Elevated the Shore Excursion Program 900% net profit per passenger, making it the highest generator of on-board revenue, by establishing the pricing and vendor payment agreements, researching and introducing new excursions, creating marketing materials, and soliciting input from passengers and Cruise Directors.
- Negotiated with the Port of Miami to homeport the S.V. Legacy there, the first time the company had brought a ship to the mainland US in 40 years. This included responsibility for ships' agents, stevedoring and security company contracts, and compliance with associated US Coast Guard and US Customs and Borderland Protection requirements.
- Developed a stronger, cohesive team and reduced turnover by taking a "hands-on" approach to recruiting and managing cruise directors and dive staff. Improved incentives and benefits and created a structured training program.
- Initiated and managed the development of the company's first onboard dive program. Hired certified scuba instructors, researched liability requirements, and introduced the program in stages to evaluate customer responsiveness, offering the services on just one ship and then expanding it to others. Sales doubled within one year.

LOUISE RANDALL   LouiseRandall20@aol.com   **PAGE TWO**

MANAGER, OPERATIONS & PASSENGER SERVICES, continued......

- Developed theme cruises that provided "added value" to the passengers' cruise experience, such as Taste of the Caribbean Culinary Cruise Series and Pirate Week.
- Set up and managed season programs for kids, Junior Jammers, and Teen programs, enabling the company to successfully capitalize on the booming family vacation market.
- Created a new itinerary in Kuna Yala, Panama, the first of its kind in the region. Researched legalities, analyzed costs, established a working relationship with the Kuna Council (the representative body of the indigenous population of the area), which was of mutual benefit to all parties and ensured the cultural integrity of the cruise experience.
- Engineered the promotion of pre- and post-cruise land packages that provided increased revenue for the cruise line, and greatly increased customer satisfaction.
- Worked with Groups and Incentives Department in the design and implementation of customized itineraries and cruise experiences for various corporative incentive groups and TV companies such as MARS, Computer Associates, Might Auto Parts, BBC, Food Network, and Fox Network.

SENIOR CRUISE DIRECTOR – ONBOARD   1994 – 1997
CRUISE DIRECTOR – ONBOARD   1992 – 1994

Promoted to position. In addition to providing on-board entertainment, shore excursion sales, and passenger cabin charge accounts, which were the standard responsibilities of a Cruise Director, was given added responsibility of developing the fleet's shore excursion program.

- First person promoted to this position and the only person in a "ship-based" position ever be given this level of responsibility.
- Through experimentation, identified the passengers' preference for more active and educational shore excursions and determined their willingness to pay a premium price for these activities.
- Replaced many existing tour companies with smaller, specialized tour operators that offered higher quality "customized" excursions. Due to highly increased customer satisfaction, profit margin increased while maintaining volume.
- Introduced non-profit excursions led by Cruise Directors, diversifying their role as the providers of on-board entertainment and significantly improving customer satisfaction.

Previous experience: **ENGLISH TEACHER** for the **WILLIAM SHAKESPEARE SCHOOL OF ENGLISH**, Lima Peru

EDUCATION

UNIVERSITY OF KENT AT CANTERBURY, Canterbury, Kent, UK – *Theatre & Film Studies*
INTERNATIONAL HOUSE, Barcelona, Spain – *Certificate in T.E.F.L.*

PROFESSIONAL AFFILIATIONS / COMMUNICTY ACTIVITIES

Guest Speaker – AAPA CRUISE WORKSHOP, New Orleans, LA, February 2005.
Participant – LEUKEMIA & LYMPHOMA SOCIETY'S TEAM IN TRAINING PROGRAM - raised $3500+ this year.
Volunteer – HANDS ON MIAMI – a non-profit organization working with the elderly and disadvantaged.

Written By: Joyce Fortier
Font: Tahoma

Chapter 10

▶ Resumes for

Human Resources and Training Careers

Each and every industry and profession presents unique resume writing and design challenges. If you are interested in pursuing a career in human resources or training, be certain to incorporate these important success factors:

Success Factor #1

Show your diverse skills by mentioning the different aspects of human resource management with which you have experience, for example, benefits administration, recruiting, payroll, employee relations, and training.

Success Factor #2

Mention initiatives you have developed or implemented to improve employee satisfaction and retention. This might include counseling individual employees on professional development or introducing employee incentive programs recognizing peak performance.

Success Factor #3

For trainers, include activities such as needs assessment, curriculum planning, course design, on-line instruction, classroom training, and instructional materials design.

Success Factor #4

Include information about your familiarity with time-keeping, payroll tracking software, or other enterprise software that impacts human resource operations.

Keywords and Keyword Phrases

Keywords and keyword phrases are a critical component of every successful job seeker's resume. By using just one or two words, you're able to communicate a wealth of information about your skills, qualifications, and experience. What's more, keywords are the basis for resume-scanning technology and are therefore critical to any job seeker's campaign in today's electronic-based job search market. For more information on keywords, refer back to pages 17–19 in Chapter 1.

Following are the top 20 human resources and training keywords, some of which may reflect your skills and some of which may not be appropriate for you at this time. Use these words as the foundation for developing your own list of keywords on the Professional Keyword List form in Appendix B.

Top 20 Keywords

Benefits Design and Administration

Change Management

Employee Assistance Programs

Employee Communications

Employee Relations

Employee Retention

Grievance Proceedings and Arbitration

Human Resources Administration

Labor Contract Negotiations

Leadership Development

Manpower Planning

Organizational Development

Performance Incentives

Performance Reviews and Appraisals

Recruitment and Selection

Staffing

Succession Planning

Training and Development

Union Relations

Wage Administration

Following are some excellent examples of resumes for human resources and training careers.

GEORGE R. SCHUP

190 East Primrose Lane   414-564-4141 (h)
Greendale, WI 53152   414-425-3136 (o)

grschup22@execpc.com

HUMAN RESOURCES BENEFITS ANALYST/MANAGER

Ten years of progressively responsible experience in the planning, design, implementation, and management of comprehensive employee benefit programs. Combines expert technical qualifications with solid performance in building cooperative employee relations that promote hard work and commitment. Excellent communication, organizational, and negotiation skills.

FORMAL EDUCATION

Keller University, Milwaukee, WI
MASTERS IN HUMAN RESOURCES MANAGEMENT (2005) – GPA 3.8/4.0

University of Wisconsin-Milwaukee, Milwaukee, WI
BACHELOR OF ARTS (1989) – GPA 3.3/4.0

EMPLOYMENT HISTORY

Bonanza Company, Glendale, WI   July 2000-Present
BENEFITS ANALYST – COMMUNICATIONS (May 2003-Present)
SENIOR BENEFITS SPECIALIST (July 2001-May 2003)
MANAGER OF BENEFITS/CUSTOMER SERVICE (July 2000-June 2001)

Scope: Benefits, Payroll, and International Assignment. Report to Director of Employee Services.

Benefits: Communicate benefit plan design to 40,000 union and non-union employees throughout the United States and Canada (2004), 30,000 of which are in the program. Serve as voice of Benefits Department (one-on-one and in groups). Maintain 17 benefit programs. Resolve issues and "put out fires." Serve as Acting Supervisor in absence of Manager.

Open Enrollment: Facilitate and implement open enrollments annually. Authorized to write all materials in kit, create Human Resources on-line calendar of events, develop how-to's for employee meetings/benefit fairs, and create/deliver PowerPoint presentations for all employees. Develop rate sheets, how-to-enroll guides, and "benefits at a glance."

Compliance: Meet ERISA compliance. Write Summary Plan Descriptions and Summary Materials Modification. Appeals Manager for eligibility and claims processing. Work with outside counsel and major Milwaukee law firm.

Communication: Serve as Lead on Bi-Annual Report to all covered employees. Communicate costs and benefits, including pensions and 401K projections. Update and maintain on-line "My Benefits" program accessible by employees.

Results:
- Enhanced and improved previous tools; added data for additional groups.
- "Great job," said management and employees. "Very helpful."
- Feedback on benefits has been excellent.
- Received recognition and thank-yous from internal staff and employees.
- Promotions based on work ethic, skills and abilities, and excellent performance evaluations.

Wisconsin Energy Company, Milwaukee, WI   1996-2000
BENEFITS REPRESENTATIVE (1996-2000)

Results:
- Efficiently managed COBRA enrollments and assisted with interpretation of benefits.
- Effectively maintained cash billing system for retiree medical plans.
- Member of the Technical Support Team for upgrade to Customer Service Solutions (CSS) computer program.

Written By: Doris Applebaum
Font: Arial Narrow

LILLIAN HALPERN
650 Alameda Boulevard
Houston, TX 77013
(713) 555-1212
lillyhalpern@optonline.net

SUMMARY   **Goal-oriented Human Resources Generalist** with proven capabilities in recruiting, training, benefits administration, and employee relations programs. An innovative problem-solver with the flexibility to adapt and communicate effectively with all levels of the workforce. Balanced perspective that combines a sympathetic approach when dealing with employees with loyalty to the company's position. Strong technical skills with MS Word, Excel, and PowerPoint, utilized to produce reports, charts, and graphics for corporate presentations. Accustomed to working well under pressure and multitasking in a time-sensitive environment.

PROFESSIONAL EXPERIENCE

ANDOVER PLASTICS, INC., HOUSTON, TX   1990–2006
Manufacturing facility for polyethylene products, employing 250. Positions held:

Employee Benefits and Services Administrator (1998–2006)
Employee Benefits Coordinator (1993–1998)
Human Resources Assistant (1990–1993)

Highlights of effectiveness in the following areas:

Recruiting/Training
- Administration of non-exempt and temporary applicant selection, interviewing, and testing
- Temporary job order placement and negotiations with agencies regarding invoicing
- Scheduling of pre-employment physicals and random drug testing
- Updates to policies and procedures manual
- Coordination of seminars within and outside the company

Key accomplishments:
- Prepared materials for in-house training courses in total quality management (TQM) and performance assessment.
- Revised job descriptions in compliance with ADA.
- Created and graphically presented employee turnover reports for executive meetings.

Benefits Administration
- Total administration of medical and dental benefits through PPO networks
- Insurance liaison in matters of premium payments and disputed claims
- New employee briefings regarding their benefits package
- Exit interviews to inform terminating employees of COBRA provisions

Key accomplishments:
- Researched and provided necessary information to the Vice President of Finance for the selection of a cost-effective third-party administrator for company's self-insured benefits plan.
- Following switch to new PPO networks covering three states in which the company operates, gave group presentations to introduce the plan, answered inquiries, and handled the entire enrollment process.
- Set up a log to track claims processing complaints, enabling the identification of trends and implementation of corrective actions.

LILLIAN HALPERN   Page 2
(713) 555-1212   lillyhalpern@optonline.net

Programs
- — Coordination of corporate events, incentives, and recognition luncheons
- — Performance review and salary increase processing
- — Development and editing of quarterly newsletter
- — Tuition reimbursement for employees' continuing formal education
- — Addressing of safety issues

Key accomplishments:
- Encouraged social interaction and enhanced morale among the staffs of seven buildings in the complex.
- Generated increased interest and voluntary participation from all departments in company's high-priority safety awareness program which reduced accidental injuries by 35%.

Reporting
- — Changes to employees' status on HRIS and coordination with Ceridian payroll system
- — OSHA logs and Workers' Compensation claims
- — Compliance reports to government agencies
- — E-mail dissemination of corporate memos to all applicable employees
- — Maintenance of employees' sick and vacation absence records

Key accomplishments:
- Initiated computerized compilation and tracking of all OSHA and EEOC/Affirmative Action reports, assuring their timely and accurate completion.
- Created a performance review reminder system for supervisors, resulting in more timely submission of appraisals on their employees.

EDUCATION   A.A.S. in Business Management with emphasis in Human Resources   1995
Galveston County Community College

Continuing education seminars:

- Recruiting, Interviewing, Selecting and Training Employees — AMA
- Personnel Policies for Personnel Clericals — Career Track
- Employee Benefits Administration — East Texas University
- OSHA Policies and Procedures — AMA
- Americans with Disabilities Act — Texas Department of Labor
- Human Resource Laws — AMA

Written By: Melanie Noonan
Font: Perpetua

Michelle Reinecke

7263 Callaghan Rd., San Antonio, Texas 78217   (H) 210-783-2574   (W) 210-558-6327   (C) 210-852-5237   e-mail: mreine@tisd.net

---

Senior Human Resource Manager
with thirteen years of human resource experience including a strong background in regional and corporate level support in multiple U.S. based, culturally diverse call center operations with a workforce total of up to 600 local and 2500 regional associates.

Core Professional Strengths

Human Resource Management
State / federal employment law / unemployment compensation / policy interpretation / safety & health / benefits design & administration / departmental budget / HRIMS / performance management

Recruiting
Exempt & non-exempt level sourcing / selection / on–boarding / orientation / employee relations / community relations / pre- & post-hire assessments / applicant tracking / per hire cost analysis

Training and Development
Grant attainment / instructional systems design / training facilitation / organizational development / quality improvement

Retention
Retention strategy analysis / workforce surveys / case studies / development & implementation of employee retention programs

Professional Achievements

- ❖ **Educated** the corporate sales team in the components of corporate staffing package – *Call Source Plus.*
- ❖ **Initiated $350K worth of annual bottom-line savings** by implementing employee equipment purchase programs, redesigning differential/vacation pay policies and reducing starting salaries.
- ❖ **Maximized the call-based routing** initiative of the call center group by providing human resource expertise in the area of employee profiling, behavior profiling, and pre-and post-hire assessment processes.
- ❖ **Provided human resource expertise** as part of Spherion's Customer Development Solutions sales presentation design team and facilitated the presentation on an "as-needed" basis to current and potential outsourcing clients as part of the contract retention strategy.
- ❖ **Assimilated** the division's human resources data and talent in support of the launch of the corporate HRIMS initiative, **Project Meteor.**

Professional Experience

Senior Human Resource Manager
DIGICOM TELESERVICES, INC., San Antonio, Texas—1998 to present
24X7 Inbound Customer Service Call Center servicing DigiCom calling-card and long-distance customers. The center staffs 450-600 local employees. This position is also indirectly responsible for human resources consultation for 1500-2500 regional employees.
- ❖ Awarded **CEO recognition** for representing the Customer Development Solutions Group as the subject matter expert on the **corporate team** that led the organization through the 2001/2002 **corporate payroll system implementation.**
- ❖ **Received local recognition for:** *2001 Employer of the Year* by the State of Texas; *2001 Employer of Excellence* and *2001 Transitional Employer of the Year* by Bexar County Employment Services Development Board.

Michelle Reinecke
-2-
(H) 210-783-2574 (W) 210-558-6327 (C) 210-852-5237 e-mail: mreine@tisd.net

Professional Experience - *continued*

- ❖ **Achieved 100% of hiring goals** while maintaining lowest recruiting costs of the division at $275 per hire.
- ❖ **Implemented an Integrated Voice Response** unit to capture 100% of survey data from a workforce of 2500 associates for the 2001 Associate Survey project. Achieved an above average response rate of 42%.
- ❖ **Increased associate retention by 47%** to achieve industry standard excellence rate of 53% and maintained this rate for three consecutive years.
- ❖ **Led the regional succession planning and performance management** process to ensure talent development and quality bench strength.
- ❖ **Secured $100K+ of community funds** for employee training and development programs.
- ❖ **Repeatedly achieve a win rate of 99%** on unemployment claims for three locations across the U.S., resulting in **savings of $90K** for the division.

Human Resource Supervisor / Management Trainer
GRAYSON FOODS, Rochester, New York - 1989 to 1997
Food Processing Facility - 800 Local employees
- ❖ **Managed** hiring/orientation for dayshift.
- ❖ **Facilitated 100% of management training** programs for the operation.
- ❖ **Secured $100K + of state grant** training funds.
- ❖ **Developed and implemented employee mentor program.**
- ❖ **Developed and implemented the** night shift human resources department.
- ❖ **Managed grievance process** for non-exempt employees under the UFCW union contract.

Agriculture Science Instructor
ROCHESTER INDEPENDENT SCHOOL DISTRICT, Rochester, New York - 1988 to 1989

Quality Supervisor
HENSLEY FARMS OF TEXAS, San Angelo, Texas - 1985 to 1988

Education and Professional Training

- ❖ **Master of Science - Human Resource Development** – University of Texas, 1997
- ❖ **Bachelor of Science - Agriculture Science** - Texas A&M University, 1985
- ❖ **Professional Training:**
  Vital Learning Management Development- Certified Facilitator
  Dale Carnegie - Certified Assistant

Professional Organizations

- ❖ Professional Association for Training and Development (ASTD)
- ❖ American Association of Human Resource Management (AAHRM)
- ❖ Rochester Economic Development Corporation (REDC)
- ❖ Rochester Chamber of Commerce
- ❖ Rochester Independent School District (RISD) Volunteer: Innovative Research Team – Curriculum for Real World Application

Written By: MeLisa Rogers
Font: Garamond

MARTIN A. MURRAY

94 Ellington Road
Croton, NY 95587

914.478.3422

EAMurray@aol.com

CAREER PROFILE

Strategic **Human Resources Executive** and proactive business partner to senior operating management to guide the development of performance-driven, customer-driven and market-driven organizations. Demonstrated effectiveness in providing vision and counsel in steering organizations through accelerated growth as well as in turning around under-performing businesses. Diverse background includes multinational organizations in the medical equipment and manufacturing industries.

Expertise in all Generalist HR Initiatives:

Recruitment & Employment Management ... Leadership Training & Development
Benefits & Compensation Design ... Reorganization & Culture Change ... Merger & Acquisition
Integration ... Union & Non-Union Employee Relations ... Succession Planning
Expatriate Programs ... Long-Range Business Planning ... HR Policies & Procedures

PROFESSIONAL EXPERIENCE

MARCON MANUFACTURING COMPANY, Peekskill, NY
Director, Human Resources (1996–Present)

Challenge: Recruited to build the HR organization and support business growth at a $30 million global manufacturing company with underachieving sales, exceedingly high turnover and lack of cohesive management processes among business entities in U.S. and Asia.

Actions: Partnered with the President and Board of Directors to reorganize company, reduce overhead expenses, rebuild sales and institute solid management infrastructure.

Results:
- ◆ Established HR with staff of 5, including development of policies and procedures; renegotiated cost-effective benefit programs that saved company $1.5 million annually.
- ◆ Reorganized operations and facilitated seamless integration of 150 employees from 2 new acquisitions within parent company.
- ◆ Reduced sales force turnover to nearly nonexistent and upgraded quality of candidates hired by implementing interview skills training and management development programs. Results led to improved sales performance.
- ◆ Recruited all management personnel, developed HR policies and plans, and fostered team culture at newly built Malaysian plant with 125 employees.
- ◆ Initiated business reorganization plan, resulting in consolidation of New York and Virginia operations and $6.5 million in cost reductions.

BINGHAMTON COMPANY, New York, NY
Assistant Director, Human Resources & Administration (1993–1996)

Challenge: Lead HR and Administration function supporting 1,600 employees at $500 million manufacturer of medical equipment. Support company's turnaround efforts, business unit consolidations and transition to consumer products focus.

Actions: Established cross-functional teams from each site and provided training in team building to coordinate product development efforts, implement new manufacturing processes and speed products to market. Identified cost reduction opportunities; instrumental in reorganization initiatives that included closing union plant in Texas and building new plant in North Carolina. Managed HR staff of 12.

MARTIN A. MURRAY • PAGE 2
EAMurray@aol.com

Assistant Director, Human Resources & Administration continued...

Results:
- Instituted worldwide cross-functional team culture that provided the foundation for successful new product launches and recapture of company's leading edge despite intense competition.
- Led flawless integration of 2 operations into single, cohesive European business unit, resulting in profitable business turnaround.
- Restructured and positioned HR organization in the German business unit as customer-focused partner to support European sales and marketing units.
- Initiated major benefit cost reductions of $3 million in year one and $1 million annually while gaining employee acceptance through concerted education and communications efforts.

ARCADIA CORPORATION, New York, NY
Manager, Human Resources (1990-1993)
Assistant Manager, Human Resources (1989–1990)

Challenge: HR support to corporate office and field units of an $800 million organization with 150 global operations employing 4,500 people.

Actions: Promoted from Assistant Director of HR to lead staff of 10 in all HR and labor relations functions. Established separate international recruitment function and designed staffing plan to accommodate rapid business growth. Negotiated cost-effective benefits contracts for union and non-union employees.

Results:
- Oversaw successful UAW, Teamsters and labor contract negotiations.
- Established and staffed HR function for major contract award with U.S. government agency.
- Introduced incentive plans for field unit managers and an expatriate program that attracted both internal and external candidates for international assignments in the Middle East.
- Managed HR issues associated with 2 business acquisitions while accomplishing a smooth transition and retaining all key personnel.
- Restructured HR function with no service disruption to the business while saving $500,000 annually.

EDUCATION

M.B.A., Cornell University, New York, NY
B.A., Business Administration, Amherst College, Amherst, MA

AFFILIATIONS

Society for Human Resource Management
Human Resource Council

Written By: Louise Garver
Font: Book Antiqua

SUSAN COOPER

254 Asbury Place, #5 • Melbourne, Florida 32940 • Tel: (321) 555-0555

SENIOR TRAINING MANAGER
Human Resources / Training & Development

High-impact and results-oriented professional with successful experience designing, selecting, implementing, and evaluating comprehensive learning solutions that support key performance indicators. Partner with division managers to identify critical business needs, define employee performance gaps, and recommend effective platforms to enhance organizational competencies. Combine superior business acumen, communication, and group facilitation skills with the ability to promote an all-inclusive, high-performing culture where team members embrace and leverage each others' talents and backgrounds while nourishing innovative thinking in order to achieve full potential. *Core competencies include:*

- Strategic & Tactical Planning
- Multi-Site Training Initiatives
- Technical & Human-Performance Topics
- Continuing Education & Adult Learning
- Interactive & e-learning Formats

- Financial Services Operations
- Performance Metrics
- Process Redesign & Change Management
- Human Resources/Administration
- Critical Problem Resolution

PROFESSIONAL EXPERIENCE

Senior Training Manager, 2001 – Present
KEY BANK, INC., Melbourne, FL

Oversee the analysis, design, delivery, implementation, and evaluation of adult-learning initiatives for a leading banking institution. Report directly to the V.P. of Human Resources. Collaborate with internal functional departments to conduct business and competency needs assessment and redefine and/or create highly effective learning solutions. Handle human resources functions including newsletter development and HRIS, manage new hire and benefits administration, and serve as HR generalist/advisor to HR manager. Possess strong knowledge of various corporate education topics including Ethics and Code of Conduct, Debt Collection, Management/Leadership, and Software/Technical applications.

- Spearheaded the creation and maintenance of a complex database program capturing training enrollment statistics while providing comprehensive reporting and certification documentation.
- Enhanced corporate learning levels by reinventing new training and development approaches that encapsulate vision, value, respect, and enthusiasm from all associates and department managers.
- Improved new hiring process by restructuring paperwork methodology from manual to online.
- Developed various technical workshops and management/leadership programs that surpassed company expectations and objectives.
- Recognized for displaying executive presence, poise, persuasiveness, and confidence necessary to earn credibility with senior management, while earning the trust and confidence of associates at all organizational levels.

Director, Human Resources, 2000 – 2001
MOBILE-TECHNOLOGIES, INC., Fairview Park, OH

Accountable for the design and administration of health benefits, training, 401(k), Intranet, and daily employee retention programs for a technical consulting firm. Reported directly to the Chief Executive Officer.

SUSAN COOPER

Page Two

Tel: (321) 555-0555

Professional Experience Continued

Human Resources Specialist/Instructor, 1999 – 2000
FUNDAMENTAL INVESTMENTS, INC., Avon, OH

Provided staff support services for company payroll, benefits, recruitment, and Intranet initiatives. Reported to Vice President of Human Resources.

- Successfully developed and managed in-house employee training program that included business application training for corporate headquarters.
- Managed team responsible for the integration of 400+ new employees nationwide.

Corporate Software Instructor, 1998 – 1999
HORIZONS LEARNING CENTER, Boardman, OH

Facilitated classroom instruction for 12-60 students and provided individual training to corporate business clients on proprietary and popular business software and technical applications.

- Created and implemented all curriculum and presentation materials; continually assessed learning success rate and implemented adjustments as necessary.
- Recognized as an "outstanding" instructor per student evaluations; consistently acknowledged for ability to professionally instruct adults through well-developed communication and teaching skills.

Executive Coordinator, Office of the President, CEO & Chairman, 1995 – 1998
MATRIX, INC., Boardman, OH

Conducted comprehensive training and product demonstrations for clients of a leading telecommunication solutions provider. Supported staff in areas of training, administration, scheduling, business development, competitive analysis, market research, marketing communications, events planning/coordination, in-house software training/support, information services, facilities management, and research project management.

- Established a reputation as company "expert" on multi-faceted business software including office suites, desktop publishing, graphics, and audio applications.

~ Prior Work History & Achievements (1989-1994) Available Upon Request ~

EDUCATION & PROFESSIONAL DEVELOPMENT

YOUNGSTOWN STATE UNIVERSITY
Bachelor of Arts, Human Resources Management & Organizational Development

Professional Certification:

AMERICAN SOCIETY FOR TRAINING & DEVELOPMENT
Certified Professional in Learning & Performance (CPLP)

Affiliations

Professional Member, NATIONAL SPEAKERS ASSOCIATION (NSA)

Written By: Susan Barens
Font: Book Antiqua

MARVIN TISCH

315 West 68th Street, 7B ▪ New York, NY 10023 ▪ Cell: 347-484-8007 ▪ mtisch@nyc.rr.com

ORGANIZATIONAL PSYCHOLOGIST/HR GENERALIST
Public Companies ?Private Sector Companies ?Government Agencies

Leveraging best practices in organizational diagnosis, candidate assessment, and management development to deliver consistent ROI for companies and foster employee performance and loyalty.

- Ten years' experience in the U.S. and abroad; exposure to union and non-union environments.
- Expertise administering 16 performance and psychological assessment tools.
- Track record for building trust and credibility with management and employee populations.

CORE COMPETENCIES

Organizational Assessment & Redesign/Change Management ▪ Succession Planning/Management Development ▪ Leadership Training & Executive Coaching ▪ Recruitment/Retention Strategy ▪ EAP Program Implementation ▪ Competitive Benchmarking/Job Grading ▪ Employee & Union Relations ▪ Career & Performance Counseling

Certified to Administer: Myers Briggs ▪ 16PF ▪ Hogan ▪ 19 Field Inventory ▪ Value Scales ▪ Self-Directed Search Questionnaire ▪ Vienna Dover ▪ Figure Classification Test ▪ Blox ▪ Cognitive Process Profile ▪ SHL Battery of Tests ▪ Psytech Battery of Tests ▪ Weschler ▪ Thomas International ▪ DISC

PROFESSIONAL EXPERIENCE

ADOLF RUBINS CONSULTANTS, New York, NY   2002 to Present

ORGANIZATIONAL DEVELOPMENT SPECIALIST for human resources consulting firm. Partner with small and mid-size firms to deliver assessment, recruitment, employee relations, process improvement, executive coaching, succession planning, and management development initiatives.

Slashed time spent recruiting new hires by 50% by creating formal recruitment strategy for 32-store retail chain that decreased reliance on newspaper advertisements and increased alternative sourcing channels.
- Built talent pool and improved retention metrics significantly by marketing positions on college campuses, researching best practices with similar organizations, launching targeted advertisement campaigns, and building strategic alliances with management at local shopping plazas.

Developed content for and facilitated five 2-day leadership workshops in conjunction with corporate succession planning strategy.
- Authored comprehensive workbook, facilitator's guide, and PowerPoint presentation.
- Consistently exceeded participant's expectations as evidenced by outstanding evaluations.
- Leveraged success of program to increase enrollment at other management seminars.

Recommended strategies to improve strained relations between employees and management.
- Conducted 16 in-depth (1-2 day) confidential employee interviews and delivered comprehensive report within aggressive 2-week deadline.
- Suggested initiative to increase management visibility that contributed to improved employee relations, fewer occurrences of tardiness, decreased turnover, and a new leadership initiative.

CITY OF CAPE TOWN, Cape Town, South Africa   1997 to 2002

ORGANIZATIONAL PSYCHOLOGIST for 18,500-employee Municipal Authority for the greater Cape Town metropolitan area and sole distributor of utilities to population of 3.5 million. Provided strategic and tactical support with emphasis on management development and succession planning, change management, program implementation, and agency-wide assessment/recruitment.

Ensured compliance of aggressive 3-year, government-mandated Affirmative Action Plan requiring employers to significantly increase employment, promotion, and training opportunities for minority candidates.
- Led assessments for 300 engineers to identify high-potential candidates for senior positions.
- Selected by Head of Electricity Utilities Group to participate in team tasked with assessing key training and development needs for eight of the city's business units.
- Introduced first mentoring program in agency's history and a successful apprentice program.

MARVIN TISCH

- Spearheaded 16-module, two-year management development program that contributed to promotional opportunities for 92% of participants within a 1-year period.
- Forecasted and integrated development/succession plans and skills training for 3,200 employees over a 1-year period and negotiated frequency of training with union personnel.

Enhanced service levels, productivity, job satisfaction, and employee morale of 40-person business unit by introducing an 8-stage process improvement plan.
- Orchestrated anonymous interviews and employee surveys to uncover employee issues.
- Brought in external consulting team to implement teambuilding workshops and maximized ROI of program by offering weekly group meetings and ongoing opportunities to air concerns.
- Reduced temporary employees from 80% to 7%; created improved accountability standards.
- Developed job descriptions and job grading system for 25 positions.
- Reconfigured existing office space to improve ergonomics and quality of work-life.

Pioneered a Health First Program to address employee mental and physical health issues that impacted productivity, benefits expenses, and employee morale.
- Secured senior level buy-in for program by documenting 350 counseling issues over a 2-year period and preparing cost-benefits analyses to support early intervention.
- Garnered $60,000 to train HR staff to provide counseling support and boosted HR's credibility to deliver services and maintain confidentiality.
- Overhauled Employee Assistance Program to address issues outside the realm of HR, including drug and alcohol dependency, grief counseling, and severe depression; managed EAP budget.
- Counseled employees with post-traumatic stress disorder and launched stress management training program for staff to help HR professionals recognize early signs of stress-related productivity issues.

UNIVERSITY OF PORT ELIZABETH, Port Elizabeth, South Africa   1996 to 1998
LECTURER for accredited UNISA (University of South Africa) college servicing 1,500 students. Taught Industrial Psychology, Industrial Relations, and HR Management to undergraduate population.

BRICKSTONE PERSONNEL, Port Elizabeth, South Africa   1994 to1996
PERSONNEL CONSULTANT for national Human Resources and Employment Consultancy. Recruited staff for various positions in several industries; formulated job descriptions/job analyses.

THE DILLON SCHOOL, Cape Town, South Africa   1991 to 1994
VOCATIONAL GUIDANCE COUNSELOR for private middle and high school.

EDUCATION /LICENSES

M.S., Organizational/Industrial Psychology, University of Cape Town, Cape Town, South   1992
Africa
(Post graduate two-year coursework and dissertation degree) & Honors in Social Science,
Organizational Psychology/Industrial Psychology, (Post graduate one-year coursework
degree)   1989

B.S., Social Science, University of Cape Town, Cape Town, South Africa

Registered & Licensed Organizational Psychologist with the Health Professions Council of South Africa and Society for Industrial and Organizational Psychology.

PROFESSIONAL AFFILIATIONS

President, EAPAKZN, (Employee Assistance Practitioners Association), Cape Town,   2003 to
S.A.   2004

Member, SHRM, (Society for Human Resource Management)

Member, HRNY, (Human Resources Association of New York)

TECHNOLOGY & LANGUAGE SKILLS

Microsoft Office ▪ Corel Presentation ▪ WordPerfect ▪ Quattro

Fluent in English and Afrikaans; Basic Knowledge of French

Written By: Barbara Safani
Font: Verdana

Chapter 11

▶ Resumes for

Law Enforcement and Legal Careers

Each and every industry and profession presents unique resume writing and design challenges. If you are interested in pursuing a law enforcement or legal career, be certain to incorporate these important success factors:

Success Factor #1

Credentials and certifications are key. Prominently mention firearms, special tactics, or special investigative credentials. For attorneys, list the courts and states in which you are admitted to practice.

Success Factor #2

In addition to credentials, include other professional training in areas relevant to your career path. Law enforcement and legal professions place a heavy emphasis on professional development, so be sure to include all of yours.

Success Factor #3

Be sure to mention any measures of performance. What's your success rate in cases you've tried as an attorney? As a police officer, how many arrests have you made or how has the crime rate been reduced because of your actions?

Success Factor #4

Remember to include information about the administrative aspects of your job, especially if you're interested in advancing into supervisory or management positions.

Keywords and Keyword Phrases

Keywords and keyword phrases are a critical component of every success-ful job seeker's resume. By using just one or two words, you're able to commu-nicate a wealth of information about your skills, qualifications, and experience. What's more, keywords are the basis for resume-scanning technology and are therefore critical to any job seeker's campaign in today's electronic-based job search market. For more information on keywords, refer back to pages 17–19 in Chapter 1.

Following are the top 20 law enforcement and legal keywords, some of which may reflect your skills and some of which may not be appropriate for you at this time. Use these words as the foundation for developing your own list of keywords on the Professional Keyword List form in Appendix B.

Top 20 Keywords

Arbitration	Judicial Affairs
Arrest and Prosecution	Legal Research and Analysis
Civil Law Proceedings	Legislative Review and Analysis
Corporate Law and Representation	Litigation
Courtroom Proceedings	Public Safety and Administration
Criminal Investigations	Regulatory Affairs
Depositions and Discovery	Risk Management
Due Diligence	Search & Seizure
Intellectual Property	Trademark and Copyright Law
Interrogations	Workers' Compensation

Following are some excellent examples of resumes for law enforcement and legal careers.

CARLA LYNETTE JONES

3000 LIONS GATE RD • KALAMAZOO, MICHIGAN 49042 • HOME: 269.428.9630 CELL:
269.423.1986
clj@sbcglobal.net

LAW ENFORCEMENT OFFICER

10 Years' Experience in Strengthening Community Safety & Security

Dedicated law enforcement professional with proven track record in planning and leading criminal and accident investigations, providing first-rate security to residential and commercial properties, and developing interactive public service safety programs and activities. Strong qualifications in community policing, warrant and arrest procedures, emergency response, patrol, and report preparation. **Well-versed in Michigan State Traffic Laws, Vehicle Code, and Civil and Criminal Laws.** Excellent analytical and problem-solving skills. Works effectively and congenially with fellow officers and supervisory personnel at all levels. Recognized by superiors and peers as an individual who provides motivational leadership and implements cohesive team-building strategies. Maintains strict confidentiality on sensitive information. Outstanding reputation for strong work ethic and uncompromising devotion to community service.

SPECIFIC SKILL AREAS

• Emergency Response	• Arrest Procedures	• Complaint Evaluations
• Incident, Crime, Accident, and Arrest Reports	• Crisis Intervention	• Investigative Procedures
• Field Investigations	• Physical Surveillance	• Rules of Evidence
• Suspect Interviews	• Witness Interviews	• Victim Interviews
• Illegal Activities	• Assault & Battery Cases	• Street Narcotics
• Warrants & Arrests	• Traffic Laws	• DWI Stops
• Rules of Pursuit	• Narcotic Arrests	• Domestic Disputes
• Courtroom Testimony	• Court Procedures	• Constitutional Rights
• Computer Database Searches	• Background Checks	• Criminal Checks
• Evidence Collection	• Chain of Custody	• Traffic Accident Investigation

EDUCATION & TRAINING

WESTERN MICHIGAN UNIVERSITY, Kalamazoo, Michigan
Bachelor of Science, Criminal Justice, 2004

ALBURTUS COMMUNITY COLLEGE, Albion, Michigan
Associates Degree in Law Enforcement, 1995

Selected Professional Development Coursework:

Street Crimes • High-Risk Felony Stops • Bullet-Proof Mind • Active Shooter • 15 State of Michigan Legal Update Seminars

Certifications & Licenses

• MCOLES Certified (39196)	• Firearm Certification	• Preliminary Breathalyzer
• Radar Operator	• PPCT Defensive Tactics	• Taser
• Standardized Field Sobriety Testing	• Datamaster	• HAZMAT

PROFESSIONAL EXPERIENCE

CITY OF JACKSON POLICE DEPARTMENT	August 2004 – Present
CITY OF BATTLE CREEK POLICE DEPARTMENT	January 1997 – August 2004
CITY OF THREE RIVERS POLICE DEPARTMENT	August 1995 – December 1997

Protect the lives and property of the citizens of three municipalities and enforce the laws of the local, state, and federal government. Investigate traffic accidents, public complaints, and crime scenes. Record facts and locate and preserve evidence. Respond to physical attacks, applying force and physical restraint to dangerous animals or people; arrest and process accused suspects; take photographs and fingerprints. Serve as liaison between the court, victims, witnesses, and prosecutor; testify in court when necessary.

Notable Achievements

- Led patrol division by aggressively enforcing DWI and controlled substance laws. As a result of performance, had the highest number of DWI and narcotic arrest convictions in the department (54 in 2005).

- Repeatedly recognized by citizens and supervisors for quick thinking, calm, and correct response in crisis and emergency situations. Recipient of eight Jackson Police Department Citations of Merit for Outstanding Service to the Community.

- Officer-in-Charge of six high-profile narcotic investigations.

- Firearms trainer for 32 new departmental recruits.

Written By: Richard Porter
Font: Arial

TREY B. MILLER

treymiller@tech.net   23 Terrace Circle, Houston, TX 77023   713.543.1984

PROFESSIONAL GOAL: Accident Scene Investigation

PROFESSIONAL QUALIFICATIONS

- 12 years' experience in the law enforcement profession with expertise in the areas of:
  - accident investigation
  - courtroom testimonies
  - interviews & interrogations of witnesses/suspects
  - code violations
- Certified Accident Scene Investigator with 700+ hours of specialized classroom training.
- Thorough, detail-oriented and methodical regarding all facets of accident investigation.
- Excellent working relationships with county, state, and federal attorneys, insurance companies, and law enforcement professionals from other jurisdictions.
- Extensive background and experience as an Accident Investigation Instructor and Trainer.

PROFESSIONAL EXPERIENCE

CITY OF HOUSTON, Houston, TX   1993-Present
SENIOR POLICE OFFICER III – TRAFFIC DIVISION

Accident Investigation – Hit and Runs, Serious & Fatality:
- Act as primary officer in charge of reconstructing accident scenes within the Houston city limits.
- Interview witnesses, suspects, and family members to determine causal factors of the accident.
- Collaborate with County Attorney to establish accident causation and appropriate charges, if any.
- Work closely with insurance carriers regarding retrieval of property.

Training / Instruction:
- Act as lead trainer for Accident Investigation classes at the Houston Police Academy.
- One of five instructors for Accident Investigation with the Texas Law Enforcement Academy.
- Facilitate training on city and state codes for the Houston Police Academy.

Key Results:
- Recipient of *"Beyond the Call Lifesaving Award"* in 2006 from the City of Houston Chief of Police.
- Named *"Police Officer of the Year"* in 2003 for service contributions to the department.
- Skilled in the investigation of thousands of motor vehicle accidents throughout career as a Police Officer.
- Provide expert testimony during criminal and civil trials.
- Valued in the law enforcement community for broad knowledge in the field of accident investigation.

EDUCATION

- Texas State Patrol: At-Scene Traffic Crash Investigation; Advanced Traffic Crash Investigation; Technical Accident Investigation

- Institute of Police Technology & Management, San Antonio, TX: Traffic Crash Reconstruction; Investigation of Motorcycle Crashes; Pedestrian and Bicycle Crash Investigation

- Texas Law Enforcement Academy: Photography & Traffic Investigation

- Houston Police Academy: Total Work Station – GPS Training for Accident Investigations

- **Bachelor of Science in Criminal Justice,** University of Texas, Austin, TX, 1993

Written By: Billie Ruth Sucher
Font: Palatino Linotype

Dominick Coreno

24355 Park Place Circle · Fishers, Indiana 46032
Residence: (317) 555-4211 · Cellular: (317) 555-5665

Safety & Emergency Management Professional
~ Local, County, State & Federal Agencies ~

A *top-performing*, *highly educated*, and *distinguished* professional with a 20-year record of exemplary achievements directing metropolitan law-enforcement initiatives and city-wide emergency response and safety management operations. Comprehensive knowledge of responsibilities and interrelationships between Federal, State, and local jurisdictions. Manage special projects and coordinate critical emergency-management functions to accomplish immediate and long-term goals. Excellent communicator demonstrating logic, focus, and critical thinking while exercising appropriate delegation of responsibility and authority.

CORE COMPETENCIES

- Homeland Security Directives
- Emergency Preparedness
- Infrastructure Protection & Physical Security
- Anti-Terrorism/W.M.D. Threat Analysis
- Budget & Fiscal Management

- Strategic & Tactical Planning
- Fieldwork & Investigations
- Policies, Programs & Procedures
- Government & Media Relations
- Human Resources & Administration

Training, Certifications, Credentials

U.S. Department of Homeland Security Training & Certificates (2005):

National Incident Management System · Incident Command System I-100 for Federal Disaster Workers & Law Enforcement · Incident Command System for Single Resources & Initial Action Incidents · Special Events Contingency Planning for Public Safety Agencies · Community Preparedness, Response & Recovery · Professional Development Series in Emergency Management · Weapons of Mass Destruction · Public Safety – W.M.D. Response Sampling, Techniques & Guidelines · Bioterrorism: Putting the Pieces Together in Indiana · W.M.D. for First Responder – Advanced Course · Disaster Management · First Response Strategies & Protocols for Water, Utility & Public Health Staff · Emergency Operations Center

Professional Experience

LOUISTOWN POLICE DEPARTMENT – Louistown, Indiana   20+ years
Appointed to key law enforcement and homeland security leadership positions for a major metropolitan city with over 500,000 residents.

Captain of Police & Special Project Director for Homeland Security, 2005-Present
Provide a variety of complex analytical, administrative, and technical work in the development of programs, services, policies, and procedures to devise the most efficient and effective methods of accomplishing the work of a six-district police department and the Department of Homeland Security. Perform duties and exercise the powers incidental to the office of the Chief of Police in his/her absence.

➢ Successfully reviewed and updated Homeland Security strategy for the Division of Police, as well as the Emergency Operations Plan for entire city.

➢ Act as divisional liaison representative to all government agencies involved in Homeland Security.

➢ Compile intelligence to prevent, prepare, respond, and recover from acts of terrorism.

. . . Continued . . .

Dominick Coreno • Page Two
Residence: (317) 555-4211 • Cellular: (317) 555-5665

Professional Experience Continued . . .

Chief of Police, 2002-2005
Accountable for planning, organizing, directing, and evaluating the city's police department to ensure protection of life and property in the city through law enforcement and crime prevention. Oversaw patrol activities, criminal investigations, traffic enforcement, crime prevention, education, inspection, and internal training. Ensured incorporation of modern and efficient law-enforcement technologies into the department's procedures, equipment, and methods. Forged positive partnerships with Federal, State, and local agencies.

➤ Reduced 2004 budget over 15% and supported the creation of a wide-spread after-school program.

➤ Collaborated with the U.S. Secret Service in launching the City's Electronics Crimes Task Force in 2003.

➤ *"Police Dominick Coreno developed a narcotics reorganization plan that employs a three-pronged strategy: education, enforcement, and treatment. Under his leadership, our police department, in conjunction with community agencies, groups, faith leaders, and schools, will seek to reduce the harsh impact of drug abuse on our neighborhoods and our people."*
— City Mayor, State of the City Address, 2003.

Captain of Police/Executive Officer of the Bureau of Communications/ Events Coordinator, 2000-2002
Assumed all Police Captain responsibilities as documented above, as well as all law-enforcement operations in Commander's absence. Ensured adherence to all budgetary constraints. Directed all public and media relations.

➤ Achieved "Top Score" on competitive examination.

*** Prior Appointments ***

Lieutenant of Police/Sector Supervisor/Officer-in-Charge of Complaint Investigation Unit, 1993-2000
Sergeant of Police, 1985-1993
Patrol Officer, 1981-1985

Formal Education

INDIANA STATE UNIVERSITY – **Bachelor of Science, Political Science**
STATE COMMUNITY COLLEGE – **Associate of Arts, Law Enforcement**

Honors & Professional Affiliations

Service Award Recipient, Federal Bureau of Investigations
Recipient, Distinguished Service Medal
Service Award Recipient, State High-Intensity Drug Trafficking Area Task Force
Former Executive Board Member, United Stated Department of Justice Joint Terrorist Task Force
Executive Board Member, Crimestoppers
Member, International Association of Chiefs of Police
Member, County Police Chiefs
Member, Fraternal Order of Police
Member, Metropolitan Crime Clinic, Inc.

Written By: Susan Barens
Font: Arial

MITCHELL PHILLIPS

3746 Martin Lane • New City, NY 10956
Home: 845-555-8392 • Phillpsm@isp.com • Cellular: 845-555-3827

HEAD OF SECURITY

Security Consultant ~ Security Coordinator ~ Security Investigator

Dynamic, results-oriented leader with demonstrated high standards of professional conduct and excellent skills in conflict resolution. Experienced in all aspects of professional policing including security operations for special events, risk management, investigation, and personnel management. Able to plan and create comprehensive security strategies, programs, and policies. Collaborate with various governing and community agencies to ensure public safety. Gained reputation for strong security and criminal intelligence knowledge and investigative expertise.

Areas of Expertise

- Crime Prevention & Safety
- Investigation & Crime Analysis
- Special Event Coordination
- Problem Resolution

- Security Measures
- Community Policing
- Innovative Leadership
- Strategic Planning

- Operations Management
- Personnel Management
- Team Building
- Risk Assessment

PROFESSIONAL EXPERIENCE

New York Police Department – New York, NY   **1985 – 2006**
Built solid career and outstanding reputation for providing sound leadership and innovative solutions while advancing through positions of responsibility and authority.

Patrol Borough-Queens Operations Officer/ Elections Officer (2002-2006)
Supervised 12 police precincts within the Borough comprised of 3,500 police officers; deployed manpower to outer Boroughs as needed to accommodate major events. Established mobile command posts for operations; monitored all radio communications with multiple agencies involved including Emergency Service Unit, Mounted Unit, Aviation Unit, Harbor Unit, Canine Unit, Bomb Squad, Counter Terrorism Unit, Disorder Control Unit, Fire Department, Emergency Medical Services, Transit Bureau, and Housing Bureau. Monitored all personnel assigned to elections duties; collected all votes counted and delivered to Board of Elections, the Associated Press, and 1 Police Plaza.

- Managed numerous special events involving street closures for security management; coordinated all aspects of events including mass transit and traffic rerouting, scheduling additional manpower resources, and alerting EMS and Fire Department for potential crowd issues and fire calls.

- Collaborated with political and community leaders to organize major events such as protests, parades, concerts, athletic events, the New York Mets Playoffs/World Series, the Republican National Convention, local and presidential elections, and the New York Marathon.

- Evaluated and restructured documents and forms which streamlined the process of assigning and accounting for all personnel at various operations.

- Assigned police officers to each polling site and monitored all daily activities while serving as Elections Officer. Ensured election laws were upheld and provided safe passage to and from polling locations.

- Provided dignitary protection during the United Nations General Assembly.

- Ran command and coordinated personnel from various critical agencies including the FBI, Secret Service, FEMA, OEM, Fire Department, EMS, Bomb Squad, and HazMat.

- Honored with three Commendations for outstanding police duty and service.

MITCHELL PHILLIPS

HOME: **845-555-8392** • PHILLPSM@ISP.COM • CELLULAR: **845-555-3827**

Page Two

Highway Safety Officer/ School Safety Officer/ Community Policing Officer (1992-2002)
Accountable for maintaining the 66th Precinct fleet of vehicles; scheduled routine inspections and servicing for minor repairs. Procured necessary emergency equipment needed for each vehicle. Served as School Crossing Guard Supervisor; oversaw approximately 35 guards tasked with the safe passage of 3,500 students to and from five area schools in a 3-block radius. Collaborated with principals and guidance counselors to ensure overall safety of students. Interacted with general pubic in order to gain trust and confidence. Managed numerous investigative assignments utilizing sharp analytical and problem-solving skills.

- Mediated with school officials and parents regarding issues concerning safety; implemented various strategies to effectively fight increasing violence in schools.
- Collaborated with community leaders and politicians in order to identify key quality of life problems and develop strategies to correct ongoing issues.
- Actively participated in numerous plainclothes operations involving under-age sale of alcohol and cigarettes, prostitution, sale of stolen property, and carrying out search warrants.
- Performed search and rescue, as well as conducted crowd and traffic control while under assignment at Ground Zero.

Police Officer (1986-1992)
Patrolled designated areas of the 66th Precinct; answered emergency and non-emergency calls, effected arrests, served warrants, performed security checks, and investigated motor vehicle accidents. Interacted with the general public to ensure overall safety.

- Provided security for players while assigned to the Yankee Stadium - worked the press gate; monitored doors, granted access to personnel with proper authorization, provided assistance to all stadium staff members, and dealt appropriately with problem guests.

PROFESSIONAL DEVELOPMENT & TRAINING

Police Academy

Specialized Training
Latent Prints • Sound Meter • Plainclothes • Losing Proposition • Computer Training • Board of Elections Training • Disorder Control Training • Counter Terrorism Training • Mobile Field Command Post Training • Defensive Driving • Firearms Safety • CPR & Deliberator Usage

Written By: Liz Benuscak
Font: Verdana

NANCY KREEGER, ESQ.
11 Binder Boulevard
Rye, New York 12837
(907) 283-2736
nancylawyer@rochester.rr.com

LITIGATION ATTORNEY / PERSONAL INJURY ATTORNEY
Admitted To Practice In:
US Circuit Court of Appeals - 2nd Circuit / US Federal Court / US Bankruptcy Court
New York State Supreme Court / County & Local Civil & Criminal Courts

---

Outstanding ability to manage relationships with expert witnesses including sourcing various subject experts and understanding technical issues as they relate to litigation cases. Broad knowledge of medical issues and accident reconstruction techniques.

Strong legal research capabilities with excellent track record of successful litigations and appeals in civil cases, representing both defendants and plaintiffs. Argued numerous appeals in state court. Prevailed in most cases that have reached trial.

PROFESSIONAL EXPERIENCE

Personal Injury Litigator / Associate Attorney   1991 - Present
Christopher & Hawkins, P.C., Rye, New York
- Represent plaintiffs and defendants in civil litigation including medical malpractice, motor vehicle accident, personal injury, and personal liability cases.
- Interview potential clients to evaluate cases and conduct client intake including obtaining medical records and other documentation.
- Depose clients and witnesses; file and argue a variety of motions including discovery and dispositive motions; respond to motions from opposing counsel.
- Solicit and manage relationships with expert witnesses including accident reconstruction specialists, physicians, mental health professionals, and other subject area experts.
- Conduct investigations including visiting accident scenes to gather pertinent information.
- Review and interpret medical records and other technical data as it relates to cases.
- Handle Notices of Claim and 50H Hearings for cases involving governmental agencies.
- Advise clients and negotiate equitable settlements with opposing attorneys.
- Conduct extensive legal research in support of litigations and appeals.
- Litigate cases in court and argue appeals for various personal injury and liability cases.

Staff Attorney   1990 - 1991
Greenbrier Legal Services, Rye, New York
- Practiced in all areas of the law including civil and criminal litigations.

EDUCATION

Juris Doctor   May 1988
New Town University College of Law, New Town, New York
Major Program Area - Business Organizations & Transactions
Dean's List - Three Semesters

Bachelor of Science, Mass Communications   May 1982
Buffalo College, Buffalo, New York
Dean's List - Six Semesters / Varsity Basketball (Div. III)

AFFILIATIONS

American Bar Association
New York State Bar Association
Ontario County Bar Association
- *Member of Personal Injury Defense Committee (1998)*

Written By: Arnold G. Boldt
Font: Times New Roman

JUDY SOULA, Esq.
6344 North Main Avenue, Chicago, IL   60646-2923
Home: 773-764-3576 * Cell: 773-542-6844 * Email: jsoula@quixnet.net

Assistant Corporate Counsel

Experienced attorney with 10 years of successful legal experience. Excellent background in corporate law, tax law, real estate law, arbitrations, civil litigation, and courtroom proceedings. Record of consistent wins in highly complex legal proceedings. Strong legal research, writing, and negotiations expertise.

EXEMPLARY SKILLS

Strong Research Skills	Analytical Thinking	Creative Problem Solving
Keen Litigation Knowledge	Dispute Resolution	Client Advisory Services
Credit Reporting/Fraud	High-Tech Issues	Case Management

EDUCATION

JURIS DOCTORATE, DEPAUL UNIVERSITY, COLLEGE OF LAW, CHICAGO, IL   1994

BACHELOR OF ARTS, LIBERAL ARTS, UNIVERSITY OF ILLINOIS, CHAMPAIGN, IL   1989

DETAILED CAREER HISTORY

Associate
WAKENEVER & ASSOCIATES, P.C., OAK PARK, LOMBARD, IL   2004-2006
- Researched legal issues, drafted pleadings, and appeared for motions, hearings and routine trial matters in divorce and post-decree litigation, personal injury, and child support litigation.
- Successfully defended multiple motions to dismiss in contract custody cases.

Solo Practitioner, Contract Attorney
JUDY SOULA, CHICAGO, IL   2001-2004
- Researched legal issues, drafted pleadings, and appeared for motions hearings and routine trial matters in property liens, garnishment, citations and levies. Civil litigation work included legal research, court appearances, arbitrations, depositions and discovery.
- Prepared filings to enforce judgments against debtor assets and income. Represented individuals in administrative proceedings, including subdivision of property.

Associate Attorney
LAW OFFICES OF ROBERT A. LANGENDORF, CHICAGO, IL   1996-1998
- Drafted pleadings, motions, and discovery documents on behalf of firm's clients.
- Argued motions before judges.
- Prepared all appeals and documents required with high-volume, trail-level cases in state court.

Assistant State's Attorney
TASCO COUNTY STATE'S ATTORNEY'S OFFICE, PEKIN, IL   1995-1996
- Reviewed police reports and determined whether to charge the defendant or not.
- Prepared for daily court appearances made recommendations if defendant should plead guilty.

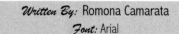
Written By: Romona Camarata
Font: Arial

RODNEY W. COLEMAN, ESQ.

902 Haverford Road
Buffalo, New York 14282
(716) 889-3828
colemanrw@frontiernet.net

Admitted to the Bar - New York State

SUMMARY

Accomplished felony prosecutor with 10-year record successfully trying a wide array of violent and non-violent felonies and misdemeanors in New York State Supreme Court, County Court, and municipal courts.

- **Demonstrated capacity to cooperate effectively with a broad array of law-enforcement agencies and prosecuting attorneys at federal, state, and local levels.**
- **Extensive experience researching, analyzing, and interpreting case law relating to both criminal and civil issues.**
- **Direct experience prosecuting firearm felonies as part of "Project Exile" task force.**
- **Highly organized with excellent time management skills and ability to balance demands of heavy caseload.**

LEGAL EXPERIENCE

NIAGARA COUNTY DISTRICT ATTORNEY'S OFFICE, Lockport, New York (1992 - Present)
Assistant District Attorney
Ten year's experience prosecuting a broad range of misdemeanor and felony cases at various levels and in various courts within the jurisdiction.

Major Felony Bureau   **June 2002 - Present**
Accountable for prosecuting violent felonies including assaults with firearms and weapons, robberies, rapes, and burglaries.
- Confer with police investigators to review case evidence.
- Appear in court and before Grand Juries to seek arraignments and indictments.
- Interview witnesses and prepare them for trial.
- Meet with defendants and defense counsel to negotiate plea agreements.
- Develop cases for trial and handle all aspects of trying cases in court.

Gun Interdiction Unit / Project Exile   **June 2000 - June 2002**
Served as member of this cross-jurisdictional task force charged with curtailing illegal firearms trafficking and illegal use of firearms in commission of other felonies.
- Collaborated with FBI, US Attorney, BATF, and state/local police agencies to further program goals.
- Conferred with representatives of other agencies to assess appropriate venue for prosecuting cases.
- Developed and managed confidential informants in conjunction with other agencies.
- Attended regular meetings to maintain rapport and enhance cooperation between agencies.

County Court - Non-Violent Felonies   **Feb. 1999 - June 2000**
Felony DWI / Fatal Traffic Accident Bureau   **Dec. 1997 - Feb. 1999**
City Court - Misdemeanors   **July 1995 - Dec. 1997**

Municipal Courts   **1992 - 1995**
In addition to criminal prosecutions, participated in Drug Diversion Court over an 8-month period. This program offered alternatives to incarceration for non-violent drug offenders with no significant criminal records.

Rodney W. Coleman, Esq.   **Résumé - Page Two**
(716) 889-3828

LEGAL EXPERIENCE (continued)

LEGAL ASSISTANCE OF THE NIAGARA FRONTIER, North Tonawanda, New York
Legal Aid Attorney   **1991**
Assisted economically disadvantaged clients with landlord/tenant issues and other routine legal matters.

US DISTRICT COURT - WESTERN DISTRICT OF NEW YORK, Buffalo, New York
Judicial Intern to Hon. Lester Riceman   **Sept. 1988 - May 1989**
Researched legal issues and drafted memoranda decisions and orders for habeas corpus petitions, civil rights actions, and Social Security actions. Discussed case decisions and rulings on motions with judge to gain further understanding of trial law and procedures.

VIRGINA DEPARTMENT OF TAXATION & FINANCE, Richmond, Virginia
Law Clerk - Litigation Division   **May 1988 - Aug. 1989**
Researched laws pertaining to real property transfer and corporate transfer taxes. Analyzed statutory and regulatory issues and prepared memoranda based on interpretations. Developed case strategies and drafted briefs and motions.

US ATTORNEY'S OFFICE – RICHMOND, SUPERIOR COURT DIV., Richmond, Virginia
Undergraduate Legal Internship   **Sept. 1986 - Dec. 1986**
Reviewed evidence, interviewed witnesses, and conducted legal research in support of attorneys preparing misdemeanor cases for trial.

EDUCATION

Juris Doctor   **June 1990**
University of Virginia, Charlottesville, Virginia

Bachelor of Science, Criminal Justice   **May 1987**
Virginia Commonwealth University, Richmond, Virginia
Graduated With Honors / GPA: 3.48

PROFESSIONAL DEVELOPMENT

Trial Advocacy II, Regional Advocacy Center, Richmond, Virginia   **Apr. 2005**
Intensive week-long program focusing on DNA, Trace, Firearm, and Psychiatric Evidence; Forensic Pathology; and Examination of Expert Witnesses. Program culminated with practical experience conducting direct and cross-examinations of experts and delivering closing arguments.

References Provided On Request

Written By: Arnold G. Boldt
Font: Tahoma

Chapter 12

▶ Resumes for

Manufacturing and Operations Careers

Each and every industry and profession presents unique resume writing and design challenges. If you are interested in pursuing a career in manufacturing or operations, be certain to incorporate these important success factors:

Success Factor #1

Highlight your experience and training in principles and methods such as Lean Manufacturing, Six Sigma, Just-In-Time inventory, TQM, SAP, and ISO standards.

Success Factor #2

Showcase information about your contributions to process improvements, scrap reduction, or other innovations that increase operating efficiency or reduce production costs. Use dollar figures or percentages whenever possible to quantify results.

Success Factor #3

Demonstrate the diversity of your skillset by mentioning the various operations/processes with which you have experience (for example, cell manufacturing, assembly line, fabrication, stamping/molding, or clean-room operations).

Success Factor #4

Include statistics about quality and customer interactions. As domestic manufacturers compete in the global market, delivering defect-free products and being attentive to customers are critical.

Keywords and Keyword Phrases

Keywords and keyword phrases are a critical component of every successful job seeker's resume. By using just one or two words, you're able to communicate a wealth of information about your skills, qualifications, and experience. What's more, keywords are the basis for resume-scanning technology and are therefore critical to any job seeker's campaign in today's electronic-based job search market. For more information on keywords, refer back to pages 17–19 in Chapter 1.

Following are the top 20 manufacturing and operations keywords, some of which may reflect your skills and some of which may not be appropriate for you at this time. Use these words as the foundation for developing your own list of keywords on the Professional Keyword List form in Appendix B.

Top 20 Keywords

Budget Planning and Administration

Continuous Process Improvement

Cost Reduction and Avoidance

Efficiency Improvement

Facilities Engineering

Inventory Planning and Control

Logistics

Manufacturing Technology

Multi-Site Operations Management

Occupational Health and Safety

Operations Re-Engineering

Plant Management

Process Automation

Productivity Improvement

Quality Assurance and Control

Resource Planning and Management

Supply Chain Management

Technology Integration

Workflow Optimization

Workforce Planning and Management

Following are some excellent examples of resumes for manufacturing and operations careers.

GIOVANNI PASSEO

2208 Covington Court • Sewell, NJ 08080 • 856-629-3259

Skills and Qualifications

- Proven ability to discover and eliminate scheduling and production inefficiencies to increase output and profits.
- Strong supervisory skills and ability to motivate employees to perform at maximum efficiency.
- Comfortable with computerized production and tracking systems, including shipping and receiving of goods.
- Excellent negotiating and interpersonal communication skills.
- Familiar with Word and UNIX database programs.
- Specialized expertise and experience in:
  - Operations
  - Personnel
  - Customer Relations
  - Inventory/Equipment Control
  - Quality Control/Assurance
  - Equipment Maintenance/Repair

Experience Using

- Numerically Controlled Machines
- Pneumatics
- Mig/Tig Welding
- Heat Treating
- Horizontal/Vertical Mills
- Sheet Metal
- Calibration
- Military Specs
- Vapor Face
- Punch Presses
- Hydraulics
- Arc Welding
- Lathes
- Surface Grinders
- Schematics
- Drafting
- Waver Soldering
- EDM

Professional Experience

Production
Facilitated staff meetings and implemented several changes which reduced downtime and increased productivity. Revised procedures that improved efficiency and reduced overhead.

Scheduling
Coordinated production schedules, material needs, and workers' shifts to meet customers' deadlines.

Quality Control
Oversaw manufacturing of product from initial to final stage of production.

Personnel Hiring, Supervision, and Training
Interviewed, hired, and trained staff in addition to supervising and evaluating the performance of 20 workers.

Sales
Recommended products to meet customers' requirements, considering features such as cost, flexibility, capacity, and economy of operation. Negotiated terms of sale and services with customers.

Equipment Repair
Repaired shop equipment such as air compressors, air conditioners, mold press and stamping machines. Performed pneumatic and hydraulic repairs as well as handled plumbing and electrical problems.

Employment History

1995 – 2006	Plant Supervisor	Marco Manufacturing Company	Philadelphia, PA
1984 – 1995	Tool and Die Maker	Budd Company	Philadelphia, PA

Written By: Johnetta Frazier
Font: Perpetua

Michael Hernandez

448 South Street Unit A
Victoria, TX 77901
(H) 361-575-2667 (pgr) 888 -932-4885
E-mail: mhern514@aol.com

SIGNIFICANT PROFESSIONAL ACHIEVEMENTS

- ✦ Launched programs and volume for Snelling's newest contact center in New York City.
- ✦ Recognized by Customer Inter@ction Solutions with the 2002 MVP Quality Award.
- ✦ Reduced agent attrition by 47%.
- ✦ Achieved a $4 million annual gross profit.
- ✦ Managed up to 25,000 calls per day while exceeding client quality standards.
- ✦ Orchestrated successful customer service programs for multiple client products.
- ✦ Increased responsiveness to customer demands through client-interfacing programs.

CORE STRENGTHS

OPERATIONS MANAGEMENT

Customer Service	Performance Improvement Management	P&L / Forecasting
Resource Management	Quality Assurance	Staff Development
Client Management	Efficiency / Productivity Enhancement	Agent Retention

TECHNOLOGY

CMS – Call Management	Performix – Performance Management	Witness Systems – Call Monitoring
IEX – Scheduling	Microsoft Office – Excel, Word, Power Point	People-Trak – Human Resources

PROFESSIONAL EXPERIENCE

SNELLING WORKFORCE – CUSTOMER CONTACT CENTER SOLUTIONS   1999–Present

Forbes Magazine recognizes Snelling as one of "America's Leading Companies". Call Center Magazine has recognized Snelling for "Best Call Center" and "Call Center of the Year." Snelling's Headquarters are located in Ft. Lauderdale, Florida and company employs more than 310K employees worldwide. The Customer Contact Center Solutions business unit has 2,000 employees in seven locations throughout the United States and abroad serving major clients such as SBC, Cingular and UPS.

Customer Contact Center Solutions - Victoria, Texas

Client – SBC / 250 Seats / 24x7
Operations Manager 2002–Present

- ▶ *Challenge*: Achieve Client Contractual Service Level Goals of 80/20.
- ▶ *Action:* Required management/supervisory teams to constantly track service level performance at half-hour intervals.
- ▶ *Result:* Year-end result = 87.7% thus meeting client expectations and increasing profit performance.

▶ *Challenge*: Meet Client Quality standards yielding Quality Scores of 93%.
▶ *Action*: The quality department's target is to monitor 5 calls per week for every newly hired agent on a probationary period as well as those agents who are not meeting the minimum average of 85%. Agents that are not meeting the minimum average goal are placed on performance counseling until their averages are above the minimum average.
▶ *Result*: Far exceeded client expectations by achieving external (client) monitor scores in excess of 96% and an annual internal quality monitoring average of 93.48%.

▶ *Challenge*: Employee development
▶ *Action*: 100% of support staff was informed of the expectations set forth by the client. Communication was cascaded down to the agent level emphasizing the importance of meeting the operational performance goals and objectives. Additionally, the exempt staff was required to attend client calibration calls in order to maintain compliance with client goals as well as a weekly roundtable discussion with the client in order to discuss past performance, future projects, and current concerns.
▶ *Result*: Cascading Goals were achieved and Assistant Site Managers were cognizant of all of the reports to be submitted to the client. Examples of these reports are: Monthly Deck Report / GPPC Report / Call Tracker Report / UK Amex Report / Monthly Invoice.

Assistant Site Manager – Operations 2000–2002

- Managed a supervisory team in regards to workflow allocation, performance appraisals, training and development, and salary recommendations.
- Coordinated the daily operational objectives of performing departmental functions in an efficient and timely manner while meeting quality performance standards.
- Resolved customer and agent challenges through proactive investigation of issues in a liaison role while partnering with other departments and the client.
- Planned and implemented new projects and procedures as a result of a continuous review of current operating methods in relation to client/customer objectives.
- Regulated expenditures, structured budget, and reconciled P&L to meet organizational objectives.

Fraud Prevention Manager – Administrative Operations 1999–2000

- Developed and implemented fraud prevention policy and procedures, resulting in the lowest chargeback percentage among all call centers (half of one percent).
- Established customer service guidelines in the Administrative Operations Department.
- Monitored the productivity of the Outbound Sales Department.
- Trained and managed a staff of 45 agents and supervisors in the following departments: Fraud Prevention, Administrative Operations, and Outbound Sales.
- Served the center in the capacity of Assistant Site Manager in the absence of the permanent ASM.

DIRECT LINK TELESERVICES – MONTOGOMERY, Florida   1996-1999
Quality Assurance Supervisor

- Developed fraud prevention guidelines.
- Corresponded to all chargeback issues.
- Managed customer complaint issues.
- Trained agents on quality assurance procedures.
- Supervised the call center on demand.

EDUCATION

UNIVERSITY OF CENTRAL ALABAMA   1996
Bachelor of Arts Psychology: National Honor Societies - Golden Key and Psi Chi

Written By: Melisa Rogers
Font: Franklin Gothic Medium Condensed

JOYCE ONER

123 Freetown Court
Reston, VA 20191

(703) 995-0706 — Home
(202) 346-8888 — Work
gone@cwla.org

A TELLING PERFORMANCE

From 2005 Evaluation:

"Joyce has an exceptional knowledge of printing and production and uses [it] to make seemingly impossible projects possible."

"Planning and organizing is Joyce's strongest asset."

"Joyce cut costs this year up to $8,000 on one printing job."

From Current Vendors:

"Joyce is patient. She understands mechanical and people problems."

"She is flexible and realistic about deadlines."
> H. Artison
> ABS Printing

"Joyce doesn't panic. She knows the reality [of the creative and the production process]."
> W. Stetson
> Printing Network

"Joyce has a realistic view of the vendor/client relationship."
> O. Kirk
> Smith Litho

From Previous Employers:

"Joyce is a person I would choose to have on any staff at any company."
(MCI-WorldCom Supervisor)

"She understands the larger picture of the company's needs and can bring it down to a smaller, functional picture, to accomplish what is needed."
(MCI-WorldCom Supervisor)

PRODUCTION COORDINATOR

Objective: To use my creative and organizational skills for publishers or agencies focused on the very best in print buying and production.

CAREER SUMMARY

Expert production manager and art coordinator with 10+ years' experience. Articulate writer and speaker with solid vendor relationships. Delivers quality, end-to-end production and creative management in a friendly, "on time-in budget" atmosphere. Reputation for "ace-ing" every job and making order out of chaos.

EXPERTISE / ACCOMPLISHMENTS

Production (10+ years)
- Purchases printing for 40-page glossy magazines and scholarly trade journals with up to 20,000+ circulation.
- Triples distribution and production of children's books and adult imprints in one year, without adding staff.
- Produces billboards, phone cards, CDs, folders, and print ads in foreign languages (Japanese, NorweJoycean, Swedish, Pilipino, and Asian).

Inventory management (10 years)
- Monitors inventory of 500+ client packages, books, and Joycefts.
- Coordinates Joycefts and packages to avoid out-of-stock status.
- Centralizes division inventory for association members and develops reorder points.
- Reviews annual physical inventory with fulfillment house.

Art Coordinator (5+ years)
- Oversees and advises on development and use of branding / corporate identity including logos, taglines, trademarks and copyrights, colors, and corporate stationery.
- Purchases printing for 20+ books per year including covers, layouts, and sizes, while handling reprints of 200 existing publications.
- Advisor and liaison to graphic artists, designers, editors, and marketing staff. Educates others in production process.

Purchasing (10 years)
- Selects local and specialty printers to maximize quality and turnaround of printing and design projects.
- Buys paper by the carload—direct from the paper mill.
- Knows the market to maximize value for every project.
- Understands technology and how it affects the quality of each project.
- Manages annual budget of $2M.

Supervision & Vendor Relationships (10 years)
- Closely partners with vendors to ensure ongoing relationships, quality, and on time-in budget deliverables.
- Creates comprehensive job-tracking files / reports encompassing cost, timeline, challenges, and status of design, editing, layout, and production for 200+ jobs.

JOYCE ONER
Page Two

HONORS

Earned award for outstanding corporate communications during MCI-WorldCom merger. (1999)

Has never missed a deadline!

NAME CLIENTS

National Geographic
AAFES (U. S. Army)
Japan Airlines
MCI-WorldCom
AARP
Child Welfare League
Prudential
Intl Assn. of Chiefs of Police

Career History

CHILD WELFARE LEAGUE OF AMERICA—WASHINGTON, DC
Production Manager   01/02 to Present
- Plan, manage, and purchase all printing for annual production of two periodicals, five new children's books, 20 other books, 14 newsletters, 75 conference items, 500,000 direct-mail pieces, and ad-hoc specialty items.
- Produce two bi-monthly publications—one glossy magazine and one journal for practitioners in the field of child welfare.
- Monitor inventory, initiate reprints, and manage production of new books, conference, and direct-mail materials.
- Administer nonprofit production budget of $2M.

MCI WORLDCOM, LTD.—ARLINGTON, VA
Production Manager   09/95 to 12/01
- Purchased printing for, outsourced, and managed the creative process for $1.5 billion printing / promotion contract for the U.S. Army—from logo creation to billboards and phone cards. This AAFES contract was the largest every awarded to MCI.
- Promoted web training content for National Geographic contract, including purchasing printing for the joint Marco Polo project.
- Grew print production by 50% in two years—from 300 to 450+ jobs.

C. G. SLOAN & COMPANY—BETHESDA, MD
Art Director   06/93 to 08/95
- Core contact for ads and catalogs from concept to delivery.
- Produced 200+ page auction catalogs and 8-page marketing brochures every five weeks.
- Redesigned auction catalog.

ADVANCED MARINE ENTERPRISES, INC.—CRYSTAL CITY, VA
Purchasing Specialist   02/90 to 06/93
- Assisted 4 designers and art staff in the preparation and editing of marketing collateral.
- Managed all printing, billing, and vendor outsourcing.

AMERICAN ASSOCIATION OF RETIRED PERSONS—ALEXANDRIA, VA
Publications Production Manager   1986 to 1990
- Centralized production of Membership Division collateral.
- Managed three staff and published 500+ magazines, audiovisuals, and program kits each year.
- Tripled imprints and distribution from 6 to 18 million in one year.

EDUCATION

COLUMBIA VISUAL ARTS COLLEGE—COLUMBIA, MD
Master of Arts Degree

GEORGETOWN UNIVERSITY—WASHINGTON, DC
Publication Specialist Certificate

NORTHWESTERN UNIVERSITY—CHICAGO, IL
Bachelor of Arts Degree, French

COMPUTER SKILLS
MS Word, Excel, Quark Express, FileMaker Pro, E-mail, Web browsers, and Windows.

Written By: Helen Oliff
Font: Tahoma

JOB ID: 4774

Pete Astrud
inventory manager

4114 North Carlton Street
Kansas City, Missouri 64101
☎ 816.989.3827 (cell) – 816.226.3827 (Home)
📧 peteastrud6290@yahoo.com

WHAT I CAN OFFER TopLINE

❑ Proven track record in maximizing ROI...in people, software, stock levels, and policies.

❑ Documented skill at finding and fixing inventory and logistics problems with solutions that work over the long haul.

❑ Practiced ability to train others in best practices.

RECENT WORK HISTORY WITH EXAMPLES OF PROBLEMS SOLVED

❑ Independent **Logistics Contractor**, McConnell Air Force Base, Kansas   Jul 03 – Present

❑ **Logistics Contractor**, Airside, Inc., McConnell Air Force Base, Kansas   Dec 02 – Jun 03

Helped support a full-service outpatient clinic employing 300 professionals who serve a population of 41,000.

More than 10 years of increasingly responsible logistics experience on active duty with the United States Air Force including these most recent assignments:

❑ *Promoted by name at the request of the Chief of Medical Logistics to serve as* **Medical Logistics Manager,** Yigo, Guam   Nov 00 – Oct 02

Served as direct reporting official for eight professionals including an assistant chief of medical logistics, an acquisitions manager, a warehouse manager, and purchasing specialists. Took on additional responsibilities as the Director of the Logistics Disaster Team. **Built, defended, and managed an annual budget of $960K.**

Inherited an organization that had needed improvement in accountability and inventory control for two years. Others tried adding more people, but that approach failed. Soon uncovered the real problem: improper training. *Outcomes:* Designed, built, and delivered solid training **without spending an extra dime**. We went from near the bottom of *more* than 15 organizations **right to the top**—and we stayed there.

Found a much better way to get management the logistics reports they needed to support our mission. Replaced cumbersome text format with an easy-to-use, concise PowerPoint presentation. *Outcomes:* The leadership liked the reports so much, my format **became the corporate standard**. What **once took 40 hours** a month to compile, **now done in an hour.**

Asked to build one of the very first logistics plans in support of homeland defense—after $250K worth of material had already arrived. My baseline audit, done **single-handedly**, corrected dozens of errors in five weeks of nights and weekend work. *Outcomes:* By redistributing several line items, support improved quickly. **Saved $10K a year.**

More indicators of performance TopLine can use ...

| Pete Astrud | **Inventory Manager** | 816.989.3827 (Cell) |

Did the work of 2 people to get our $1.1M inventory back under control. *Outcomes:* My new policies brought these advantages: **accuracy rose to 99.9 percent** (nearly 5 percent above the corporate standard); inventories increased from 1 to 4 times a year; time to complete each inventory fell from 6 man weeks to 12 man hours.

Trained the staff to transition to a much more responsive inventory control—even though I had no experience or training in that system. Mastered the subject so well, I soon trained 54 customer representatives. *Outcomes:* Organization's **average delivery time fell from 65 to 8 days.**

❑ *Sought out for promotion by senior management to serve as* **Quality Assurance Manager,** United States Embassy, Cairo, Egypt   Nov 98 – Oct 00

Helped support 200 directly assigned staff and an additional 40 contractors at four sites spread over hundreds of miles of empty desert in four countries.

Restored accountability measures to the system used to evaluate contractors' performance. *Outcomes:* **Miscalibration rate fell** from 12 percent to 0; **$10K saved** in transportation costs, **availability** of parts **rose 25 percent**—and all this done in 60 days.

Recovered value from expired stock by finding a market for those products. *Outcomes:* **Recovered $75K** in one line item category alone.

❑ *Promoted to* **Medical Systems Analyst** and Section Training Manager, McConnell Air Force Base, Kansas   Sep 94 – Nov 98

Chosen by the most senior management to **lead a team** that did **breakthrough work on usage rates.** With nothing but the broadest guidance, recruited an interdisciplinary team of 12. *Outcomes:* Our software test produced **such flawless results that it's still in use** today. Brought in this 90-day project **20 days early.** Decorated for this achievement.

EDUCATION AND PROFESSIONAL DEVELOPMENT

❑ Associates Degree, Management, Empire State College of New York, Saratoga Springs, New York   2003
Earned this degree while working 40 hours a week. Completed eight hours toward a B.S. in management at the same school.

❑ Associates Degree in Logistics, Community College of the Air Force, Maxwell Air Force Base, Alabama   1998

❑ "Acquisition Planning – Under Development: Determination of Need, Market Research & Analysis Requirements," two days, Federal Acquisition Institute   2001

COMPUTER SKILLS

❑ Near expert in a proprietary inventory control, accounting, purchasing, shipping, and report generator **logistics software suite.**

❑ Proficient in Word, Excel, PowerPoint, and advanced Internet search protocols.

❑ Working knowledge of Access and UNIX.

Page two

Written By: Don Orlando
Font: Book Antiqua

SHARON C. CLEMENTS
2721 Abernathy Drive, Columbia, MD 21044
(410) 997-7521 Home ▪ (703) 771-8113 Mobile ▪ sharonclem@newmedia.com

OPERATIONS & MANAGEMENT EXECUTIVE
Regional Director ▪ General Manager ▪ Operations Manager

General/Operations Management professional with proven expertise in expanding product/program lines, increasing revenue streams, and capturing market share in highly competitive Health and Fitness industry. Doubled membership income and gross revenues within one year (2004-2005). Leadership role in health and fitness clubs expansion (15 greenfields and 10 acquisitions).

Hands-on P&L role in strategic planning and initiative management, multi-site operations, recruitment and training (60 management and 1000 line staff), team building, and project management. Met or exceeded revenue/development expectations for 20+ years. Experienced in:

☑ Revenue & Market Expansion	☑ Change Management	☑ Start-ups & Acquisitions
☑ Staff & Management Development	☑ Sales & Marketing	☑ Business Development
☑ Budget & Financial Performance	☑ HR Management	☑ Branding & Technology

PROFESSIONAL EXPERIENCE

FITNESS CLUBS INTERNATIONAL, Washington, DC (corporate headquarters)   1984 – 2006
Leader in Health & Fitness Industry, ranked 2nd in U.S. and 7th worldwide (based on revenues) with 365,000 members at 132 clubs and 7,200 employees.

General Manager – Columbia Fitness Club (CFC), Columbia, MD (2003-2006)
Full P&L responsibility for sports club ranked 1st in suburban DC market. Managed 20,000 SF club with 2000 members, and supervised 40 management and line staff. Key player in strategic planning, business development, operations, sales and marketing, brand building, PR and community relations, customer service/retention, HR, administration, and technology performance.

ACCOMPLISHMENTS
Challenged in company restructure and brand-building initiative to deliver smooth-running, profitable operations and sales in high-profile fitness club facility. By 2005, voted "Best Health Club" in DC Metro area. Key contributor to market dominance on East Coast. Introduced new product and service lines, negotiated cost reductions (from 10% to cost of item), collaborated in succession planning and team building, and led revenue and profitability increases (demonstrated by financial metrics below):

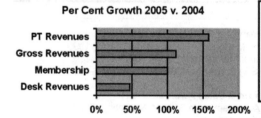

Per Cent Growth 2005 v. 2004

2005 v. 2004
PT Revenues: $509,136 v. $197,225
Gross Revenues: $1,863,790 v. $881,506
Membership: $1,544,748 v. $768,564
Desk Revenues: $27,541 v. $18,774

SHARON C. CLEMENTS   Page 2
(410) 997-7521 Home ▪ (703) 771-8113 Mobile ▪ sharonclem@newmedia.com

Area Manager – CFC, Columbia, MD (1999-2003)
Oversaw operations and explosive growth of suburban DC clubs. Full P&L responsibility for sales and marketing, systems, finance, SOP, customer service, multi-unit management, HR, initiative management, succession planning, recruiting, training, and management development.

- **Start-up and Acquisition.** Delivered strong revenues and development results in soft market: spearheaded growth from 1 club with 500 members (starting revenues of $1.4M) to 6 clubs with 13,200 members and annual revenues of $14.5M (2003). Clubs ranged in size from 20,000 sf to 200,000 sf on 23 acres. Managed and motivated team that grew to 550 employees. Chosen as member of Washington, DC Mayor's Health & Fitness Council Committee in 2003.

- **Technology Improvements.** Played key team role in 2002-2003 rollout of Club Networks, integrated enterprise software solution for sales reporting with online point-of-sale/real-time sales, tracking, financial, and reporting capability. In 2000 successfully launched automated Fitness Database as well as online direct payroll processing IT system (Kronos).

General Manager – Washington, DC Fitness Club (DCFC), Washington, DC (1990-1999)
Directed operations of largest sports club in DC market (8 locations). Full P&L responsibility. Supervised 30-60 management and line staff, including recruitment, training, and staff development.

- **Acquisitions and Revitalization.** Designated Lead Management Trainer for new manager orientation. Initiated employee cross-training programs, new employee and customer service seminars, monthly performance incentives, and SOP guidelines for training, operations, maintenance, tracking, and production. Negotiated cost-saving contracts with outside vendors. Oversaw multi-million-dollar club renovations.

- **New Technology and Products.** In 1997 transitioned club from manual to computerized system for sales tracking (sales, leads, and management system software), increasing accuracy and turnaround time for sales reporting. First to introduce electronic funds transfer.

Previous FCI Career History:
Progressive promotions from Sales Consultant through Sales Supervisor to Area Membership Supervisor (supervised 36) as company grew from 3 to 9 locations. Set year-over-year sales records, pre-sold and assisted in opening 7 clubs, and initiated performance improvement processes.

EDUCATION & AWARDS

Bachelor's Degree Program, University of Maryland, College Park, MD
Certificate, Managing Performance, American Management Association (AMA), 1999
Certificate, The Manager's Role in Professional Management, AMA, 1998
International Racquet Sports Association (IRSA) Conventions & Seminars, 1986-1998

Fitness Clubs International (FCI) Management & Sales Awards
Service Recognition Award for Outstanding Achievement in Sales & Marketing, 2003
Certificate of Achievement "Employee Primer" Award, 1997
Certificate of Achievement for "greatest drop in cancellation percentage", 1996

Written By: Susan Guameri
Font: Arial

WALTER ROBERTS

PRODUCTION MANAGEMENT

Highly regarded manager whose accomplishments reflect strong leadership ability, an organized, solution-oriented mindset, and the ability to recognize and act on improvement opportunities.

SUMMARY OF QUALIFICATIONS

- Solid record of accomplishment initiating operational / organizational changes to improve performance.
- Organized and systematic. Go-getter who gets the job done, remaining calm and cool under pressure.
- Effective, hands-on manager. Able to capitalize on individual strengths and build productive teams.
- Respected leader who readily takes initiative to solve problems and improve business operations.
- Demonstrated commitment to maximizing efficiency and productivity in the workplace.

PROFESSIONAL EXPERIENCE

JOHNSON FOODS, Mount Laurel, NJ   1985 to present
Production Supervisor (1995 to present)
Monitor daily operations, setting schedules for blending and production while supervising 39 production workers.

- Currently assigned to finishing plant; effectively schedule blending, packaging, and labeling of products in 6-day, 24-hour operation that produces an average of 500,000 packages daily. Capably troubleshoot problems and resolve issues related to mechanical systems, supplies, computer systems, and personnel.
- Manage dispatch for fleet of 20 drivers, capably coordinating pickups and deliveries while competently dealing with problems related to truck breakdowns, driver illnesses, and schedule changes.
- Mobilized management team to reach mandated cost-savings objective of $8,000/week. Organized brainstorming sessions that identified improvement opportunities, leading team to successfully reach target within four months.
- Introduced new schedule that reduced the number of employees assigned to Saturday clean-up. With more man-hours available for daily production, win-win situation saved $360,000 in overtime costs.
- Established training program for new employees, regularly evaluating performance to gauge progress.
- Created fact book that detailed production operations, procedures, and configurations for various plant products. Well-received manual is currently used as a training and reference tool for plant personnel.
- Earned reputation for commitment to operations improvement. Routinely and proactively implement new procedures, improving efficiency and productivity while reducing waste and costs.

Warehouse Manager (1990 to 1995)
- Reduced workforce 20% while increasing productivity by redesigning labor-intensive operation.
- Developed recommendation for cost-saving pallet control program.
- Implemented bar code system that automated inventory control and improved accuracy.

Shipping Supervisor (1988 to 1990)
Working Foreman (1986 to 1988)

PROFESSIONAL DEVELOPMENT

Completed training in: TQM, Reliability Centered Management, Supervision & Management

Computer skills: Word, Excel, AS400, Internet, Email

35 WALNUT ROAD ◆ MOUNT LAUREL, NJ 08054 ◆ (856) 235-4190

roberts@aol.com

Written By: Carol Altomare
Font: Arial Narrow

Stephen J. Morris

5870 Dover Court, Carmel, Indiana 46033
Tel: (317) 861-2943   Cell: (317) 940-5279   s.morris@yahoo.com

MANUFACTURING MANAGEMENT PROFESSIONAL

Delivers strong and sustainable improvements in efficiency, productivity, quality, and profits through aggressive turnaround leadership, product development innovations, best-in-class operations, and cost-reduction initiatives.

Increased sales 150% while improving 48% profit margin 48% in less than three years.

PROFESSIONAL EXPERIENCE:

Lantz Industries, Indianapolis, Indiana, 2002 – 2006
(Manufacturer of high-quality industrial & commercial abrasive products)

Consultant

- Purchased and tested competitors' products to develop new product lines for roll-coating manufacturing company. Researched product combinations, determined most cost-effective alternatives, and added new manufacturing processes. New products increased annual revenues by $7 million in 2 ½ years.

- Responded to global competition by investigating new suppliers with consistent level of high quality and low cost. Personally traveled to foreign countries, evaluated and modified existing raw materials, and built strong company-supplier relationships. Reduced raw material cost by as much as 40% on select product lines.

- Demonstrated exceptional ability to significantly raise the level of product quality in production operations at fast-paced manufacturing facility. Personally led and inspired staff and crews to embrace the importance of quality improvement, lifelong learning, and personal development. Reduced non-standard product costs by $500K annually.

3M Abrasives, St. Paul, Minnesota, 1989 - 2002
(Worldwide distributor of abrasive products with over $3 billion in annual sales)

Plant Manager, Manufacturing, Tonawanda, New York, 2000 - 2002

- Managed multiple areas of manufacturing by leading, training, advising, and scheduling all production operations. Identified bottlenecks to attaining goals and focused on each obstacle individually. Created satisfied customers and increased business by improving on-time delivery rate from 92% to 98%.

- Reduced inventory and improved JIT manufacturing. Coordinated manufacturing operations, quality, and supplies with headquarters' master schedulers at affiliate site. Reduced inventory by 50% while achieving 98% on-time delivery.

Film Products Manager, Manufacturing, 1995 - 2000

- Assigned to underperforming union manufacturing department. Reorganized assignments, plant layout, and written work instructions. Improved sales and profits by more than 100% in three years, increasing total sales from $1.5 million to $3.8 million while achieving a 48% profit margin.

EDUCATION: **Bachelor of Science,** *Business Administration,* 1989
BALL STATE UNIVERSITY, Muncie, Indiana

Written By: Michael S. Davis
Font: Bookman Old Style

WILLIAM T. PARKERSON

35 Sunderland Drive　　　　　　　　　　　　　　　　　　　　　Home: 201.339.6755
Cedar Grove, NJ 07005　　　　E-mail: parkersonw@comcast.net　　Mobile: 201.568.3390

PLANT / OPERATIONS / GENERAL MANAGEMENT EXECUTIVE

Multi-site manufacturing plant/general management career building and leading high-growth, transition and start-up operations in domestic and international environments with annual revenues of up to $680 million.

Expertise: Organizational Development • Productivity & Cost Reduction Improvement • Supply Chain Management • Acquisitions & Divestitures • IPOs • Plant Rationalizations • Safety Performance • Customer Relations • Change Agent

---

CORE COMPETENCIES

Manufacturing Leadership—Strong P&L track record with functional management experience in all disciplines of manufacturing operations • Developing and managing operating budgets • Spearheading restructuring and rationalization of plants and contracted distribution facilities • Initiating lean manufacturing processes utilizing SMED principles • Establishing performance metrics and supply chain management teams.

Continuous Improvement & Training—Designing and instituting leadership enhancement training program for all key plant management • Instituting Total Quality System (TQS) process in domestic plants to promote the business culture of continuous improvement • Leading ISO 9001 certification process.

New Product Development—Initiating plant-based "New Product Development Think Tank" that developed 130 new products for marketing review, resulting in the successful launch of 5 new products in 2000.

Engineering Management—Oversight of corporate machine design and development teams • Developing 3-year operating plan • Directing the design, fabrication and installation of several proprietary machines • Creating project cost-tracking systems and introducing ROI accountability.

PROFESSIONAL EXPERIENCE

BEACON INDUSTRIES, INC., Cedar Grove, NJ (1997–Present)
Record of continuous promotions to executive-level position in manufacturing and operations management despite periods of transition/acquisition at a $680 million, Fortune 500 international manufacturing company. Career highlights include:

Vice President of Manufacturing (1997–Present)
Senior Operating Executive responsible for the performance of 7 manufacturing/distribution facilities for company that experienced rapid growth from 4 plants generating $350 million in annual revenues to 14 manufacturing facilities with revenues of $680 million. Charged with driving the organization to become a low-cost producer. Established performance indicators, operating goals, realignment initiatives, productivity improvements and cost-reduction programs that consistently improved product output, product quality and customer satisfaction.

Achievements:

- Selected to lead corporate team in developing and driving forward cost-reduction initiatives that will result in $21 million saved over the next 3 years through capital infusion, process automation and additional rationalizations.

- Saved $13 million annually by reducing fixed spending 11% and variable overhead spending 18% through effective utilization of operating resources and cost-improvement initiatives.

- Cut workers' compensation costs 40% ($750,000 annually) by implementing effective health and safety plans, employee training, management accountability and equipment safeguarding. Led company to achieve recognition as "Best in Industry" regarding OSHA frequency and Loss Workday Incident rates.

- Reduced waste generation 31%, saving $1 million in material usage by optimizing manufacturing processes as well as instituting controls and accountability.

- Enhanced customer service satisfaction 3% annually during past year (measured by order fill and on-time delivery percentage) through supply chain management initiatives, inventory control and flexible manufacturing practices.

- Trimmed manufacturing and shipping related credits to customers from 1.04% to .5% of total sales in 1999, representing annual $1.8 million reduction.

- Decreased total inventories 43% from 1997 base through combination of supply chain management, purchasing, master scheduling and global utilization initiatives.

- Rationalized 3 manufacturing plants and 6 distribution facilities, saving $6 million over 3 years.

General Manager, Northeast (1994–1997)

Assumed full P&L responsibility of 2 manufacturing facilities and a $20 million annual operating budget. Directly supervised facility managers and indirectly 250 employees in a multi-line, multicultural manufacturing environment. Planned and realigned organizational structure and operations to position company for high growth as a result of acquiring a major account, 2 new product lines and 800 additional SKUs.

Achievements:

- Reduced operating costs by $4.5 million through consolidation of 2 distribution locations without adverse impact on customer service.
- Accomplished the start-up of 2 new manufacturing operations, which encompassed a plant closing and the integration of acquired equipment into existing production lines for 2 new product lines without interruption to customer service. Achieved 2 months ahead of target and $400,000 below budget.
- Increased operating performance by 15% while reducing labor costs by $540,000.
- Reduced frequency and severity of accidents by 50% in 3 years, contributing to a workers' compensation and cost avoidance reduction of $1 million.
- Decreased operating waste by 2% for an annual cost savings of $800,000 in 2 manufacturing facilities.
- Negotiated turnkey contracts for 2 distribution warehouses to meet expanded volume requirements.
- Maintained general management and administrative cost (GMA) at a flat rate as sales grew by 25% annually over 3 years.

ROMELARD CORPORATION, Detroit, MI (1980–1994)
Division Manufacturing Director (1989–1994)

Fast-track advancement in engineering, manufacturing and operations management to division-level position. Retained by new corporate owners and promoted in 1994 based on consistent contributions to revenue growth, profit improvements and cost reduction. Scope of responsibility encompassed P&L for 3 manufacturing facilities and a distribution center with 500 employees in production, quality, distribution, inventory control and maintenance.

Achievements:

- Delivered strong and sustainable operating gains: increased customer fill rate by 18%; improved operating performance by 20%; reduced operating waste by 15%; reduced inventory by $6 million.
- Justified, sourced and directed the installation of $10 million of automated plant equipment.
- Implemented and managed a centralized master scheduling for all manufacturing facilities.
- Reduced annual workers' compensation costs by $600,000.
- Created Customer Satisfaction Initiative program to identify areas of concern and implemented recommendations, significantly improving customer satisfaction.

Prior Positions: Manufacturing Manager (1987–1989); Plant Manager (1986–1987); Engineering Manager (1984–1986); Plant Industrial Engineer (1980–1984).

EDUCATION & PROFESSIONAL DEVELOPMENT

Bachelor of Science in Manufacturing Engineering, 1979
Syracuse University, Syracuse, NY

Continuing professional development programs in
Executive Management, Leadership and Finance

Written By: Louise Garver
Font: Times New Roman

Chapter 13

▶ Resumes for

Sales, Marketing, and Customer Service Careers

Each and every industry and profession presents unique resume writing and design challenges. If you are interested in pursuing a career in sales, marketing, or customer service, be certain to incorporate these important success factors:

** Success Factor #1**

Use statistics to quantify your achievements whenever possible. Show percentage increases in revenues, ranking among other sales associates, or number of new accounts, to demonstrate how you've added value. If you're a marketing professional, how much was market share or sales volume increased based on the campaign(s) you recommended?

** Success Factor #2**

Show your versatility by including the different categories of products/services you have experience representing or types of customers you have served (for example, business-to-business or direct-to-consumer).

** Success Factor #3**

Highlight consultative selling and relationship-building skills. In today's environment, connecting with customers, assessing their needs, and recommending solutions are highly valued in sales and customer service professionals.

** Success Factor #4**

Mention your technology skills, especially presentation software or contact management applications that help sales professionals do their jobs more efficiently. For customer service people, experience with various order entry/tracking software is important.

Keywords and Keyword Phrases

Keywords and keyword phrases are a critical component of every successful job seeker's resume. By using just one or two words, you're able to communicate a wealth of information about your skills, qualifications, and experience. What's more, keywords are the basis for resume-scanning technology and are therefore critical to any job seeker's campaign in today's electronic-based job search market. For more information on keywords, refer back to pages 17–19 in Chapter 1.

Following are the top 20 sales, marketing, and customer service keywords, some of which may reflect your skills and some of which may not be appropriate for you at this time. Use these words as the foundation for developing your own list of keywords on the Professional Keyword List form in Appendix B.

Top 20 Keywords

Brand Development and Launch

Competitive Market Intelligence

Contract Negotiations

Corporate Communications

Customer Relationship Management

Customer Service and Retention

E-Commerce

International Trade

Key Account Management

Media Affairs and Press Relations

Multi-Channel Marketing

Multimedia Marketing and Promotion

Product and Market Positioning

Product Lifecycle Management

Public Relations

Sales Administration

Sales Presentations

Sales Training

Solutions Selling

Time and Territory Management

Following are some excellent examples of resumes for sales, marketing, and customer service careers.

MARILYN WALTON

"Committed to exceeding performance expectations."

111 Main Street
Laguna Hills, CA 92653

949.292.0983
marilynwalton@internet.com

OBJECTIVE

Certified Surgical Technologist, Medical Assistant and Licensed Medical Aesthetician uniquely qualified for **Outside Sales** position with a skin care products or medical equipment company seeking to increase market share, revenue and profits.

PROFILE

- *Professional image* combined with *persuasive communication, presentation* and *interpersonal skills.*
- *Excellent skin care and plastic surgery background* strengthened by practical medical procedures experience.
- *Well-versed in presentation* and *closing strategies* for diverse products and medical procedures.
- *Reputation for organization, time management, reliability, results* and *integrity.*
- Separated from others by *intensity of commitment to growing revenue* and providing *superior customer service.*

KEY COMPETENCIES

Client Focus ♦ Consultative Sales Approach ♦ Customer Retention

Overcoming Objections

EDUCATION, LICENSE AND CERTIFICATIONS

Valley Beauty College – Laguna Hills, CA   2005
Medical Aesthetician

Health Care College – Santa Ana, CA   1997
Surgical Technologist

Beach City Medical Careers – Laguna Beach, CA   1996
Medical Assistant

California Medical License – **Medical Aesthetician**
California Certified **Surgical Technologist, Medical Assistant** and **Phlebotomist**

CAREER BACKGROUND

Modern Medical Clinic – Newport Beach, CA   2001 – Present
Surgical Technologist

Family Hospital – Laguna Hills, CA   1998 – 2001
Surgical Technologist

Dermatology and Laser Center – Dana Point, CA   1996 – 1997
Medical Assistant

Written By: James A. Swanson
Font: Times New Roman

ALLAN WILDER

212-476-0090   AllanWilderPro@comcast.net

22 Rood Street
Bronxville, NY 11100

MARKET RESEARCH ANALYST

Fast-track professional with over five years of experience in conducting market research and analysis on electronic products in international markets. Key strengths lie in brand labeling, strategic sales planning and client relationship management. Technically proficient with Microsoft Office and DTP software. Fluent in Japanese and conversant in German.

Representative Achievements:

✓ Recognized by Japan's leading economic magazine, *Outstanding Business Practices*, by winning the 2001 New Business Plan Award for pioneering new market penetration matrix.

✓ First and youngest-ever company representative to earn coveted MVP award for playing pivotal role in launch of a new hand-held data set that outperformed sales forecasts by 25%.

✓ Acted as liaison between Japanese headquarters and newly formed US branch that enabled North American markets to exceed benchmark goals.

PROFESSIONAL EXPERIENCE

PROFILES PLUS, New York, NY   2000 to Present
Marketing Representative & Coordinator, North America (2003 to Present)
Conduct market research and analysis including brand recognition and technology trends to determine marketing strategy for North American sector. Develop new sales channels in United States; establish pricing, planning and sales promotion tools. Design advertisements and exhibitions with media agencies publishers. Analyze market needs and serve as a liaison to Japan headquarters.

• **Fast-tracked to position as the most junior person in the company's history** to land promotion prior to completing five-year track at the assistant level.

• **Researched and uncovered new market segments that helped company capture #2 position** in the industry within only six months.

• **Created a branding strategy that enabled sales force to tap into new Canadian marketplace** and effectively positioned the subsidiary for triple digit growth over a five-year period.

Sales & Promotion Marketing Assistant, International Division (2000 - 2003)
Created a unified user database for the overseas market and introduced a product modification plan that transformed hard-copy manuals into online references. Prepared presentation materials and organized Asian distributor meetings. Maintained meeting notes and agendas for distribution company-wide. Analyzed market trends and research new opportunities. Assisted with new product sales collateral.

• **Asked by senior management team to participate in a presentation on innovative marketing strategies** for post Y2K in electronics markets internationally.

• **Oriented and trained new marketing interns** that resulted in the placement of four new professionals globally within eight months.

EDUCATION

INTERNATIONAL UNIVERSITY, Osaka, Japan - **Bachelor of Arts in Marketing**, 1999

Written By: Jill Grindle
Font: Book Antiqua

LISA COLAVITO

18 Center Drive ♦ Madison, NJ 07940
(973) 377-3349 ♦ lisacola@aol.com

TOP-NOTCH ACCOUNT MANAGER
"A true professional and role model who sets the standards for others"

SUMMARY OF QUALIFICATIONS

Performance-driven sales professional with a wealth of sales experience and proven achievements in account management and client retention. Stellar performance record. Consistently recognized for excellence in achieving and exceeding goals. Knowledgeable business partner with consultative approach. Able to accurately assess client needs and identify best-fit solutions. Highly customer-focused. Valued for exceptional relationship-building skills and ability to leverage customer service expertise to gain sales. Intensely driven to succeed.

PROFESSIONAL EXPERIENCE

DIGITAL SOLUTIONS, New York, NY   1987 to present
A leader in document management offering innovative technology, products, and services
Account Manager
Manage $2 million territory, marketing and selling high-end products and services to client base that includes large law firms, major accounting firms, and other corporate clients. Drive all aspects of sales process. Service accounts, cultivating strong relationships to maintain client business long term.

Sales Highlights

- Consistently rank among company's top producers, profitably selling value in highly competitive, price-sensitive market while retaining accounts long term. Among award-winning successes, achieved #2 national ranking in 2003 with sales that reached 311% of quota.
- Brought on key national account worth more than $1 million, displacing major competitor. Won account based on effectiveness in selling value and service to client.
- Leveraged company's competitive advantage and cutting-edge solutions to dramatically increase law firm sales by exploiting key opportunity opened by mandates to move to digital environment.
- Maintain active pipeline for new sales, earning repeat business when customers are not in buy mode by keeping them informed of new technologies, emerging industry trends, and new solutions.

Service Excellence

- Gain confidence of client and win sales by conducting extensive pre-sale research using internal and third-party resources to identify best-fit technology solutions customized to specific needs.
- Practicing customer-first philosophy, proactively mobilize internal resources to address and resolve customer problems to achieve outstanding customer satisfaction ratings. Earned special kudos from accounting clients for success in keeping equipment running during critical, high-volume periods.
- Spearhead planning and implementation of all post-sale installations, going above and beyond in coordinating resources to ensure flawless execution and customer delight.

EDUCATION & TRAINING

RUTGERS UNIVERSITY, New Brunswick, NJ
Bachelor of Science Degree in Marketing

Completed extensive sales training. Well-versed in many document management technologies.

Written By: Carol Altomare
Font: Baskerville Old Face

GERALD STOREY

DRIVING EARLY- TO MID-STAGE SOFTWARE COMPANIES TO MARKET DOMINANCE

55 Lansing Street
Philadelphia, PA 1 9120
267-555-9726
TopSales99@hotmail.com

SALES EXECUTIVE – SOFTWARE INDUSTRY

SALES & SALES MANAGEMENT
ALLIANCE-BUILDING
NEW PRODUCT LAUNCH
STRATEGIC PLANNING

TOP PERFORMING SALES MANAGER AND MULTIMILLION-DOLLAR INDIVIDUAL CONTRIBUTOR with 12 years' experience selling innovative products and professional services into the enterprise software space. Fast-track career (6 promotions in 6 years). Played key role in growing company from start-up to $189 million in annual sales. Inspirational manager with a record of building loyal, high-performance teams. Communicate effectively up and down the organization. Passionate, competitive, and driven-to-succeed. MBA degree.

Regional Director MVP Award	Q3 - 2005, Q4 - 2005, Q2 - 2006, Q3- 2006
Proclub	2001 - 2005 (all years measured)
#1 Sales Rep #1; Sales Manager; #1 Sales Director	2000 - 2006

PROFESSIONAL EXPERIENCE

NETDOMINANT, Philadelphia, PA   1999 – Present
Played key strategic sales role in growing company from 1 customer to 825 corporate accounts and achieving #2 position in emerging market of identity and access management solutions – out of 20 rivals (IBM, Sun, Novell, etc.).

Director of Sales – Northeast Region (2005 – Present)
Promoted to reenergize the strategically critical Northeast territory. Direct 8 sales reps and 6 sales engineers.
- Built and stabilized a high-powered team. Restructured existing staff and hired/mentored 4 sales representatives, one of whom closed the 2 largest deals in the company's history.
- Achieved impressive metrics for both contribution margin and overall revenue attainment.

Sales Metrics for Team	2005	2006
Sales Revenue	$21.23M	$28.77M
Quota Attainment	140%	130%
Profitability	#1 out of 7 Regions	#1 out of 7 regions
Proclub Attainment	Highest % in North America	Highest % in North America
Forecast Accuracy	#1	#1

Director of Sales – Firewall Sales/Corporate Sales (2004 – 2005)
Tapped to lead development of inside sales/corporate sales model. Full P&L accountability for $2 million product line.
- Re-envisioned and rebuilt the call center. Developed/implemented a call center automation system.
- Devised online tools and strategies that enabled the company to sell technical products over the phone.
- Built team of 8. Established call metrics and targets. Doubled productivity per sales rep in one quarter.
- Grew call center business to one of company's top revenue generators at $1.4 million in Q2 2004 sales.
- Ramped up to $1.2 million per quarter within 2 quarters. Slashed sales cycle by 78% (vs. outside sales).
- Revamped firewall sales business, increasing profits by $110,000. Improved forecasting accuracy.
- Dramatically increased lead generation and sales of maintenance agreements.

GERALD STOREY - TopSales99@hotmail.com

NETDOMINANT (Continued)
Director of Alliances and Channel Sales (2003 – 2004)
Promoted to accomplish a 3-fold mission: design and execute a comprehensive OEM channel strategy; develop the CRM/ERP Solutions Program; and eventually develop the System Integrator Alliances Program. Managed team of 5.

- Managed OEM program to a sustainable $600,000 per quarter.
- Developed a groundbreaking CRM/ERP Solutions Program to provide integration of access management software with ERP systems.
- Accelerated quarterly revenue achievement in the CRM/ERP Solutions Program from $100,000 to $1 million.
- Built alliances with system integrators that yielded $7+ million in indirect or influenced revenue.
- Implemented a training program, delivering over 1,000 trained system integration consultants.

Director of Sales – Strategic Global Accounts (2002 – 2003)
Challenged to develop a global accounts region across North America. Managed 30 Fortune 500 accounts. Hired and managed team of 3 sales reps and 3 sales engineers.

- Earned top ranking out of 8 regions as measured by percentage of goal achieved through 1st half of 2003.
- Drove $11 million in 2002 revenue with 11 assigned accounts.
- Contributed 20% of total corporate revenue (including maintenance renewals).
- Played integral role in producing 400% corporate growth in 2002.

Sales Executive/Manager – Northeast Region (1999 – 2002)
Launched the Major Accounts Program. Evangelized innovative software solutions to major corporations.

- Signed many of the company's first and largest customers – FAA, Tokai, GE, The Hartford, Liberty Mutual, Electronic Payment Services, Cigna, Akamai, CVS, State of NY, Xerox, Paychex, United Technology.
- Closed company's first $500,000 and $1 million deals.
- Delivered watershed account valued at $2 million with follow-on revenue of $25 million.
- Exceeded quota in all 13 quarters.
- Achieved 200% of goal in 2002 and 30% in 2001.
- Leveraged partner relationships to accelerate growth into new accounts and grow size of deals.
- Established the company's most profitable territory based on resource-to-revenue ratio.

TITAN SOFTWARE, INC., Philadelphia, PA   1997 – 1999
Global provider of enterprise fax and forms solutions for AS/400 systems.

Corporate Sales Manager
Built strategic relationships with major software firms to leverage the business model.

- Ranked #1 or #2 out of a field of 8 reps for 10 straight quarters. Responsible for 30% of all new business.
- Generated over $450,000 in gross margin in 1998.

Education and Professional Development

UNIVERSITY OF PENNSYLVANIA, Philadelphia, PA
Master of Business Administration   1999
Bachelor of Science: Business Management   1995

Written By: Jean Cummings
Font: Arial Narrow

WILLIAM A. MROZ

811 66th Avenue North
Myrtle Beach, SC 29578

(843) 650-0072
wam@aol.com

EXPERIENCED TERRITORY MANAGER / ACCOUNT EXECUTIVE

High-performance individual with a record of success for securing new business and developing other sales professionals.
Offering well-developed negotiation skills, productive work methods and high personal performance standards.

Proven sales leader with a strong background in business-to-business sales and a demonstrated ability to drive business despite aggressive competition and price-driven market conditions. Able to establish mutually respectful, client-loyal relationships through an accessible service orientation and honest representation. Regarded as a diligent problem solver who is able to provide highly specialized service while balancing competing demands. Consistently able to exceed goals through intensive prospecting, effective entry strategies, a consultative sales approach and strong "big-picture" presentation skills.

Sales & Territory Management Strengths	Staff Management / Leadership Competencies
▪ Deal Origination / Contract Structuring / Pricing Strategies	▪ Sales Training / Team Development / Hiring
▪ New Product & Service Introductions	▪ Morale Building, Mentoring & Coaching
▪ Negotiating Terms, Rates & Service Conditions	▪ Strategic Sales Planning / Meeting Facilitation
▪ Prospecting / Cold Calling / Customer Retention Strategies	▪ Solutions Selling / Sales & Market Analysis

EMPLOYMENT EXPERIENCE

MOHAWK TELEPHONE, *Mohawk, NY*   **2002 to Present**
Retention Manager (2005 - Present)
Initially recruited to expand company presence and develop new revenue streams (DSL, telephone, Internet). After 18 months of active selling (adding 2,000 access lines), selected to become Retention Manager with the challenge to solidify existing customer relationships and profitably manage the company's 32,000 service contracts. Investigate customer complaints on a constant basis, taking appropriate steps to resolve issues, ensure service quality standards and retain critical accounts.

Sales Manager—Mohawk Valley Region (2003 to 2005)
Sales Representative—Mohawk Valley Region (2002 to 2003)
Managed the entire sales process and provided sales support/guidance for up to 11 sales representatives. Maintained a comprehensive knowledge of company services as well as a deep understanding of each client's business in an effort to accurately identify needs, anticipate problems, overcome possible objections and educate clients on new services.

In addition to securing and servicing business, maintained full responsibility for responding to client inquiries and disseminating service changes. Guided sales agents by establishing goals, conducting field training, boosting morale and developing sales techniques that facilitated a high level of attention and follow-up.

- Maintained a $480,000 monthly territory business while limiting attrition to less than 1%.
- Personal client base had the highest level of retention *and* the highest number of clients *not* locked into a contract.
- Built new account business to $100,000 monthly sales within 18 months.
- Credited with having the highest number of "quality accounts" and one of the most profitable assignments in the company.

CINGULAR WIRELESS, *Utica, NY*   **2001 to 2002**
Major Market Representative
Key relationship manager with full responsibility for prospecting, needs analysis, sales presentations, price negotiations and closing for Herkimer County. Operated territory autonomously, developing strategies to increase account base, improve profitability and build retention while maintaining servicing relationships for established accounts.

- Launched a new business division and the start-up of a new office while simultaneously building sales.
- Expanded client base and penetrated accounts despite significant market saturation.
- Consistently exceeded established goals for profitability, loss/ratio, sales and customer satisfaction.

EDUCATION

B.S., **Human Resource Management,** Syracuse State University, *Syracuse, NY*

John Belmont

978.555.8113

E-mail: jbelmont@aol.com

177 Washington Avenue • Boston, MA 95818

Sales Management

Delivering consistent and sustainable revenue gains, profit growth and market-share increases through strategic sales leadership of multi-site branch locations. Valued offered:

- ✓ Driver of innovative programs that provide a competitive edge and establish company as market leader.
- ✓ Creative problem solver who develops solutions that save time, cut costs and ensure consistent product quality.
- ✓ Empowering leader who recruits, develops, coaches, motivates and inspires sales teams to top performance.
- ✓ Innovative in developing win-win solutions to maximize account expansion, retention and satisfaction.

Selected Career Achievements

RANFORD COMPANY • Boston, MA   1990 to 2006

As Branch Manager, reinvigorated the sales organization, growing company revenues from $9MM to $11MM, expanding account base from 450 to 680 and increasing market share 15%. Established new performance benchmark and trained sales team on implementing sales-building customer inventory rationalization programs.

- **Revitalized and restored profitability of 2 underperforming territories** by coaching and developing territory reps.

- **Penetrated 2 new markets and secured a lucrative market niche in abrasive products.** Staffed, opened and managed the 2 branch locations in New Jersey—one of which alone produced $3MM+ over 3 years.

- **Initiated and advanced the skills of sales force to effectively promote and sell increasingly technical product lines** in response to changing market demands.

Increased profit margins and dollar volume through product mix diversification and expansion. Created product catalogs and marketing literature.

- **Ensured company maintained its competitive edge in the marketplace** by adding cross-functional product lines.

- **Led highly profitable new product introduction with 40% profit margin** that produced $100K in new business.

BERLIN COMPANY • Worcester, MA   1985 to 1990

As Account Executive, rejuvenated sales performance of a stagnant territory. Turned around customer perception by cultivating exceptional relationships through solutions-based selling and delivering value-added service. Recognized as a peak performer company-wide who consistently ranked #1 in sales and #1 in profits.

- **Positioned and established company as a full-service supplier** to drive sales revenues by translating customer needs to product solutions.

- **More than doubled territory sales from $700K to $1.6MM** during tenure and grew account base from 80 to 125 through new market penetration. **Landed and managed 3 of company's 6 largest accounts** and grew remaining 3.

- **Mentored new and existing territory reps** on customer relationship management, solutions-selling strategies, advanced product knowledge and customer programs.

Education

B.S. in Business Management—Rhode Island University, Providence, RI

Written By: Louise Garver
Font: Arial Narrow

Alicia T. Crawford

634 Maplebrook Drive • Ada, MI 49301
616-555-4982
atcrawf@isp.com

Profile

EXPERTISE   **Customer Service & Client Relationship-Building • Inside & Outside Sales • Merchandising • Office Administration**

QUALIFICATIONS

Customer Service: Track record of building strong and lasting relationships by providing excellent customer service after the sale to ensure satisfaction and build repeat business.

Sales: Able to win over the gatekeepers and counter objections. Capable negotiator. Experienced in making cold calls and interpreting customer needs.

Product Knowledge: Emphasize features and value compared to competitors' products. Understand and effectively communicate scientific and technical information to general audiences. Possess creativity in *thought* as well as with *things*.

Administration: Excel at training and motivating staff. Lead by example.

Personal: Accustomed to working in fast-paced, intense environments resulting in decisiveness and ability to prioritize. Highly organized. Demonstrate strong work ethic. Committed to performing beyond expectations.

Technology: Windows • Microsoft Office • Internet

Employment

JC PENNEY • Grand Rapids, Michigan

2005-Present   **Merchandising Team Member**
- Coordinate physical appearance of men's department. Stock merchandise on sales floor and create displays based on corporate plans.
- Organize and track inventory.
- Provide merchandising support to additional departments as needed.

2004   **Estee Lauder Cosmetics Consultant**
- Provided individualized sales and customer service.
- Demonstrated products for customers; developed personal product plans.
- Utilized relationship-management strategies to develop large customer base.

2003-2004   **Seasonal Display Coordinator**
- Created, stocked and maintained 25+ unique holiday merchandise displays spread throughout the store.

RIVERSIDE ANIMAL HOSPITAL • Ada, Michigan

2003   **Customer Service Manager**
- Provided overall practice management including financial, human resources and client management responsibilities.
- Hired, trained, scheduled, motivated and supervised 20+ front-end and clinical staff members.
- Ordered products and supplies; tracked inventory of both. Met with sales reps.
- Coordinated all aspects of customer service.

2002-2003   **Customer Service Representative**
- Interacted with clients at appointment check-in and departure.
- Assisted veterinary staff with patients before and after procedures.

Alicia T. Crawford   616-555-4982
                                                                                                  Page 2

Employment (continued)

VETERINARY SPECIALISTS OF WEST MICHIGAN • Comstock Park, Michigan
     2000-2002   **Client Care Coordinator**
- Managed front-desk activities including scheduling appointments, generating estimates, collecting payments, communicating with clients and trouble-shooting problems. Supervised daily accounting procedures.
- Monitored/coordinated work flow in clinical areas.
- Acted as liaison between medical staff, clients and vendors.
- Developed and implemented marketing concepts and plans.

POLE'S SKI SHOP • Portage, Michigan
     1993-2000   **Assistant to Soft Goods Manager/Sales Associate**
- Created displays and merchandised sales floor. Monitored inventory.
- Trained and motivated sales staff.
- Coordinated product training sessions with sales representatives.
- Assisted sales reps at trade shows.
- Established and maintained loyal customer base.
- Developed mutually beneficial relationships with community organizations to sponsor presentations and product demonstrations to the public.

BAYER PHARMACEUTICALS • Kalamazoo, Michigan
     2000   **Pharmaceutical Representative (Intern)**
- Completed month-long comprehensive product knowledge and sales training.
- Independently conducted and documented an average of 10 calls per day to private practices, pharmacies and hospitals. Delivered product information and samples to physicians, medical support staff and pharmacists.
- Generated new accounts and managed existing accounts.

Education

WESTERN MICHIGAN UNIVERSITY • Kalamazoo, Michigan
     2000   **Bachelor of Science – Animal Science**

- References available on request -

Written By: Janet L. Beckstrom
Font: Arial

Sheraton

Connie Rodriguez

727 N. 51ˢᵗ Dr., Phoenix, AZ 85051 / H: 602-543-6227 / Cell: 928-457-2220 / Email – crodriguez@yahoo.com

CUSTOMER SERVICE MANAGEMENT PROFESSIONAL

OFFERS TWENTY YEARS OF PROVEN EXPERIENCE MANAGING OPERATIONS FOR MAJOR BRANDS IN THE TRAVEL, HOSPITALITY, UTILITIES AND COMMUNICATION INDUSTRIES.

P&L / Quality Assurance/ Resource Allocation / Incoming Call Routing / Reservations / Food Service

SIGNIFICANT PROFESSIONAL ACHIEVEMENTS

- Managed operations budget *within 5% variance* for annual forecasting.
- *Improved employee retention by 40%* in a multi-shift, 8K calls per month operation.
- Implemented customer service incentives to *exceed 100%* of client metrics.
- Launched programs to *increase customer tracking* and *agent customer service skills.*
- Orchestrated successful customer service programs for *multiple client products.*
- *Increased responsiveness to customer demands* through client interfacing programs.

CORE STRENGTHS

OPERATIONS MANAGEMENT

Recruiting / Selection	Performance Improvement Management	Forecasting
Training & Development	Assessment Administration	Purchasing
Client Metric Management	Efficiency / Productivity Enhancement	Agent Retention

TECHNOLOGY

CMS/ Performix / Witness Systems / IEX / Nice / Sabre Airline Reservation System / Microsoft Office Suite

PROFESSIONAL EXPERIENCE

SPACEY CUSTOMER CONTACT CENTER SOLUTIONS   September 1997– February 2006

Forbes Magazine recognizes Spacey as one of "America's Leading Companies". *Call Center Magazine* has recognized Spacey for "Best Call Center" and "Call Center of the Year." Spacey is headquartered in Atlanta and has 310K+ employees worldwide. The Customer Contact Center Solutions business unit has seven locations throughout the United States and abroad serving major clients such as AT&T, Sprint and Cisco.

SITE OPERATIONS MANAGER -Yuma, Arizona - July 2000– February 2006
Client – Arizona Public Service
Scope of Operations: 120 Seats / 15 Hr. shifts / 4-8 supervisors dictated by seasonal volume

- Build and implement strategies to meet financial and quality objectives that support business unit goals.
- Develop, manage and motivate a strong, effective management team. Maintain the Spacey Customer Solutions quality system which focuses on continual improvement and employee involvement.
- Design and implement planning activities that ensure a successful operation including business forecasting, internal and external client communications, and policy development/improvement.
- Coordinate with resource management to accurately determine resource and capacity requirements, including telecom, facilities and staffing.
- Create/maintain a healthy and productive environment for associates, guaranteeing fair, consistent, equitable treatment in a safe environment, operating efficiently and balancing costs and quality performance.

CONNIE RODRIQUEZ – Page 2   crodriguez@yahoo.com

ASSISTANT SITE MANAGER – Tucson, Arizona – December 1999 – June 2000
Client – American Express Corporate Travel
Scope of Operations: 120 Agents / 15 Hr. shifts / 8 supervisors / Customer - PriceWaterhouse
- Managed a supervisory team in regards to workflow, performance appraisals, training and compensation.
- Implemented and planned new projects and procedures as a result of a continuous review of current operating methods in relation to client/customer objectives.
- Regulated expenditures, structured budget and reconciled P&L to meet annual organizational objectives.

TRAINER / SUPERVISOR – Tucson, Arizona – September 1997 – November 1999
Client - AT&T / SmartTalk / Western Pacific Airlines
Scope of Operations: 249 seats /250-250 / 24 x 7
- Trained new hires on airline reservation system exclusive for discount airline ticket company, utilizing Sabre Airline reservation system
- Partnered with calling card client to create training curriculum to "ramp up" 400 new hires in 90 days.

FIRST UNITED CHRISTIAN CHURCH – August 1995 – April 1995
First United Christian Church is a 500,000 - member congregation located in Tucson, Arizona which housed a full service kitchen, dining hall and banquet room.

DIRECTOR OF FOOD SERVICE – Tucson, Arizona
- Estimated food and beverage costs, requisitioning and purchasing supplies.
- Directed, hired and assigned food preparation personnel and volunteers to plan menus and events.
- Investigated and resolved food quality and service complaints.
- Trained and managed all food servers, from 3-40 depending on size of function, and facilitated a "Food Handlers" training course to all church members assisting in the church kitchen.

SHERATON   June 1990 – December 1993
Sheraton has more than 400 hotels and resorts in over 70 countries. As the largest of the Starwood® Hotels & Resorts Worldwide, Inc. brands, Sheraton serves the needs of both business and leisure travelers in locations from Argentina to Zimbabwe.

Catering Sales Assistant – Phoenix, Arizona – December 1991 – December 1993
- Coordinated staff and convention personnel to make arrangements for meetings and conventions.
- Consulted with representatives of group and organization to plan details, such as number of persons expected, display space desired and food service schedule.
- Directed workers in preparing banquet and convention rooms and erecting displays and exhibits.
- Inspected rooms and displays for conformance to needs and desires of group.

Reservations Sales Agent / Front Desk Clerk – Tucson, Arizona – June 1990 – December 1991
Greeted, registered and assigned rooms to guests in non-computerized, 200-room hotel. Offered information pertaining to available services and facilities of hotel, points of interest and entertainment attractions; Worked toward goal to achieve 100% occupancy each night.

JUNIOR GROCERY AND PROCESSING   January 1982 – August 1997
A Family Owned Business servicing the grocery retail needs of Tucson, AZ

EDUCATION

UNIVERSITY OF YUMA - 2004
Bachelor of Science – Business Management

Written By: MeLisa Rogers
Font: Garamond

Chapter **14**

▶ Resumes for

Skilled Trades Careers

Each and every industry and profession presents unique resume writing and design challenges. If you are interested in pursuing a career in the skilled trades, be certain to incorporate these important success factors:

Success Factor #1

In the "Training & Education" section of your resume, be sure to include information about your apprenticeships—both classroom and hands-on experiences—and highlight any additional certifications or licenses you have earned, such as welding and HVAC.

Success Factor #2

Show your range of experience. For example: framing, roofing, finish cabinetry work (carpenter); 120-volts, 480-volts, network cabling (electrician); pneumatics, hydraulics, high-pressure lines (plumber).

Success Factor #3

Remember to mention special skills that set you apart (for example, conduit bending, fiber-optic installation, EDM processes, and compound and progressive die building and repair).

Success Factor #4

Highlight your familiarity with the latest technology. Do you use CAD/ CAM software, CNC programming, or other technology tools and aids?

Keywords and Keyword Phrases

Keywords and keyword phrases are a critical component of every successful job seeker's resume. By using just one or two words, you're able to communicate a wealth of information about your skills, qualifications, and experience. What's more, keywords are the basis for resume-scanning technology and are therefore critical to any job seeker's campaign in today's electronic-based job search market. For more information on keywords, refer back to pages 17–19 in Chapter 1.

Following are the top 20 keywords for careers in the skilled trades, some of which may reflect your skills and some of which may not be appropriate for you at this time. Use these words as the foundation for developing your own list of keywords on the Professional Keyword List form in Appendix B.

Top 20 Keywords

Blueprints and Drawings

Contract Administration

Crew Supervision

Customer Relations

Electrical, Plumbing and HVAC

Fault Isolation and Analysis

Maintenance and Repair

Material Management

Preventative Maintenance

Project Management

Project Scheduling and Documentation

Project Specifications

Regulatory Compliance

Residential and Commercial Projects

Scope-of-Work Documents

Security Systems Installation

Testing and Troubleshooting

Tools and Equipment Control

Training and Apprenticeships

Work Site Safety

Following are some excellent examples of resumes for skilled trades careers.

LOUIS G. WESTER

2229 N. Avondale Dr. #212
Phoenix, AZ 85000

312/555-2222   web@e-mail.com

PROFILE

A conscientious, team-centered **Machinist** with focus on **prototype engineering**, offering more than 10 years' experience. Knowledge / expertise in:

- CNC Programming
- Research & Development
- Quality Assurance Inspections
- Process Flow / Improvement

- Tear Down / Reverse Engineering
- ISO Standards
- Safety
- Blueprint Reading

Detail-oriented with strong organizational and problem-solving abilities, as well as sound judgment in establishing priorities, maximizing productivity and introducing improvements.

Equipment: CNC / manual mills, lathes, general cutting tools
Forklift Certified

EXPERIENCE

03/00 - Present	ROBOBA INSTRUMENTS, INC., Crystal Division **Machinist Technician I**	Phoenix, Arizona

Fabricate and inspect materials to engineering specifications / ISO standards, ensuring customer satisfaction. Set up, program and operate CNC milling center for optimum productivity and process flow.

- Measure and record ambient parameters to maintain proper crystal growth and maximize product yield.
- Polish and assemble components, then, using computer with photo-multiplier tube, perform testing to meet or exceed specifications.
- Troubleshoot and resolve operational issues in a timely manner; serve as point of contact for any outsourced machine maintenance / repair.
- Develop ongoing process flow improvements, consolidating steps while maintaining the highest-quality product.

08/98 -
12/00

W.T.S., Automotive Safety Bag Division   Phoenix, Arizona
Tech 3 Prototype Machinist / Engineering
Assembled fixtures and tooling for mounting devices to facilitate engineering tests.

- Conducted manual quality control inspections of product to ensure fabrication to engineering specifications / blueprints.
- Orchestrated departmental team to achieve greater efficiency and organization which significantly increased workflow and productivity.

08/97 -
08/98

BOEING, Helicopter Division   Phoenix, Arizona
Machinist Technician
Operated CNC mills, manual lathes, shears and saws to fabricate fixturing for military applications.

- Communicated effectively with engineers, providing feedback to effect both process and quality improvements.

Prior

Machinist Tech, Bartleman Bearing Inc.   Courtland, Wisconsin
Machinist Tech, Metro Design   Hartford, Wisconsin

EDUCATION

ARIZONA COMMUNITY COLLEGE   Phoenix, Arizona
A.A. - Interdisciplinary Studies / Business

DANIEL J. BOLLINGER, JR.

8862 Mundania Press Road • Heatherville, Ohio 45002
djbollinger@printedpages.com • (513) 598-9100

PROFILE

Skilled plumber, pipefitter, and welder with diversified experience including new construction and renovations, industrial, commercial and residential projects. Innate mechanical aptitude, enhanced by comprehensive training, a "can-do" attitude and strong work ethic. Skilled in operating construction equipment such as bobcats, backhoes, forklifts and freeze machines. Accustomed to working outside in all types of weather conditions. Proven ability to complete all assigned jobs accurately, safely, and on time. Trained in first aid and CPR. Excellent safety and work attendance record. Skills include:

• Blueprint Reading	• Plumbing System Maintenance	• Troubleshooting
• Fabrication	• HVAC System Installation	• Diagnostics
• Plumbing System Installation	• Safety	• Problem-Solving

LICENSES & CERTIFICATIONS

- Licensed Master Plumber, City of Heatherville
- Certified Stick Welder, State of Ohio
- Certified TIG Welder, State of Ohio
- 1X Brazer, ASME
- 6010 Installer, ASSE

EDUCATION

ANDREW GREGORY VOCATIONAL SCHOOL, Heatherville, OH   1998 – 2002
Plumber/Pipefitter Training
Completed comprehensive 5-year program, including a 2-year apprenticeship.

ST. NICHOLAS HIGH SCHOOL, East Megantown, OH
Diploma   1998

EXPERIENCE

Worked all overtime requested by management. Consistently met deadlines and quality standards without compromising safety.

BENJAMIN MECHANICAL, Cincinnati, OH   11/03 – Present
Plumber/Pipefitter
Installed plumbing systems for institutional customers across the tri-state including: Jennifer-Jessica Art Center, St. Michael Hospital, Joshua Rehabilitation Center and City of Katiesburg Police and Fire Departments. Assisted in training new/apprentice plumbers.
- Achieved "Outstanding" (highest rating) in all 10 categories on performance review, 2005.

THE JEANSTER COMPANY, Cincinnati, OH   6/98 – 11/03
Welder/Pipefitter
Worked with other trades on new residential construction in Mary Edie Estates, Harry Hills and Moose Gardens Condominiums. Installed new heating and cooling system at Sanders Manufacturing. Retrofitted plumbing on renovation project at Jesse Lee Gregory Office Park.
- Earned 2 Perfect Attendance Awards, 1999 and 2000.

Written By: Michelle Reitz
Font: Times New Roman

Charles T. Stiller
8567 Kings Road, St. Petersburg, VA 23806
(804) 524-5555 Home ▪ charleststiller@popmail.com

Manager, Alarm / Mechanical Trades

Highlights of Qualifications

☑ Well-qualified Master Plumber and Certified Inspector with extensive mechanical trades' knowledge, 18 years' experience in plumbing and heating, ventilating and air conditioning (HVAC), as well as general contracting construction and maintenance experience.

☑ Demonstrated skills in supervision and project management / coordination. Track record of working cooperatively and productively with diverse personalities, within tight deadlines.

☑ Proven ability to set priorities, assume responsibility, make effective decisions and give directions, organizing workflow, ideas, materials and time for cost-efficient projects. Take pride in achieving the best possible results, within budget and timelines.

Professional Registration – Certifications and Licenses
Kings County Vocational School Black Seal Certification – 2006
Virginia State Inspector's I.C.S. License – 2002
Virginia Master Plumbing License – 1988

Professional Experience

Manager and Owner, Stiller Plumbing and Heating, St. Petersburg, VA   1988 – present

Plumbing and HVAC - Install and maintain plumbing and heating systems for residential and commercial clients. Direct maintenance, repair and construction of multi-trade projects, including hiring, training, supervising and evaluating trades' employees. Read and interpret blueprints, plans and specifications, and comply with safety, environmental and technical regulations. Representative client projects include:

- **Virginia State Central Motor Pool**, Richmond, VA
  Plumbing contractor on call for 180,000 square foot facility (for 18 years)

- **WaterWorks Plant**, Richmond – $125,000 plumbing / heating system renovation and update

- **Kingstown Learning Center**, Kingstown – 40,000 square foot plumbing system installation

- **University Plaza**, Richmond – New plumbing system construction for four office buildings

- **Washington Correction Facility**, Norfolk – Plumbing / heating system renovation

General Contracting – Oversee project management of construction and renovation projects for new homes (up to $525,000), utilizing thorough knowledge of construction standards and practices, tools, methods and materials. Supervised 12 contractors, with 40 indirect reports in the construction trades, ensuring optimum scheduling and workflow.

Education & Training
Diploma – Plumbing (4-year program), Kings County Vocational School, St. Petersburg, VA
High School Diploma, St. Paul High School, Washington Township, VA
Computer Skills: Windows 2003, MS Word, MS Excel, Internet, email

---

Written By: Susan Guameri
Font: Book Antiqua

ANDREW PAUL

111 Main Street
Laguna Hills, CA 92653

949.242.8355
andrewpaul@internet.com

REGISTERED SPECIAL INSPECTOR

I.C.B.O. CERTIFICATIONS

REINFORCED CONCRETE ♦ STRUCTURAL MASONRY ♦ STRUCTURAL STEEL AND WELDING

Well-respected throughout the construction industry by contractors, tradesman, public inspectors and clients. Experience includes wide range of new construction and remodeling projects including luxury residential to large commercial developments. Expert in blueprint reading, construction processes, inspection procedures, laboratory testing and all building codes. Conscientious, responsible professional known for having a "construction attitude" and the ability to "do it right the first time."

CAREER BACKGROUND

Andrew Paul Inspection Services – Laguna Hills, CA   **2003 – Present**

Founded this privately held firm providing inspection services for construction projects throughout California. The firm's reputation is based on delivering the highest levels of technical expertise and timely resolution of issues affecting specifications, project cost and schedules.

Registered Special Inspector

- ♦ Interact with general and subcontractors, architects and crews to coordinate projects on-site, from blueprints to completion, while meeting schedule and project specifications.

- ♦ Investigate and resolve issues related to project / material specifications and code compliance.

- ♦ Conduct field material sample testing as well as welding inspections.

- ♦ Document and approve all aspects of projects related to time, materials, specifications and code compliance.

Construction Union, Local 449 – Los Angeles, CA   1985 – 2003

Journeyman Welder / Foreman

- ♦ Started as an apprentice and learned all aspects of the trade while working on diverse projects including high-rise developments.

- ♦ Led training programs covering industry standards, best practices and safety procedures.

AFFILIATIONS

American Welding Society   ♦   Association of Builders and Contractors

National Precast Concrete Association

Written By: James A. Swanson
Font: Times New Roman

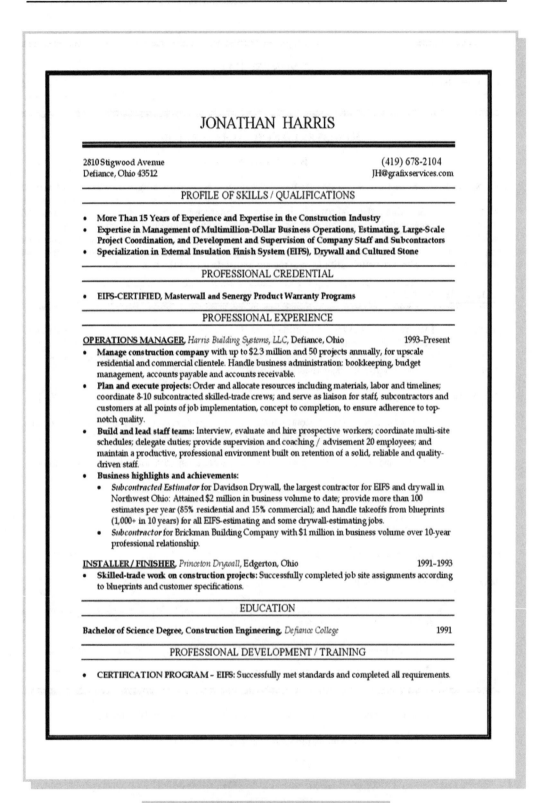

JONATHAN HARRIS

2810 Stigwood Avenue   (419) 678-2104
Defiance, Ohio 43512   JH@grafixservices.com

PROFILE OF SKILLS / QUALIFICATIONS

- More Than 15 Years of Experience and Expertise in the Construction Industry
- Expertise in Management of Multimillion-Dollar Business Operations, Estimating, Large-Scale Project Coordination, and Development and Supervision of Company Staff and Subcontractors
- Specialization in External Insulation Finish System (EIFS), Drywall and Cultured Stone

PROFESSIONAL CREDENTIAL

- EIFS-CERTIFIED, Masterwall and Senergy Product Warranty Programs

PROFESSIONAL EXPERIENCE

OPERATIONS MANAGER, *Harris Building Systems, LLC*, Defiance, Ohio   1993–Present
- **Manage construction company** with up to $2.3 million and 50 projects annually, for upscale residential and commercial clientele. Handle business administration: bookkeeping, budget management, accounts payable and accounts receivable.
- **Plan and execute projects:** Order and allocate resources including materials, labor and timelines; coordinate 8-10 subcontracted skilled-trade crews; and serve as liaison for staff, subcontractors and customers at all points of job implementation, concept to completion, to ensure adherence to top-notch quality.
- **Build and lead staff teams:** Interview, evaluate and hire prospective workers; coordinate multi-site schedules; delegate duties; provide supervision and coaching / advisement 20 employees; and maintain a productive, professional environment built on retention of a solid, reliable and quality-driven staff.
- **Business highlights and achievements:**
  - *Subcontracted Estimator* for Davidson Drywall, the largest contractor for EIFS and drywall in Northwest Ohio: Attained $2 million in business volume to date; provide more than 100 estimates per year (85% residential and 15% commercial); and handle takeoffs from blueprints (1,000+ in 10 years) for all EIFS-estimating and some drywall-estimating jobs.
  - *Subcontractor* for Brickman Building Company with $1 million in business volume over 10-year professional relationship.

INSTALLER / FINISHER, *Princeton Drywall*, Edgerton, Ohio   1991–1993
- **Skilled-trade work on construction projects:** Successfully completed job site assignments according to blueprints and customer specifications.

EDUCATION

Bachelor of Science Degree, Construction Engineering, *Defiance College*   1991

PROFESSIONAL DEVELOPMENT / TRAINING

- **CERTIFICATION PROGRAM – EIFS:** Successfully met standards and completed all requirements.

Written By: Lee Anne Grundish
Font: Book Antiqua

Steven J. Sommers

17 Savannah Lane • Charleston, SC 29402
843 292 1938 • steven_sommers@myemail.com

CONSTRUCTION PROJECT MANAGEMENT
Residential · Multi-Family · Commercial · Military · School

☐ Highly skilled in technical and business aspects of construction
☐ Strong communicator, successful at negotiations
☐ Personable, forthright, equitable and creative
☐ Background includes: New construction, renovation and remodeling; facilities maintenance; government-financed projects; ISO 14001 as well as in-house quality management programs

HIGHLIGHTS OF PROFESSIONAL EXPERIENCE

CORINTH CONSTRUCTION COMPANY, Southeast Division – Charleston, SC
Headquartered in Arizona, the firm hired key people from competitors to break into the multi-family market, a first for Corinth. Success in that area drove company to compete for and win its first military housing project. Division has grown from 60 to 200 staff and a backlog of contracted work from $40M (multi-family) to $1.4B (military housing).

Key member of new business unit; promoted to APM and asked to relocate to Charleston to supervise first military housing project. Acclimated new Project Manager and trained two Project Engineers and Intern. Atypically assigned project manager duties due to project size and complexity. Received praise from VP, significant salary increase, and bonuses for successful completion of previous projects. Acting Project Manager since early 2005.

Assistant Project Manager/Acting Project Manager, Military Housing Business Unit 2003 to present
Charleston Army Airfield –Charleston, SC
- New construction of a $302M 1,865-unit quadplex/duplex/single family housing development in numerous neighborhoods; six scheduled for completion by year-end 2006.
- Report to Unit VP and Project Manager; supervise Project Engineer and Intern.
- Assist with architectural and civil reviews to final design while completing multi-family projects.
- Oversee product selection in accordance with Community Development and Management Plan and Army's Residential Community Initiative design/specification standards.
- Monitor and manage project scope, negotiate cost claims, and oversee contracts, dealing with five general superintendents and 60+ subcontractors and suppliers.
- Manage submittal process, RFIs, owner billing, and subcontractor pay application processes.
- Coordinate with third-party inspector for lender on billing review and approval.
- Track and monitor material expediting.
- Research and resolve warranty issues with owner's project director.
- Interface with Army's Department of Public Works on wet utility issues and the National Resource Conservation Society and State of Georgia EPD on erosion and sedimentation matters.
- Run bi-weekly staff meetings, owner meetings and design team meetings.
- Delegate Project Engineer to coordinate and attend subcontractor staff meetings.
- Report to VP on factors measured by balanced score card system reviewed at C-level monthly business unit meetings.

Project Engineer, Multi-Family Business Unit 2002 to 2003

Summit Homes at Georgetown – Georgetown, SC
- New construction of a $15.5M 300-unit apartment complex with clubhouse.
- Completed buyout process; managed request for information tracking, control and approval.

Sanctuary at Orangeburg, Phase II – Orangeburg, SC
- New construction of a $7.9M 160-unit apartment complex with pool house.
- Coordinated close-out procedures; completed submittal application and approval process.

STERNS USA – Atlanta, GA
Recognized global leader in construction management. Firm has serious commitment to environmental awareness and protection; ISO 14001 certified.

Promoted after first five months with company. Salary increased by more than 18% during tenure. Tapped to be division's Environmental Compliance Officer; assigned project passed corporate-level audit.

Project/Office Engineer	2000 to 2002
Internal Environmental Compliance and Control Inspector	2001 to 2002

Fayette County Schools – GA
- Renovation and remodeling at 50 schools throughout the county; $18.5M five-year project.
- Involved in all facets of the project; completed all tasks saving owner more than $2M.
- Clarified scope of work and prepared budgets for 1,000 future projects at 36 school sites.

Marion County Schools – GA
- New construction of an elementary school; $11M, 104,000 SF project.
- Completed submittal process and expedited material deliveries.
- Reduced project schedule by more than one month.

Bibb County Schools – GA
- New construction of an elementary school; $12.5M 112,000 SF project.
- Monitored and reported impact of new federal guidelines for National Pollution Distribution Elimination System as a test site for State of Georgia.
- Coordinated submittal process and owner and subcontractor billing requests.

Preconstruction Services Department
- Upgraded subcontractor database (3,000) in software conversion from Bid Fax to Win Fax.
- Resolved dispute between project owner and subcontractor.

HABITAT FOR HUMANITY – Atlanta, GA

Construction Supervisor (through AmeriCorps)	1998 to 2000

- Supervised as many as 40 volunteers (adults of all ages) constructing affordable housing on a 144-lot subdivision project and other smaller concurrent projects.
- Delegated tasks to and trained volunteers of varying skill levels in all facets of non-mechanical construction. Maintained quality and safety standards.

US DEPARTMENT OF THE INTERIOR, National Parks Service

Independent Architectural Contractor	Summer 1998

- Documented historic cotton mill facilities for the Historic American Engineering Record.
- Prepared architectural drawings which are archived in Library of Congress.

EDUCATION & PROFESSIONAL DEVELOPMENT

Bachelor of Science, Architecture: George Washington University – Washington, DC; 1998
- **Study Abroad, Historic Preservation:** Yorkshire, England; 1997
- **Historic Preservation Project:** Victorian hotel, Asbury Park, NJ; 1997

Business Management Training: Corinth; 2004 to present (monthly)
Grid Leadership Development Seminar; October 2004 + ongoing training sessions
Grid Modeling Partnering Program; Summer 2004
Project Management Training: Skill Path; 2003
Safety Training: Sterns USA; 2001-2002
Office Engineer/Project Engineer Training: Sterns USA; 2001

COMPUTER SKILLS

Microsoft Excel, Word, Outlook · Lotus IRIS Docs, Lotus Notes · Expedition, ConstructWare (Internet-based Project Management Software) · JD Edwards (Accounting Software) · Primavera P3 · Sure Track

Written By: Salome A. Farraro
Font: Arial

Chapter 15

▶ # Resumes for

Teaching and Education Careers

Each and every industry and profession presents unique resume writing and design challenges. If you are interested in pursuing a career in teaching and education, be certain to incorporate these important success factors:

Success Factor #1

List your credentials/certifications prominently, possibly right after your contact information. Principals and administrators want to see right away what subject areas or grade levels you are qualified to teach and/or administer.

Success Factor #2

Mention the classes you have taught, including grade levels and subjects. Include any information about special lesson plans or field trips related to a particular subject area to illustrate your ingenuity and creativity in bringing the subject matter alive for your students.

Success Factor #3

Highlight any committees you have been a member of or student activities for which you have served as an advisor (for example, Science Curriculum Committee; Olympics of the Mind Advisor).

Success Factor #4

Include travel or other enriching activities that provide you with added perspective in the classroom. A social studies teacher who has spent extensive time exploring Europe or Native American cultures in the Southwest can be a much more fascinating candidate than someone who hasn't had similar experiences.

Keywords and Keyword Phrases

Keywords and keyword phrases are a critical component of every successful job seeker's resume. By using just one or two words, you're able to communicate a wealth of information about your skills, qualifications, and experience. What's more, keywords are the basis for resume-scanning technology and are therefore critical to any job seeker's campaign in today's electronic-based job search market. For more information on keywords, refer back to pages 17–19 in Chapter 1.

Following are the top 20 teaching and education keywords, some of which may reflect your skills and some of which may not be appropriate for you at this time. Use these words as the foundation for developing your own list of keywords on the Professional Keyword List form in Appendix B.

Top 20 Keywords

Accreditation	Parent-Teacher Relations
Academic Advising	Research and Publishing
Academic Standards	School Administration
Classroom Management	Student Advisement
Course Design	Student Placement
Curriculum Development	Student Recruitment
Educational Services Administration	Student Relations
Higher Education	Teacher Training and Instruction
Instructional Materials	Testing and Evaluation
Multimedia Learning Methodologies	Textbook Review and Selection

Following are some excellent examples of resumes for teaching and education careers.

KATLINA NOBELSON

2387 East Nine Mile Road • Brighton, MI 48114

h: 810.299.6811 • c: 810.455.4550   KatlinaNobelson@gmail.com

PROFILE

Dedicated classroom teaching assistant with outstanding performance in classroom management, student teaching, student testing, learner retention, curriculum development, instructional materials design, and special events planning/management. Thrive in challenging, fast-paced classrooms. A keen commitment to fostering growth and educational excellence within our student populations.

- Self-motivated professional who pays attention to detail, is student-oriented, and is well organized and efficient.
- Skilled at planning and coordinating multiple tasks concurrently.
- Experience in data entry and MS Word.
- Excellent communication skills and the ability to work independently or in a team environment as the situation requires.

EXPERIENCE

Teacher Aide • 2001–present — CROSSROADS PRESCHOOL
Direct hands-on involvement supporting a classroom of 20, 3-year-old children. Provide a safe, nurturing, and supportive environment while promoting social, emotional, motor, and cognitive development. Help with group play, art, and life skills. Perform recordkeeping and interact with parents.

Teacher's Assistant • 2004–present — ST. VINCENT ACADEMY
Manage an afternoon session of private preschool children ages 3- to 4-years old. Adhere to teacher's curriculum and provide individualized instruction on projects. Create a learning environment that fosters creativity while promoting self-dependency.

Customer Service Agent • 1991–96 — FEDERAL EXPRESS (FedEx)
Managed material and logistics in busy Customer Service Center for provider of global transportation, business, and related information services. Handled customer relations and tracked expedited shipments both domestically and internationally. Accountable and responsible for routing, tracking and tracing, customer follow up, and overall accountability for customers freight.

Prior experience includes entrepreneurial home-based businesses.

OTHER EXPERIENCE

Chair of Fundraising Committee • 2003–present — ST. VINCENT ACADEMY
Head fundraising campaigns including volunteer recruitment, training, and direction. Make decisions on product sales, contact local business for support, organize sales, and control finances.

Volunteer • 2000–03 — MAYBERRY PARK
Team Leader for up to eight volunteers caring for ailing and rescued horses. Responsible for feeding, medication preparation, and application; stall, barn, and pasture maintenance for up to 20 horses.

Written By: Lorie Lebert
Font: Tahoma

JULIO MIGUEL DIAZ
987 Brennan Drive
Mansfield, Pennsylvania 16534
717-321-4567
diazjm@stny.rr.com

Pennsylvania State Provisional Teaching Certification, Elementary Education (N-6)

EDUCATION

Pennsylvania State University, State College, Pennsylvania
Master of Science, Education   May 2006
Elementary Concentration – GPA – 3.84

Significant Courses:

Reading for Special Needs Students	Advanced Child Psychology
Nature Needs of Special Ed. Students	Curriculum Organization – Elementary
Health Education & Child Abuse	Methods (Math, Science, Social Studies)

Swarthmore College, Swarthmore, Pennsylvania
Bachelor of Science, Business Administration   May 1993
Finance Concentration

TEACHING EXPERIENCE

BRADFORD CENTRAL SCHOOL DISTRICT, State College, PA   Spring 2006
Per Diem Substitute for the following elementary schools:

Northwood Elementary / George Washington Elementary

- Provided instruction to classes at all grade levels (K-6) following regular teachers' established lesson plans.
- Served as substitute in a 3-1-1 behavior management class with emotionally disturbed and learning disabled students.
- Engaged students and set daily goals; employed peer instruction strategies.

Lakeland Elementary

- Spent five days teaching sixth-grade class with mix of suburban and urban students.
- Addressed classroom management and discipline issues.
- Built rapport with students to foster productive learning environment.

SUGARWOOD ELEMENTARY SCHOOL, Mansfield, PA   Spring 2005
Student Teacher – Third Grade

- Taught students with learning disabilities, emotional needs, and autism.
- Collaborated with a teacher's aide and Math and Reading specialists to develop individualized instruction that met the needs of each student.
- Created an interdisciplinary thematic unit on the solar system that incorporated interactive activities and student research projects.

SPECIAL SKILLS

Computers: *Macintosh and IBM* - Microsoft Word, WordPerfect, Excel
Languages: Speak and understand basic American Sign Language

Written By: Arnold G. Boldt
Font: Arial

Evelyn C. Jensen

1055 East Capitol Street, Washington, DC 20013
(202) 200-3927 /// evelyncj@yahoo.com

||||||||||||||||||||||||||||||||||||||||||||||||||||||||||||||||||||||||||||||||||||||||

CAREER GOAL

To reenter the teaching profession in a position that will utilize training and experience in special education. Mission to strengthen and expand the potential of students varying in learning ability by providing a safe and nonjudgmental educational environment based on mutual respect.

EDUCATION and CREDENTIALS

AMERICAN UNIVERSITY, WASHINGTON, DC
B.A. Elementary Education, *magna cum laude,* 1986
Concentration in Reading and Language Arts

District of Columbia Elementary Teacher Certification, K-8
District of Columbia Special Education Certification, K-12

PROFILE of QUALIFICATIONS

- Exposure to all childhood developmental stages from infancy through adolescence gained from prior teaching background, volunteer activities, and raising three children.
- Patient and adaptable teaching style utilized in reaching special needs students that are classified ADD/ADHD, emotionally disturbed, developmentally delayed, dyslexic, socially maladjusted, or neurologically, perceptually, speech, or language impaired.
- Major strength in championing students to triumph over their weaknesses, develop other talents, and strive for attainable goals.
- Knowledgeable of current teaching methodologies, including situational learning, interactive lessons, co-op education, multisensory experiences, and language arts combining phonics; computer literate.
- Successful in using a reward system to encourage positive behavior and raise expectation levels.

PROFESSIONAL EXPERIENCE

THE TRENT SCHOOL, Arlington, VA   1986–2006
Private school for the learning disabled
Resource Room Teacher, grades K through 8
Classroom Teacher, grades 1, 2, 6 and 7
- Concentrated heavily on language arts, particularly the etiology of words, providing students with a solid foundation for vocabulary building and reading comprehension.
- Worked one-on-one with a 6-year-old child whose kindergarten teacher reported was uneducable and displayed behavioral problems. Recognized child's frustration was due to full mirror reversal disorder and applied appropriate techniques, preparing him to be mainstreamed into public school.
- Developed a science curriculum where no formal program or books previously existed.
- Contributed to interdisciplinary teams and development of group and individual education plans.

COMMUNITY SERVICE and VOLUNTEER WORK

- Advocate for parents with learning disabled children, bringing their issues to the attention of school system officials.
- Boy Scout Leader for troop of 12 boys. In addition to required activities of the organization, provided guidance on moral issues and personal problems faced during preadolescent years
- Coordinator for Special Olympics for 5 years, receiving award for dedication to the program.
- Liaison with principal, parents, and teachers to ease children's transition into elementary school.

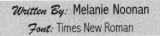

Written By: Melanie Noonan
Font: Times New Roman

Mark Jonas

CARPENTRY INSTRUCTOR

Box 48, Ingleside, ON K0E 1J0
Home: (613) 469-3825 ♦ Cell: (613) 469-9511

Professional carpenter with 13+ years successful experience in all phases of construction in progressively responsible positions. Strong background teaching at the college level, demonstrating proficiency in developing effective curriculum and authentic assessment models. Innovative educator skilled at building positive rapport with students and colleagues.

Professional Strengths:

- Developing Curricula & Teaching Methods
- Student Relationship Building
- Professional Demeanour & Attentiveness
- Influential Communications Skills

- Knowledge of Ontario Apprenticeship Program
- Licensed Red-Seal Carpenter since 1991
- Practical Acumen with Construction Technology
- Educational Fairs & Student Recruitment

Key Qualifications:

➤ Effective teaching, advising, and assessment skills within academic settings.
➤ Strong professional links to Apprenticeship Program with the Ontario Ministry of Training, Colleges, & Universities.
➤ Ability to create innovative programs and conduct extracurricular activities for students to maximize performance outcomes.
➤ Proactive leadership skills, exhibiting positive coaching and motivational practices.
➤ Strong interpersonal relations, coupled with talent for troubleshooting and making maximum use of available resources.
➤ Strong work ethic, personal drive and dedication, reflected in compelling desire to promote professionalism throughout the construction industry.

Uses Softplan on job and PowerPoint in classroom.

TEACHING & INSTRUCTING FAMILIARITY

Key member of teaching staff, charged with the development, direction, and implementation of programs within the apprenticeship program. Ability to maintain active, disciplined classroom while activities occurred simultaneously. Consistently posts 90% on teacher evaluations, driven by strong student relationships and open-door communication policy. *Actual teaching experience includes:*

Carpentry Teacher (part-time) – Peterborough College, Ottawa, ON 1996-present

Carpentry Teacher – Round Lake Reserve, 2001

Carpentry Teacher – Champlain Reserve, 1999

PROFESSIONAL CONSTRUCTION EXPERIENCE

Successful construction career cumulating in supervision and management of large residential renovation projects. Possesses knowledge of building practices and codes. Interacted directly with clients regarding design, construction, material, and decorating requirements. Superior hands-on experience through all phases of construction from start to completion – framing, remodeling, drywall, interior and exterior trim, plumbing, electrical, siding, decks and roofing. *Summary of work assignments includes:*

Owner ♦ Operator – Jonas Renovations, Ottawa, ON 1995 - present

Lead Hand – Marvel Carpentry, Ottawa, ON 1993 - 1995

Written By: George Dutch
Font: Garamond

LANIE CLARK

LClark@comcast.net

333 American Ave, West Islip, NY 11795   631.445.1996 / 631.524.0206 (Cell)

READINESS LANGUAGE DEVELOPMENT TEACHER
~Elementary Teacher~

Recognized leader in the strategic development and implementation of the latest and most-effective instructional teaching tools to produce winning programs for students and staff. Thrive in challenging atmospheres where resourceful and organized determination transforms chaos into order. Successfully structure areas of safety, discipline, testing and integrating programs including Academic English Master Program (AEMP), Title 1 and English Language Development test (ELD). Continue to look for new and creative techniques to enhance an over 20+ year span of teaching English to elementary children.

SELECTED SKILLS AND ACCOMPLISHMENTS

CLASSROOM ASSISTANCE
- Provided classroom observations and next-step support for teachers.
- Assisted in teaching the full implementation of the District's adopted reading/language art programs.
- Managed the administration of State and District assessments and kept current with new program initiatives.
- Planned and scheduled special event programs, including winter and cultural celebrations.

STAFF DEVELOPMENT
- Conducted monthly meetings and District-wide parent workshops.
- Arranged all Title 1 and school-wide curriculum trips for the teachers.
- Planned and implemented all Professional Staff Development workshops for teachers, paraprofessionals and parent volunteers to ensure effectiveness of the program.
- Oversaw all Title1 Parent Advisory Council meetings.
- Member of the Instructional Audit Team.

CURRICULUM DEVELOPMENT
- Updated School Site Safety Plans.
- Assisted in development of School-wide Discipline Plan.
- Member of Immediate Intervention for Under Performing Schools Program Team.
- Participated in the development of the Learn Site Action Plan.
- Aided in the development and implementation of Saturday School Extended Learning Program for low-performing students.
- Evaluated, recommended, purchased and distributed textbooks, materials and equipment.

PROFESSIONAL EXPERIENCE

West Islip School District, Islip, NY   2000 to Present
LITERACY COACH ADVISOR
Coordinate the Academic English Mastery Program, Language Literacy Program, and Open Court Reading Program serving as a knowledgeable resource for teachers and staff to ensure implementation of all facets of the various program components. Observe classrooms, provide necessary support and lead parent volunteer and staff off-site development programs. Manage accurate form, records and report completions.
- Assisted teachers in applying appropriate instructional strategies resulting in improved achievements for English learners, standard learners, and English learners enrolled in special education programs.

Continued...

LANIE CLARK
631.524.0206

-Page 2-

Collier Elementary School, Huntington, NY   1997 to 2000
CATEGORICAL PROGRAM ADVISOR

Coordinated student testing, scheduled yearly assessments and input documentation into the school's student information system. Kept current on all compliances issues for Title 1 and the bilingual program. Attended training for Title 1 coordinators and taught mandated teacher, parent volunteer and staff workshops. Worked with administration evaluating textbook purchases, organizing special programs and planning cultural celebrations.

◆ Member of several teams including Learning Walk Team, Instructional Audit Team and High-Performing Schools Grant Team.

Jefferson Elementary School, Melville, NY   1978 to 1997
ELEMENTARY TEACHER

Provided a stimulating learning environment for teaching first through fifth grades. Developed curriculum and daily lesson plan generating interest and providing thought-provoking tools to maintain interest. Instilled self-confidence, disciplined and maintained order, and worked to cultivate a life-long love of reading and learning. Provided instruction and guidance for parent volunteers and para-educators.

◆ Participated in the creation of the Learn Site Action Plan.
◆ Active member of the School Student Success Team and the School-wide Discipline Plan committee.
◆ Acted as Master Teacher and liaison for student teachers enrolled at Grossmont College.
◆ Created and managed English Language Development Program for children and families of the school.

EDUCATION AND TRAINING

NEW YORK STATE UNIVERSITY, NY
Preliminary Administrative Credential Candidate

DOWLING COLLEGE, OAKDALE, NY
MS, Early Childhood Education

DOWLING COLLEGE, OAKDALE, NY
BS, Sociology

Certifications

Leadership Development, Harcourt Mathematics Training, Organizational Management, Waterford Computer Training, Open Court Reading Training

Associations
International Membership Committee, Pi Beta Omega Chapter, New York City
Member, Top Ladies of Distinction, West Islip, NY
Member, The Loxx; Supporting Babies with Aids, West Islip, NY

Written By: Kris Plantrich
Font: Garamond

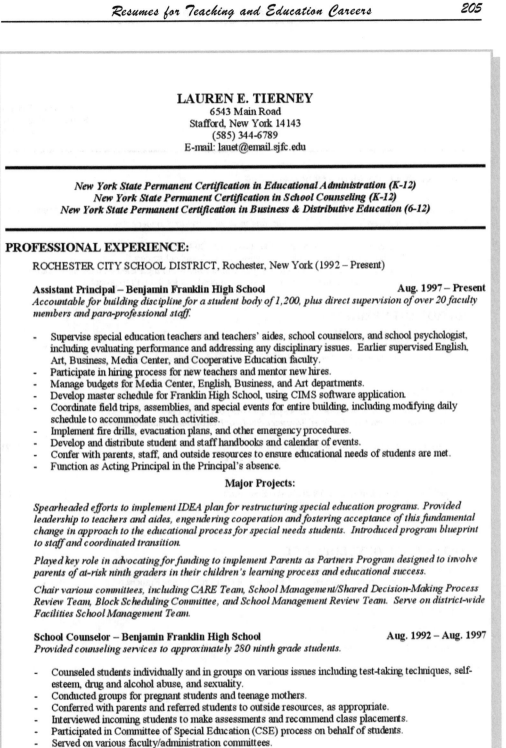

LAUREN E. TIERNEY
6543 Main Road
Stafford, New York 14143
(585) 344-6789
E-mail: lauet@email.sjfc.edu

New York State Permanent Certification in Educational Administration (K-12)
New York State Permanent Certification in School Counseling (K-12)
New York State Permanent Certification in Business & Distributive Education (6-12)

PROFESSIONAL EXPERIENCE:

ROCHESTER CITY SCHOOL DISTRICT, Rochester, New York (1992 – Present)

Assistant Principal – Benjamin Franklin High School   Aug. 1997 – Present
Accountable for building discipline for a student body of 1,200, plus direct supervision of over 20 faculty members and para-professional staff.

- Supervise special education teachers and teachers' aides, school counselors, and school psychologist, including evaluating performance and addressing any disciplinary issues. Earlier supervised English, Art, Business, Media Center, and Cooperative Education faculty.
- Participate in hiring process for new teachers and mentor new hires.
- Manage budgets for Media Center, English, Business, and Art departments.
- Develop master schedule for Franklin High School, using CIMS software application.
- Coordinate field trips, assemblies, and special events for entire building, including modifying daily schedule to accommodate such activities.
- Implement fire drills, evacuation plans, and other emergency procedures.
- Develop and distribute student and staff handbooks and calendar of events.
- Confer with parents, staff, and outside resources to ensure educational needs of students are met.
- Function as Acting Principal in the Principal's absence.

Major Projects:

Spearheaded efforts to implement IDEA plan for restructuring special education programs. Provided leadership to teachers and aides, engendering cooperation and fostering acceptance of this fundamental change in approach to the educational process for special needs students. Introduced program blueprint to staff and coordinated transition.

Played key role in advocating for funding to implement Parents as Partners Program designed to involve parents of at-risk ninth graders in their children's learning process and educational success.

Chair various committees, including CARE Team, School Management/Shared Decision-Making Process Review Team, Block Scheduling Committee, and School Management Review Team. Serve on district-wide Facilities School Management Team.

School Counselor – Benjamin Franklin High School   Aug. 1992 – Aug. 1997
Provided counseling services to approximately 280 ninth grade students.

- Counseled students individually and in groups on various issues including test-taking techniques, self-esteem, drug and alcohol abuse, and sexuality.
- Conducted groups for pregnant students and teenage mothers.
- Conferred with parents and referred students to outside resources, as appropriate.
- Interviewed incoming students to make assessments and recommend class placements.
- Participated in Committee of Special Education (CSE) process on behalf of students.
- Served on various faculty/administration committees.
- Served as advisor to Class of 1996 and Students Against Drunk Driving (SADD).

Lauren E. Tierney
Résumé – Page Two
(585) 344-6789

PROFESSIONAL EXPERIENCE (continued):

MONROE COUNTY #1 BOCES, Fairport, New York
Business Education Teacher   1991 – 1992
Instructed vocational students in data entry and medical secretarial subject areas.

- Provided classroom instruction to inclusion classes with 20 to 30 students.
- Designed career exploration program for Option III middle-school students.
- Participated in county-wide Tech Prep Group in conjunction with Finger Lakes Community College.
- Wrote learning outcomes and authentic assessment procedures for Tech Prep program.

ADDITIONAL EXPERIENCE:

STATE UNIVERSITY OF NEW YORK at Brockport, Brockport, New York
Adjunct Instructor   1995 – 1996
Taught Introduction to Psychology and Childhood & Adolescent Psychology.

EDUCATION:

State University of New York at Brockport; Brockport, New York   1998
*Coursework toward **Certificate of Advanced Study** in **Educational Administration***

Master of Science, Education (Counseling)   1991
ST. JOHN FISHER COLLEGE, Rochester, New York
GPA: 3.60

Bachelor of Arts, Business & Distributive Education   1988
ROBERTS WESLEYAN COLLEGE, Rochester, New York
Dean's List / Wegmans Teachers Scholarship

PROFESSIONAL DEVELOPMENT:

IDEA Conference (1998), Denver, Colorado
Women in Administration Conference; University of California at San Francisco

New Learning Standards   Cognitive Coaching
Life Space Intervention   Block Scheduling

Training in American Sign Language

Computer Skills: Windows XP, Microsoft Office XP, CIMS

REFERENCES:

Available Upon Request

Written By: Arnold G. Boldt
Font: CG Times

Chapter 16

▶ Resumes for

Technology, Science, and Engineering Careers

Each and every industry and profession presents unique resume writing and design challenges. If you are interested in pursuing a career in technology, science, or engineering, be certain to incorporate these important success factors:

Ⅹ **Success Factor #1**

Technology, science, and engineering careers all require knowledge of technical equipment, computer systems, and software. Be comprehensive in including *all* of your technical knowledge (for example, scientific/ laboratory equipment, computer software and hardware, operating systems, and networks).

Ⅹ **Success Factor #2**

Document any research papers, studies, or patents in which you have participated. In addition, be sure to incorporate any results or outcomes of those projects that added value to your organization.

Ⅹ **Success Factor #3**

Highlight projects on which you have worked and discuss how your participation contributed to the success of those projects (for example, under budget, ahead of schedule, exceeded customer expectations, or upgraded organizational capabilities).

Ⅹ **Success Factor #4**

Showcase all of your *extra* professional activities, which may include public speaking, professional affiliations, publications, teaching/training, and more.

Keywords and Keyword Phrases

Keywords and keyword phrases are a critical component of every successful job seeker's resume. By using just one or two words, you're able to communicate a wealth of information about your skills, qualifications, and experience. What's more, keywords are the basis for resume-scanning technology and are therefore critical to any job seeker's campaign in today's electronic-based job search market. For more information on keywords, refer back to pages 17–19 in Chapter 1.

Following are the top 20 technology, science, and engineering keywords, some of which may reflect your skills and some of which may not be appropriate for you at this time. Use these words as the foundation for developing your own list of keywords on the Professional Keyword List form in Appendix B.

Top 20 Keywords

Applications Development	Project Planning and Management
Capital Projects	Prototype Development and Testing
E-Commerce	Research and Experimentation
Engineering Design	Scientific Methodologies
Fault Isolation and Analysis	Systems Engineering
Information Services Management	Technical Writing
Information Technology	Technology Transfer
Multimedia Technology Integration	User Training and Support
Network Design and Technology	VOIP Technology
Performance Optimization	Website Design and Management

Following are some excellent examples of resumes for technology, science, and engineering careers.

DONALD L. FISHER

7721 Lost Tree Trail
Athens, GA 30605

(706) 223-7566
dfisher@bellsouth.net

SUMMARY

Innovative IT Professional with experience in diverse business environments. Key strengths in technology design, development and implementation. A focused, self-motivated team member who takes pride in solving complex technology problems and delivering user-friendly solutions.

TECHNICAL SKILLS

Databases	Operating Systems Languages and Utilities	C.A.S.E. Tools
Microsoft SQL Server 7.0/2000	Microsoft NT/XP, T-SQL, DTS	ERWin
ORACLE V4 - V8	UNIX shell, SQL*Plus, PL/SQL	System Architect

PROFESSIONAL EXPERIENCE

QUALITY INFORMATION SYSTEMS, Atlanta, GA   1998 - 2006

IT Project Manager, Health Systems, Atlanta, GA   2003 - 2006

Scheduled daily production of reports, processes and data transfers from internal and external systems for IT hardware, software and project administration.

- Developed and implemented the database components of an IT Project Administration system that automated time, labor and other costs as they related to programs, projects and plans. The system greatly reduced manual documentation, saved administrative costs and improved the timeliness of project reporting.

- Developed and implemented the database components of an IT Assets Management system to track more than $40 million in hardware and software, identifying location, status, usability and configuration. Project significantly improved accountability and delivery of information services.

IT Project Analyst, Health Foundations of Florida, Miami, FL   2001 - 2003

Worked with systems analyst to design and implement advanced database systems, components and applications.

- Designed and implemented the database to create the Coordination of Benefits system, saving administrative time and reducing cost of claims.

Senior Programmer-Analyst, ITP Health Systems, Tampa, FL   1998 - 2001

Developed the supporting databases for the upgrade and expansion of pre-paid calling cards, handling all the functional aspects of the cards including managing production scheduling and execution, tracking customer accounts, balances and usage, providing essential details for new product offerings and generating management reports.

- Implemented replication and partition options (dual-master sites) that increased the volume from 10 million to 40 million phone cards while maintaining responsiveness and reliability.

EDUCATION

B.S., Electrical Engineering Technology, De Vry Institute of Technology, Chicago, IL, 1998

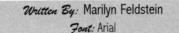

Written By: Marilyn Feldstein
Font: Arial

J O H N   D .   B R A D O V I C H

4560 Great Mountain Street   Telephone: (515) 211 3444
Des Moines, IA 50312   ■ ■ ■   Email: johndbrady@gmail.com

NETWORK ADMINISTRATOR | NETWORK ENGINEER | SYSTEMS ADMINISTRATOR
SYSTEMS ANALYST | INFORMATION ANALYST | OPERATING SYSTEMS SPECIALIST
• Professional Certifications • Masters Degree in Information Systems

"He not only showed extraordinary initiative in solving problems, but he also looked ahead toward better ways of doing things and making those available." —C.R. O'Dell, Distinguished Research Professor

Network professional with finely honed talents in network infrastructure, system security, and high-level troubleshooting. Persistent and in-depth problem-solver; acknowledged for capacity to source and resolve hidden issues eluding the most dedicated trouble-shooter, while simultaneously considering the impact of actions on end-users and the business bottom-line. Deadline, budget, and quality driven; expert in prioritizing tasks, analyzing the options, setting goals, and delivering on promises. Intuitive in exposing security vulnerabilities, and inspired by harnessing the power of technology to refine networks, automate and streamline systems, boost productivity, and eliminate errors. Bi-lingual: English and Russian.

Value Offered:

▪ Systems Design & Analysis	▪ Technical Support	▪ Network & Server Configurations
▪ Fault Identification & Resolution	▪ Data Communication Analysis	▪ Database Management
▪ IT Needs Analysis	▪ Network Security	▪ IT Security Policy Development
▪ Disaster Recovery Planning	▪ Strategic & Project Planning	▪ Capacity Planning
▪ Client & Staff Training	▪ Platform Enhancements	▪ Multi-Site Network Administration

TECHNOLOGY SNAPSHOT

Network Services and Applications	Apache, BIND, DHCP, FreeS/WAN, FTP, ipchains, IP Filter, IPSec, iptables, LDAP, Majordomo, NAT, Nessus, NFS, NIS, nmap, NTP, POP3/IMAP4, Postfix, Samba, Sendmail, Snort, snoop, socks, Squid, SSH, tcpdump
Networking	CIDR, Ethernet, IPv6, NDP, RDISC, RIP, RIPNG, TCP/IP, Token Ring, VLSM, VLAN
Operating Systems	Linux, Mac OS X, MS Windows, Sun OE, Sun Solaris
Back-up Utilities	dd, fssnap, tar, ufsdump, Backup Exec
Office Suites	OpenOffice, MS Office, Macintosh AppleWorks, StarOffice
Programming	Assembly 80x86, C/C++, Java, Visual Basic
Web Programming	PHP, HTML
Database Technologies	MySQL, PL/SQL, Postgre SQL
Documenting Tools	LaTeX, LyX, TeX
Mathematical Software	Matlab, Mathematica, Maple
Antivirus/Malware	Ad-Aware, McAfee, MS AntiSpyware, Spybot, Symantec

EXPERIENCE NARRATIVE

MILROY AND SONS/ACADEMIC SABBATICAL, Moscow   8/2005–Present
Successfully completed two Sun Solaris classes in Moscow and configured several network services (Apache, DNS, FTP, NFS, NIS) for Milroy and Sons sponsoring the training.

⇒ Introduced IP Filter firewalls, installed software patches, ensured NTP service synchronized time, created secure passwords in NIS, and streamlined DNS security.

⇒ Passed three certifying exams with a score of 84% to secure two Sun certifications.

⇒ Translated more than 100 pages of technical text spanning the company's user software manual, online help pages, and internal labels from English to Russian for US-based company, HiTown Software Inc.

UNIVERSITY OF TENNESSEE, TN   9/2003–8/2005
Computer Systems Administrator II, Microcomputer Laboratories
Supported 300 faculty and staff. Environment: 2000-node network with 500 new nodes annually.

Commenced engagement during peak period where new admissions and commencement of classes were the immediate priority of staff. With no supervision or direction available, personally researched the role, sourced, secured, and reviewed employee orientation information, and jump-started introductions with key stakeholders in assigned departments.

Quickly mastered the nuances of the system and daily operations and, within three weeks, management was receiving positive feedback from end-users praising expertise in sourcing answers and devising solutions.

⇒ Eliminated end-user apathy surrounding the creation of passwords, and enforced the adoption of "strong" passwords. Configured Linux to check passwords, ensuring compliance with security standards.

John D. Bradovich | Experienced Network Administrator | Page 1 | Confidential | johndbrady@gmail.com

University of Tennessee (Continued)

⇒ Created script to identify inappropriate use of copyrighted music and movie materials stored on University server. Automated script searched system weekly on suspected abuse of servers for investigation.

⇒ Served 300+ end users in a non-tiered support environment where issues could range from the routine to the complex on Linux, Unix, Windows, and Macintosh operating systems, server-based applications including Sendmail, Apache, and SpamAssassin, and end user-based MS Office, Mathematica, Matlab, Mulberry, McAfee, and Symantec.

⇒ Planned, developed, and implemented a $30K, 3-server solution to overcome the severe overloading of the main server due to processor-intensive mathematical computations being conducted in tandem with email and web operations. Three-server solution offered low-cost alternative to commercial offerings by spreading the load across three servers and was delivered in just four days—a week less than forecasted deadlines.

⇒ Defeated technological issues in transferring users and file directories from outdated Linux-based servers to new servers through a strategic, multi-phase, shell script that offered simplicity to end users.

⇒ Pioneered remote kernel of Mathematica application that allowed end users to access the application on individual computers but send time- and processor-consuming calculations to a remote server in one click.

⇒ Identified licensing issue with Matlab physics software and wrote script to assess registered user numbers. Findings prompted vendor negotiations to secure bulk licenses saving the university $12,000K annually.

⇒ Oriented staff to *Blackboard*—an online classroom software package. Presented to faculty in formal classroom settings twice a day, three times a week for three weeks.

⇒ Assigned mathematics and physics departments spanning three sites as part of a 10-person team challenged to upgrade, troubleshoot, support, and add nodes to the 2000-node network. Sole support person for Linux, Unix, Matlab, and Mathematica installation and configuration issues.

⇒ Tightened security surrounding remote access to the system. Disabled FTP and Telnet for off-campus users and replaced with secure counterparts: SCP and SSH.

UNIVERSITY OF FLORIDA, FL   9/2001–8/2002
Assistant System Administrator, Office of Information Technology
Environment: 1800 PCs, 90 printers.
An inquisitive mindset, coupled with a capacity to intuitively probe and troubleshoot network issues, gained the attention of the System Administrator, prompting an offer to share the system workload. Entrusted with access to all passwords and system configurations, quickly mastered the nuances of the system and end users, and gained a reputation for swift communications and command of system troubleshooting.

⇒ One of two employees handpicked by management for a two-week special assignment in Arizona. With an "impossible" deadline of 24 hours to assemble 2 network computer labs with 26 computers and a printer in each, delivered the turnkey project on time.

⇒ Circumvented system downtime of 1800 computers across 5 buildings—conducting an upgrade of the main domain controller from Windows NT to Windows 2000. Extensive research underscored extreme tactical planning for the project that was delivered to specification within just six hours and in readiness for daily operations.

⇒ Distinguished as the first at the university to implement new features—Active Directory group policies and organizational units. Initiative introduced concept of shared administrative rights across campus and allowed rapid troubleshooting by new administrators able to address smaller-scale problems locally. Pioneering efforts delivered productivity boosts of 30%, elevated IT support response times by 20%, and won praise by management.

⇒ Created the first system back-ups for the university—researching best options for failsafe data recording and restoration. Presented and won the green light from manager to purchase Veritas Backup Exec and devised and scheduled automated nightly backups for two servers.

——————————————— **EDUCATION | CERTIFICATIONS** ———————————————

Master of Science, *Major: Computer Information Systems*   2003
Bachelor of Science, *Major: Business Administration. Dean's List*   2001
University of California

Certifications: ?SCNA (Sun Certified Network Administrator for Solaris 10 OS) ?SCSA (Sun Certified Systems Administrator for Solaris 10 OS) ?RHCE (Red Hat Certified Engineer) ?RHCT (Red Hat Certified Technician) ?Network+ (CompTIA Certified Network Administrator) ?A+ (CompTIA Certified Technician).

Training: Solaris 9 OE: Advanced System Administration and Network Administration. Linux Network Security and Firewalls, Red Hat Linux System Administration and Networking.

John D. Bradovich | Experienced Network Administrator | Page 2| Confidential | johndbrady@gmail.com

Written By: Gayle Howard
Font: Times New Roman

Mary Ella Johnson, MBA

4000 Randall wood Place   (216) 333-1245
Cleveland, Ohio 44122   johnme@msn.com

PROJECT MANAGER

Achieved cost savings of $1M per year.

Decisive , action-oriented and results-focused professional with eight years of outstanding project planning, execution, monitoring and resource balancing skills with ability to support multiple simultaneous projects in a matrix-organizational structure. Offering exemplary communication skills demonstrated through successful meetings with stakeholders to provide accurate reporting and information regarding ongoing projects and initiatives.

- Financial Reporting and Analysis
- Strategic Thinking and Global Management
- Scheduling and Cost Control
- Financial Risk Management
- Strategy Formulation and Implementation
- Global Project Management

Information and Operations Management Background:

- Coordinate and negotiate offshore and vendor resources in support of timelines and project deliverables.
- Proven leadership and collaboration skills in both technical and cross-functional teams.
- Established and managed the operations of an offshore team charged with providing application support and services in a 24x7 environment for over 35 systems.
- Developed and implemented training programs to enhance testing standards and procedures.

EDUCATION

Master of Business Administration (MBA)   Cleveland State University
BA Justice Administration   Ohio State University

PROFESSIONAL BACKGROUND

Viacom- Shaker Heights, OH 2002- PRESENT
Systems Engineer- Account and Program Manager

Manage and track the activities and progress of over 40 mid-sized to large and moderately complex information technology projects from product inception to production deployment in a cross-functional environment. Project-managed efforts to ensure deliverables are on time and within budget. Liaison between information technology and client organizations. Work directly with internal and external clients to define and manage their needs. Resolve system implementation issues providing status reports to all stakeholders. Manage a staff of 6 system testers.

- Reduced production implementation slippage by over 30 percent.
- Increased the effectiveness of testing team by reducing software defects by more than 35 percent.
- Developed a methodology for knowledge transfer to new team members, and ensured their integration with their US-based peers.
- Provided leadership and direction to team in resolving complex technical issues.

Bell - Cleveland, OH 1997- 2002
Software Engineer – System Administrator

Strategically worked both independently and in a creative, friendly team environment with a cutting-edge engineering staff. Exceptional record of increasing operating efficiency and boosting profitability through expertise in computer software engineering, operations management, project management, and staff supervision.

- Led team that designed and implemented a web interface electronic software distribution (ESD) site for customers to download company products.
- Led team that designed and implemented an electronic software download manager that allows customers to select, download, and install specific products simultaneously.

Written By: Brenda Thompson
Font: Times New Roman

JOHN LAURENT

487 Royal Place
Royal Oak, MI 48135

jlaurent2005@yahoo.com

Home: 777.222.0001
Cell: 333.888.6999

CHEMICAL LABORATORY TECHNICIAN

Skilled Lab Technician with 15 years experience working in chemical and R&D laboratories. Expertise in molten salt technology and corrosion testing. Creative problem solver who applies technical skills and business knowledge to achieve improved research and product results. Able to manage multiple projects simultaneously. Productive in both individual contributor and team environments. Excellent communication and relationship-building skills.

Chemical Analysis ~ R&D ~ Research ~ Customer Relations ~ Chemical Processes ~ Presentations
Record Keeping ~ Report Development & Analysis ~ Data Gathering & Analysis ~ Wet Chemistry Techniques
Quality Assurance ~ Regulatory Compliance ~ Medical Lab ~ Equipment Maintenance ~ Sales ~ Patents

WORK HISTORY

CRANDALL CORPORATION, Detroit, MI   1990 - 2006
Company sells chemicals, equipment, and services for metal surface technologies
APPLICATIONS SPECIALIST (LAB TECHNICIAN)

Responsible for analyzing customer parts, with metal/resin surfaces, that are in need of chemical applications. Determined the correct process needed, gathered all the data for engineering and sales staff, wrote laboratory reports, and returned the parts to the customers. Handled the process from beginning to end, in addition to maintaining all the equipment.

- Cleaned up the chemical lab within one month, organizing it, instituting a 24-hour turnaround policy (that had previously taken weeks), and streamlining procedures. Cleaned up the R&D lab, going in and organizing it, making it ready for extensive customer contact.
- Reinvented a product, putting it together, obtaining a patent, and marketing it quickly to beat the competition. This product produced a big revenue stream and replaced the competitor's old product.
- Readied both labs for ISO 9001 compliance, establishing a routine, documenting it, and setting up policies and procedures for the R&D lab. Complemented for efforts by management and the ISO auditors.
- Handled customer demos because of extensive knowledge of the processes and the ability to communicate well with others.
- Complied with all OSHA safety standards, always passing inspections.

LAKE SHORE CLINICAL, Dearborn, MI   1986 – 1990
A medical lab that conducted blood analysis for doctors' offices
MEDICAL LAB ASSISTANT

Handled all the blood chemistries, analyzing the samples and maintaining the equipment. Ensured that all controls were within specification and drew blood samples from patients.

- Maintained quality control for all blood chemistries.
- Kept up all equipment to make sure high-quality standards were met.
- Provided a 24-hour turnaround time to doctors, issuing reports on sample results. Interfaced with doctors and answered any questions on test results.

EDUCATION / AFFILIATIONS

Biomedical Engineering, SCHOOLCRAFT COLLEGE, Livonia, MI

Diploma – *Material Science*, MATERIALS ENGINEERING INSTITUTE, six-month program
Diploma – *Medical Laboratory Assistant*, CARNEGIE INSTITUTE OF DETROIT, one-year program

Member – American Society of Metals (ASM)
Member – Heat Treat Society (HTS)

Written By: Joyce Fortier
Font: Arial

MARGARET BOLING
boling@verizon.net

27735 Goldcrest Road   661 435-3671
Valencia, California 91355   Cellular: 661 435-0393

FIELD SERVICE ENGINEER
Providing outstanding quality and customer assurance

Dynamic, self-directed, goal-oriented, hands-on professional with a varied background in leading-edge technologies as well as **extensive experience in client relations across broad industries.** Successful track record of maximizing resources to increase production capacity with the ability to analytically troubleshoot / identify problems and implement solutions in a timely manner while keeping an eye on the company's bottom-line. Excellent problem-solving skills with a strong orientation in customer service / satisfaction. Able to work under pressure in fast-paced, time-sensitive environments.

Demonstrated ability in assessing problem areas and offering recommendations resulting in increases in productivity and profitability. Background encompasses strong leadership as well as the ability to establish and build positive, solid relationships with clients and all levels of management. Effectively interface with executives, line staff, and people of diverse socioeconomic backgrounds and cultures. Able to work well in self-managed and team-based environments. Liaison between clients, engineers, and customer support personnel. Highly adaptable to new systems and processes.

- Project Design & Management
- Engineering Management
- Estimating, Budgeting, and P&L
- Field Installation Management

- Resource Planning & Management
- Client Presentations & Negotiations
- Vendor Selection & Negotiation
- Material Selection & Management

Technically proficient, detail oriented, and accurate. Proven expertise in assembling and organizing data. Patient and persistent; excellent interpersonal and communication skills. Well-organized and adept at multitasking. Extensive background working with cross-functional scientific and research teams. Foster environments of high productivity and team orientation. Train end-users on equipment operation. **Strong work ethic.**

Expertise
Thorough knowledge of good manufacturing / laboratory practices such as **CGMP, ISO 9000-9002, USP <788> Supplemental 28,** and **FDA 21CFR Part 11 compliance** as well as **ISO 14644-1** and **Fed-Std-209E calculations.**
Read schematics; pneumatic and mechanical knowledge; use of voltmeter, oscilloscope, PHA (pulse height analyzer), USP Calibration (previously all in liquid and air; now all laser), HPLC (high-performance liquid chromatography), Orbisphere, Anatel (TOC), flow cytometry, IQOQ, SOPs, clean-room environment.

Computer Skills
ORACLE and work-specific software
Microsoft Word and Excel
Built entire computers from parts; loaded software in Windows 2000 XP.

Language Skills: Basic conversational Spanish

ACCOMPLISHMENTS / AWARDS
Who's Who in Worldwide Registry
Employee of the Month, 1991 (Pacific Scientific)

MARGARET BOLING – Page 2 – **boling@verizon.net**

PROFESSIONAL EXPERIENCE

SENIOR FIELD SERVICE ENGINEER   2005 - Present
Southern California Edison Company - Los Angeles, CA

Recruited by former employer to direct the Southern California customer base. Work in clean-room environments using all laser-driven equipment. Involved with semiconductor manufacturing, aerospace, industrial, pharmaceutical, research, and filter testing. Calibrated on site to NIST traceable methods for pharmaceutical companies, advise clients on proper usage application, and train end-users on operation while ensuring ISO 9000-9002 procedures, FDA 21 CFR part 11, and clients' SOPs (Standard Operating Procedures) are met with satisfaction.

Provide technical and engineering assistance to teams and participate in client presentations / contract negotiations. Lead cross-functional teams of software, electronic, and mechanical engineers throughout entire project cycle. Manage relationships with project managers and plant managers at client sites. Interact daily with clients. Calibrate on clients' sites.

SENIOR FIELD SERVICE ENGINEER   2003 - 2005
Scientific Fields - Hacienda Heights, CA

Scheduled all appointments and closed service orders using ORACLE. Operated fluorospheres (flow check) standards to verify optics alignment and fluidics of the systems. Used Argon laser in clinical work for flow cytometry and mechanical, pneumatic, and electronics on equipment to detect AIDS, leukemia, Lymphoma, Marine Biology, and DNA.

SENIOR FIELD SERVICE ENGINEER   1998 - 2003
Fisher Concepts - Pittsburgh, PA

Promoted from Field Service Engineer. Handled mostly research and production for pharmaceuticals. Conducted HPLC based on chemistry: ensured instrumentation was running properly, Installed and performed preventive maintenance, IQOQ, calibration, and repair.

Adhered to clients' specifications and FDA CFR 21 Part 11 compliance procedures through USP pharmacopoeia. Amgen Inc, Wyeth Pharmaceutical, Gilead Sciences, and cosmetic companies were some clients among others.

FIELD SERVICE ENGINEER   1985 - 1998
Halcium - Silver Spring, MD (covered Western Region including Hawaii and Mexico)

Worked in clean-room environments. Involved with semiconductor manufacturing, aerospace, industrial, pharmaceutical, research, and filter testing. Calibrated on site to NIST traceable methods and performed USP<788> 28 calibration (indictable) for pharmaceutical companies.

Systems used were laser-based halogen lamps and light-scattering methods with RS232 communication ports controlling equipment. Some systems had temperature, relative humidity, air velocity, and air differential pressure.

Scheduled all appointments and maintained accurate spare parts inventory. Serviced all Western Regional companies holding service contracts and some that didn't. Out of state calls constituted 40% of workload.

EDUCATION

Associate of Science, Electronic Engineering, with Honors, ITT Technical Institute, Sylmar, CA

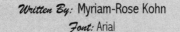

Written By: Myriam-Rose Kohn
Font: Arial

DANIEL F. SMYTH

6145 COLUMBUS AVENUE • KALAMAZOO, MICHIGAN 49002 • 269.483.6319 • dfsmyth@charter.net

LEAD PHARMACEUTICAL ANALYST

*Five Years of Diversified Analytical Experience and Documented Contributions as a
Method Development / Validation Chemist, R&D Chemist, and Laboratory Trainer in a CRO Environment.*

Professional Profile

➤ Quality-focused laboratory lead analyst with proven expertise in HPLC and GC methodologies and instrumentation; data collection and analysis; and project management. Highly experienced using a wide range of ChemServ instrumentation and software.

➤ Proven expertise in ChemServ Millennium v. 6.0, Beckmart Gold, Ageus ChemistryStation (for HPLC and GC), and Parkin Elvis Turbochem analytical software systems.

➤ Extensive knowledge of FDA GMP/GLP guidelines and regulations.

➤ Excels in fast-paced laboratory environments where leadership skills are the keys to success. Recognized by management and peers as a focused laboratory professional who is goal- and project-driven.

➤ Exhibits keen organizational and problem-solving skills, with proven ability to coordinate multiple projects and meet deadlines under pressure.

Areas of Expertise

➤ Developing & Validating Analytical Methods & Techniques

➤ Pharmaceutical R&D and Product Testing

➤ Laboratory Instrumentation

➤ Method Development

➤ Instrument Calibration/Troubleshooting

➤ Team Member Training & Development

➤ Regulatory Compliance & Record Keeping

➤ SOP/Report Preparation

➤ Workflow Planning & Prioritization

➤ Multi-Task Management

➤ Client Communication and Interaction

➤ Service Quality Improvement

PROFESSIONAL EXPERIENCE

CDI Laboratories, Inc., Grand Rapids, Michigan   **July 1999 – Present**
(Privately owned laboratory providing state-of-the-art contract analytical services to the prescription pharmaceutical industry)

Analyst II (August 2003 – Present)

Maintains full lead analyst responsibilities for the laboratory. Analyzes organic compounds in clients' pharmaceutical samples using sophisticated HPLC and GC technologies. Performs method development and validation for product testing methods and dose formulation studies. Writes and updates SOPs for analytical procedures. Successfully maintains accurate and complete laboratory records including supporting calculations for analytical results. Ensures that tests are performed according to stability protocols. Possesses strong ability to analyze data to recognize trends in assay performance, QC controls, and reference or laboratory standards. Corrects identified problems to minimize delays in project completion. Calibrates and maintains pH meters, balances, HPLC, and GC instrumentation. Effectively identifies problem areas and concerns and independently pursues corrective actions while keeping management fully informed of project status.

Key Achievements

➤ Considered the company's in-house expert on ChemServ Millennium software. Responsible for maintaining validation of the system and developing training programs for new employees.

➤ Successfully troubleshot and repaired several laboratory instruments saving the company more than $15,000 in service calls over the previous year.

➤ Served as lead analyst on more than 10 method validation projects for major pharmaceutical companies that are currently using these methods in their manufacturing processes.

➤ Developed and currently validating specialized laboratory method using a headspace analyzer attached to a GC.

DANIEL F. SMYTH

PROFESSIONAL EXPERIENCE (CONT.)

CDI Laboratories, Inc. (cont.)

Analyst I (February 2000 – August 2003)

Performed bioanalytical and product testing method development as required according to GLP and GMP regulations. Conducted validation studies of new analytical methods used for drug analysis in various biomatrices and finished pharmaceuticals, as required. Maintained, calibrated, and troubleshot HPLC and GC equipment used in the analytical methods. Established and maintained appropriate records and laboratory standards to recognize trends in laboratory performance.

Key Achievements

> ➢ Demonstrated advanced knowledge of laboratory methods, procedures, and terminology.
> ➢ Successfully managed 15 assigned projects and maintained consistent analytical results.
> ➢ Developed and implemented Excel spreadsheets with complex equations. Initiated the use of graphs and charts to monitor and recognize patterns in R&D analytical results.
> ➢ Recognized for laboratory proficiency, maturity, professionalism, positive mental attitude, and commitment to excellence; promoted to Analyst II.

Entry-Level Analyst (July 1999 – February 2000)

Analyzed pharmaceutical samples in company's dose formulations department using HPLC and GC instrumentation. Successfully maintained accurate and complete laboratory records including supporting calculations for analytical results. Corrected identified problems to minimize delays in project completion. Calibrated and troubleshot all laboratory instruments. Effectively identified problem areas and concerns and independently pursued corrective actions while keeping management fully informed of project status. Made suggestions to superiors regarding ways to improve techniques (or procedures) within established company and client guidelines.

Key Achievements

> ➢ Demonstrated extensive working knowledge of analytical principles and methods of qualitative and quantitative chemical analysis.
> ➢ Successfully conducted all laboratory activities in accordance with company SOPs to meet FDA and clients' requirements.
> ➢ Assisted in the preparation of SOPs for various laboratory instruments and procedures.
> ➢ Proactively supported other staff analysts with training and technical support.

EDUCATION

WESTERN MICHIGAN UNIVERSITY
Kalamazoo, Michigan
Bachelor of Science, 1999
Biomedical Science/Chemistry

PROFESSIONAL AFFILIATIONS

American Chemical Society

Written By: Richard Porter
Font: Arial

Résumé

THOMAS BARNES, MSc

Telephones:
home: (08) 8398 6666
work: (08) 8238 9087
email: barney@biglake.com.au

21 Battunga Road
Mt BARKER South Australia 5251

POSITION SOUGHT

Biotechnology Research

- Research Organisation - Tertiary Institution - Pharmaceutical Company

CAREER OVERVIEW

Degree of Bachelor of Medical and Pharmaceutical Biotechnology and a Graduate Diploma in Medical Laboratory Science from the University of South Australia with a Masters Degree in Biotechnology from Flinders University and a total of six years post-graduate experience in applied pharmaceutical research. Spent one year as the Visiting Research Scientist at a major pharmaceutical research laboratory in South Africa with responsibility for the field collection and testing of soil samples for new strains of microbes, leading to the identification of two new genera of filamentous bacteria currently being assessed for pharmaceutical applications. Established new protocols for the inter-laboratory transport of microbes drawing on earlier experience working in Quality Control with *Australian Grain Exporters*. Currently completing a five-year contract with *Barker Microbiology Research* in South Australia collaborating in field-based research throughout Australia and South-east Asia.

KEY COMPETENCIES

- Research Skills - Computing - Reporting
- Problem Solving - Prioritizing - Organising - Collaborating
- Team Work - Lateral Thinking - Implementing - Planning

PROFESSIONAL STRENGTHS

- Field collection, laboratory isolation, identification and testing for microbial activity
- Setting up database using Paradox for Windows for recording and searching isolates data
- Shipping overseas of microbial samples – quarantine issues, permits, couriers, shipping agents
- Designing new protocols for isolation and preservation of microbial isolates
- Working collaboratively with commercial, academic and medical stakeholders
- Strong laboratory skills with experience in major hospital and commercial laboratories
- Able to adapt quickly to new research environments and work under extreme field conditions
- Up-to-date knowledge of laboratory techniques, practices and equipment

THOMAS BARNES _____ **2**

RELATED ACHIEVEMENTS

- Undertook 12-month post-graduate research position with leading South African pharmaceutical development company *Pharmaceutical Vectors Corporation* leading to the identification of two new strains of microbes from sample of 6,000 isolates of soil collected during trips to the Natal Province.

- Recognised problems with the existing protocols used by *Pharmaceutical Vectors Corporation* for freezing microbial samples and initiated new quality control procedures, decreasing contamination rate and making strains more viable for transport to other laboratories.

- Planned and undertook several major field trips in outback Australia and South Africa to collect samples for microbial isolation, living under canvass for several weeks at a time while establishing strong working bonds with support crew.

- Tested nitrogen levels in grain samples for the *Australian Grain Exporters* to establish correct payment to growers, processing approximately 500 samples per day for two months during harvest, demonstrating the ability to work accurately under pressure.

CAREER HISTORY

Research Scientist Biotechnology
Barker Microbiology Research Ltd, Mt Barker, South Australia   2001–present

> Responsibilities: *Facilitating field-based applied research with Universities, medical research laboratories and other stakeholders throughout Australia and Southeast Asia; field collection of samples; isolation and identification of microbial isolates for production of new useful strains for pharmaceutical applications.*

Visiting Research Scientist
Pharmaceutical Vectors Corporation, South Africa   1998

> Responsibilities: *Field collection and testing of soil samples for new strains of microbes; isolation and identification of microbial isolates; development of new protocols for the isolation, preservation and inter-laboratory transport of microbial isolates.*

Quality Control Chemist (part-time)
Australian Grain Exporters, Adelaide, South Australia   1993–1997

> Responsibilities: *Quality control testing; operating ECO 428 Nitrogen Determinator; identification of grain type; automated determination of amylase; infra-red analysis for moisture testing; training of staff; knowledge of export shipping procedures.*

EDUCATIONAL QUALIFICATIONS

Masters Degree in Biotechnology
Flinders University of South Australia   2001

Graduate Diploma in Medical Laboratory Science
School of Pharmacy, University of South Australia   1997

Bachelor of Medical and Pharmaceutical Biotechnology
University of South Australia   1996

Written By: Brian Leeson
Font: Times New Roman

OLIVIA GRACE

76 Columbia Street   (315) 844-2505
Mohawk, NY 13407   grace@yahoo.com

PRODUCT DEVELOPMENT & INNOVATION

Offering a well-documented record for delivering leading edge, creative liquid concepts that exceed consumer expectations. Combines international and multicultural expertise with strong technical qualifications and a mastery of marketing principles.

- Qualitative & Quantitative Research Analysis
- Ideation / Prototype Development / Risk Management
- Applications & Technology Assessment
- Production Process Flow (HACCP & QACCP)

- Shelf-Life Studies / Focus Group Studies
- US & International Production Operations
- Sensory Evaluation / Novel Ingredient Functionality
- Raw Materials Sourcing / Regulatory Compliance

HIGHLIGHTS OF QUALIFICATIONS

- Career reflects effective use of innovation and creativity from concept to launch *and* an expert ability to translate strategic business needs into high-quality liquid solutions that consistently become commercially viable and successful products.

- Highly skilled at recognizing emerging trends and identifying market gaps in both international and domestic markets.

- Proven ability to leverage internal and external creative and technical capabilities to develop break-through products. Equally skilled at leveraging supplier competencies to maximize delivery and meet regulatory standards.

- Experienced project manager who is able to facilitate multinational teams towards creative resolution and consensus.

- Able to establish a network of industry contacts to help drive forward development and advance the production process.

PROFESSIONAL EXPERIENCE

International Spirits Company   **1998 to Present**
GLOBAL BRAND INNOVATION GROUP—WHITE PLAINS, NY
Product Innovation Manager (2/04 to Present)   Product Innovation Senior Technologist (5/02 to 2/04)

Lead teams to develop innovation projects in premixed cocktails, flavored malt beverages and luxury spirits. Manage product development of innovation projects across a wide range of projects including ready-to-drink, flavored vodkas and premix cocktails. Work closely with Marketing on innovation concept development and positioning. Collaborate with global partners and North America Supply on commercialization efforts, including shelf-life studies, raw materials sourcing and BATF registration.

GLOBAL BRAND INNOVATION GROUP—HONG KONG, CHINA
Product Innovation Senior Technologist (10/00 to 5/02)

Worked closely with Marketing and Consumer Planning on concept and proposition development. Networked and managed ingredient suppliers worldwide in product development. Served as a direct liaison with global suppliers to ensure efficient commercialization according to product specifications.

SELECTED PROJECTS & HIGHLIGHTS

- Established two liquid satellite labs (Hong Kong, United States) from start-up to user-friendly facilities that fully support concept development and meet global standards in terms of equipment, processes and work tools.

- Championed the development and execution of a flavored malt beverage line that became No. 2 in the category as well as another product which received the prestigious Gold Medal in the San Francisco Spirits competition.

- Honored by ISC North America for the "Best Innovation Project" and awarded the Brand Group's Double Eagle award for "Best Product Launch" of a successful product line.

- Managed the product development of innovation projects for carbonated and non-carbonated ready-to-drink and whisky from concept to commercialization in several key markets (Australia, Thailand, Taiwan, Japan, Korea and the Philippines).

- Selected to manage two key strategic innovation initiatives to address the low carb/calorie and African-American markets.

OLIVIA GRACE

(315) 844-2505

PROFESSIONAL EXPERIENCE CONTINUED

International Spirits Company continued

BRAND INNOVATION GROUP—UNITED KINGDOM
Product Development Technologist (6/98 to 9/00)

Extensively involved with managing projects involved with the product development and commercialization of a variety of new drink products including ready-to-drink, liqueurs, cream liqueurs, spirits (vodka, whisky and gin) and low-alcohol wine. Completed extensive training in whisky, gin and cream liqueur technologies. Acquired significant experience in technical project management, risk management, shelf-life testing, technical troubleshooting, pilot plant and factory trials.

Coca-Cola International Holdings, Ltd.   1997 TO 1998

HONG KONG
Research Technologist I

Served as a project leader with direct responsibility for overseeing all stages of beverage development projects including concept and prototype development, production trial runs, specification set-up, shelf-life study, profit improvement, and troubleshooting. Audited new raw materials and set up quality control specifications. Conducted and supervised in-plant and field taste tests. Provided nutrition data on products and involved with labeling and regulatory issues. Worked with other departments to provide technical support on specific projects.

EDUCATIONAL SUMMARY

EDUCATION
Carolina State University, *Conway, SC, USA*
M.S. in Food Science & Technology GPA: 3.96 (1997)
B.S. in Food Science & Technology GPA: 4.0 (1996)

THESIS
"Growth Development & Growth Location Effects on Thermal Properties of Starch from Mutant & Exotic Corn"

ACADEMIC HONORS
- Top Graduating Scholar in Food Science
- Top Graduating Scholar in College of Agriculture
- American Association of Cereal Chemists' Graduate Scholarship
- Ranked in the University's Top 2% (1993, 1994, 1996)
- Academic All-American Scholar (1995)
- Institute of Food Technologists' TJ Lipton Scholarship (1995)
- International Student Academic Recognition Scholarship (4 year

ADDITIONAL INFORMATION

CAROLINA STATE UNIVERSITY ASSISTANTSHIPS
Teaching Assistant (Spring 1997)
Supported teaching and preparation efforts for a junior- and senior-level sensory evaluation class.

Research Assistant (Fall 1994 to Spring 1997)
Conducted ongoing research projects which included:
proximate analysis, gel strength determination, thermal analysis
amylose and amylopectin determination of starch.

PROFESSIONAL AFFILIATION
Institute of Food Technologists

COMPUTER PROFICIENCIES
Microsoft Word / Excel / PowerPoint / Project / Access
Platforms: PC and Macintosh

Written By: Kristen Coleman
Font: Times New Roman

▶ Resume Writing Worksheet

You can use this handy worksheet as a guide to gathering the critical information you will need to develop your resume:

NAME: _____

ADDRESS: _____

_____

CITY: _____ STATE: _____ ZIP: _____

PHONE: (Home) _____ (Cell) _____

E-MAIL ADDRESS: _____

CAREER OBJECTIVE(S): 1) _____

2) _____

EMPLOYMENT HISTORY:

FROM: _____ / _____ TO: _____ / _____ JOB TITLE: _____

COMPANY: _____ CITY: _____ STATE: _____

KEY DUTIES: _____

_____

_____

_____

_____

ACCOMPLISHMENTS: _____

_____

_____

_____

_____

EMPLOYMENT HISTORY:

FROM: _____ / _____ TO: _____ / _____ JOB TITLE: _____

COMPANY: _____ CITY: _____ STATE: _____

KEY DUTIES: _____

_____

_____

_____

_____

ACCOMPLISHMENTS: _____

_____

_____

_____

_____

(Use additional sheets, if necessary, to capture more of your work history)

MILITARY SERVICE: FROM:_____ /_____ TO:_____ /_____

BRANCH:_____ RANK:_____

SPECIALTY (MOS):_____ UNIT: _____

COMMENDATIONS: _____

EDUCATION:

SCHOOL: _____ GRAD. (SEP.) _____ /_____

DEGREE: _____ MAJOR: _____

LOCATION: _____

SIGNIFICANT COURSEWORK: _____

HONORS/CLUBS: _____

(Use additional sheets to capture other degrees, diplomas, etc.)

PROFESSIONAL LICENSES / CERTIFICATIONS:

_____

PROFESSIONAL SEMINARS:

_____

_____

_____

COMPUTER SKILLS: TECHNICAL SKILLS:

_____   _____

_____   _____

_____   _____

_____   _____

_____   _____

FOREIGN LANGUAGES:

_____

MEMBERSHIPS / AFFILIATIONS:

_____

_____

_____

VOLUNTEER WORK / COMMUNITY INVOLVEMENT:

_____

_____

_____

PUBLICATIONS / PUBLIC SPEAKING:

_____

_____

_____

OTHER HONORS AND AWARDS:

_____

This worksheet is only intended to be a *guide* to gathering the important information you need to prepare your resume. After reading Chapters 2 and 3, which discuss designing and writing your resume, you may think of other sections that will be important for you to include, or decide that some sections shown here are not relevant to your situation.

Appendix B

▶ Professional Keyword List

Each resume example chapter in this book (Chapters 5–16) has a list of keywords relating to the particular career field or profession covered in that chapter.

Use this form to highlight all the keywords and keyword phrases that accurately reflect *your* skills, qualifications, and experience.

Appendix $\mathcal{C}$

▶ List of Contributors

The following professional resume writers have contributed their *best* resumes to this publication. All have years of experience in professional resume writing; many have earned distinguishing professional credentials that include:

CARW	Certified Advanced Resume Writer
CCM	Credentialed Career Master
CCMC	Certified Career Management Coach
CCTJ	Certified Career Transition Jumpmaster
CEIP	Certified Employment Interview Professional
CERW	Certified Expert Resume Writer
CIS	Certified Interview Strategist
CMF	Certified Fellow Practitioner
CMP	Certified Management Professional
CPBS	Certified Personal Brand Strategist
CPC	Certified Personnel Consultant
CPRW	Certified Professional Resume Writer
CTMS	Certified Transition Management Seminars
CTSB	Certified Targeted Small Business
CWDP	Certified Workforce Development Professional
FRWCC	Federal Resume Writer & Career Coach
GCDF	Global Career Development Facilitator
IJCTC	International Job & Career Transition Coach
JCTC	Job & Career Transition Coach

MBTI	(Certified in) Myers-Briggs Type Indicator
MCDP	Master Career Development Professional
NCCC	Nationally Certified Career Coach
NCRW	Nationally Certified Resume Writer
PHR	Professional in Human Resources
RPR	Registered Professional Recruiter

Carol Altomare, CPRW
World Class Resumes
Flemington, NJ
caa@worldclassresumes.com
www.worldclassresumes.com
908-237-1883

Doris Appelbaum, President
Appelbaum's Resume Prof., Inc.
Milwaukee, WI
dorisa@execpc.com
www.appelbaumresumes.com
800-619-9777
414-352-5994

Marcia Baker
MARK of Success, LLC, Waldorf, MD
resumes@markofsuccess.net
www.markofsuccess.net
301-885-2511

Laura Barbeau
Job Training Center, Red Bluff, CA
lbarbeau@ncen.org
jobtrainingcenter.org
530-529-7000

Susan Barens, CPRW, IJCTC
Career Dynamics, Olmsted Falls, OH
Careerdynamics1@aol.com
440-610-4361

Janet L. Beckstrom, CPRW
Word Crafter, Flint, MI
wordcrafter@voyager.net
800-351-9818

Liz Benuscak, CPRW, IJCTC
Bi-Coastal Resumes
New City, NY
lizb@bi-coastalresumes.com
www.bi-coastalresumes.com
800-813-1643

Laurie Berenson, CPRW
Sterling Career Concepts, LLC
Park Ridge, NJ
laurie@sterlingcareerconcepts.com
www.sterlingcareerconcepts.com
201-573-8282

Anne Brunelle, Career Transitions Coach
Making Changes, Toronto, Ontario
info@makingchanges.ca
www.makingchanges.ca
647-224-8287

Romona Camarata, GCDF, CCM, CPRW,
    MBTI
R.L. Stevens & Associates, Inc.,
    Northbrook, IL
rcamarata@rlstevens.com
www.interviewing.com
888-806-7313

Freddie Cheek, M.S. Ed., CCM, CPRW,
    CARW, CWDP
Cheek & Associates, Amherst, NY
fscheek@adelphia.net
www.cheekandassociates.com
716-835-6945

Kristin Coleman
Career Services, Poughkeepsie, NY
kristin@colemancareerservices.com
845-452-8274

Denyse Cowling, CIS, CPC, RPR
Career Intelligence Inc., Burlington, Ontario
dcowlings@cogeco.ca
866-909-0128

Jean Cummings, CPBS, CPRW, CEIP
A Resume For Today, Concord, MA
jc@AResumeForToday.com
www.aresumefortoday.com
800-324-1699

Michael S. Davis, GCDF, CPRW
Centerville, OH
msdavis49@hotmail.com
937-438-5037

George Dutch, BA, CMF, CCM, JCTC
Ottawa, Canada
george@GeorgeDutch.com
www.jobjoy.net
800-798-2696

Salome A. Farraro, CPRW
Careers TOO, Mount Morris, NY
sfarraro@careers-too.com
www.careers-too.com
877-436-9378

Marilyn Feldstein, M.P.A., JCTC, MBTI,
    PHR
Career Choices Unlimited, Jacksonville, FL
mwfeld@aol.com
www.careerchoicesunlimited.com
904-262-9470

Joyce Fortier, CCM, CPRW, CCMC, JCTC
Create Your Career, Novi, MI
careerist@aol.com
www.careerist.com
248-478-5662

Johnetta Frazier, Director of Training
Philadelphia Workforce Development Corp.
Philadelphia, PA
jfrazier@pwdc.org
215-854-1965

Louise Garver, MA, CMP, CPRW, CEIP,
    MCDP, JCTC
Career Directions LLC, Enfield, CT
LouiseGarver@cox.net
www.careerdirectionsllc.com
860-623-9476

Jill Grindle, CPRW
Resume Inkstincts, Agawam, MA
j.grindle@resumeinkstincts.com
www.resumeinkstincts.com
413-789-6046

Lee Anne Grundish
Grafix Services / ACHIEVE SUCCESS!
Toledo / Ottawa Hills, OH
GrafixServices@aol.com
www.grafixservices.com
419-534-2709

Susan Guarneri, NCCC, CCMC, CPBS,
    CERW, CCTJ
Guarneri Associates, Three Lakes, WI
Resumagic@aol.com
www.resume-magic.com
866-881-4055

Loretta Heck
All Word Services, Prospect Heights, IL
siegfried@ameritech.net
847-215-7517

Gayle M. Howard
Top Margin Resumes
Melbourne, Australia
getinterviews@topmargin.com
www.topmargin.com
+61 3 9726 6694

Erin Kennedy, CPRW
Professional Resume Services
Lapeer, MI
ekennedy@proreswriters.com
www.proreswriters.com
206-339-2876

Myriam-Rose Kohn, CPBS, CCM, CCMC,
    IJCTC, CPRW, CEIP
Jeda Enterprises, Valencia, CA
Myriam-rose@jedaenterprises.com
www.jedaenterprises.com
661-253-0801

Lorie Lebert
THE LORIEL GROUP
Brighton, MI
lorie@CoachingROI.com
www.coachingroi.com
www.domyresume.com
810-229-6811

Brian Leeson MSc
Vector Consultants Pty Ltd.
Echunga, South Australia
vector@adelaide.on.net
www.users.on.net/~ vector
+61 8 8388 8183

Marilyn McAdams, CPRW
Ms. Secretary/MS Career Service
Franklin, TN
info@mscareerservice.net
www.mscareerservice.com
615-794-3223

Melanie Noonan
Peripheral Pro, LLC,
West Paterson, NJ
PeriPro1@aol.com
973-785-3011

Helen Oliff, FRWCC, CPRW,
Certified Executive Coach
Turning Point, Reston, VA
helen@turningpointnow.com
www.turningpointnow.com
703-716-0077 (VA)
651-204-0665 (Midwest)

Don Orlando, MBA, CPRW, JCTC, CCM,
    CCMC
The McLean Group, Montgomery, AL
yourcareercoach@charterinternet.com
334-264-2020

Kris Plantrich, CPRW
ResumeWonders, Ortonville, MI
krisplantrich@charter.net
248-627-4243

Richard Porter
CareerWise Communications, LLC,
    Portage, MI
careerwise_resumes@yahoo.com
269-321-0183

Michelle Mastruserio Reitz, CPRW
Printed Pages,
Cincinnati, OH
michelle@printedpages.com
www.printedpages.com
513-598-9100

MeLisa Rogers
Ultimate Career, Scroggins, TX
mrogers@tisd.net
www.ultimatecareer.biz
903-860-3963

Barbara Safani, M.A., CERW, NCRW,
    CPRW, CCM
Career Solvers, New York, NY
info@careersolvers.com
www.careersolvers.com
866-333-1800

Bob Simmons
Career Transition Associates, Plainview, NY
ctasimmons@aol.com
careerstransition.com
516-501-0717

Tammy J. Smith
Professional Image Design, LLC, Olivet, MI
ProResumeWriter@aol.com
269-209-3539

Billie Ruth Sucher, MS, CTMS, CTSB
Billie Ruth Sucher & Associates,
    Urbandale, IA
billie@billiesucher.com
www.billiesucher.com
515-276-0061

James A. Swanson, PHR
Resume Design Studio, Rancho Santa
    Margarita, CA
jim@dosllc.com
949-766-6795

Brenda Thompson, CCMC
TH & Associates, Bowie, MD
thworks@comcast.net
www.thworks.net
301-266-1115

Donna Tucker, CPRW
CareerPRO Resume Center, Phoenix, AZ
Donna@4greatresumes.com
www.4greatresumes.com
602-788-3121

Edward Turilli, MA, CPRW
AccuWriter Resume, Writing, & Career
    Services, Bonita Springs, FL
edtur@comcast.net
239-948-7741
North Kingstown, RI
edtur@cox.net
401-268-3020

Pearl White, CPRW, JCTC, CEIP
A 1st Impression Resume & Career
    Coaching Services, Irvine, CA
Pearlwhite1@cox.net
www.a1stimpression.com
949-651-1068

*I*ndex

A

accounting career resumes, 69-81
administrative career resumes, 82-92
age, resumes and, 52-53
ageism, 52-53
ASCII text files, 58-59
attachments, e-mail, 56-58

B

banking career resumes, 69-81
Best Keywords for Resumes, Cover Letters, and Interviews, 19
burnout skills, 14
buzz words, 17-19

C

career counselors, 14
career summary on your resumes, 42-44
chronological resumes, 26-27
clerical career resumes, 82-92

contact information on your resume, 40-41
core skills, capturing your, 10
counselors, career, 14
cover letters, 24
customer service careers, resumes for, 175-187

D

design, resume, 25-38
development opportunities, 14
DISC, 14

E

education
    careers, resumes for, 197-206
    on your resume, 48-50
electronic resumes, 56-63
e-mail
    address on your resume, 41
    attachments, 56-58
engineering careers, resumes for, 207-221

F

finance career resumes, 69-81
food service careers, resumes for,
    120-134
formats, resume, 25-31
functional resumes, 28-29

G

government career resumes, 93-105

H

healthcare careers, resumes for,
    106-119
hospitality careers, resumes for,
    120-134
human resources careers, resumes
    for, 135-147
hybrid resumes, 30-31

I

interests, identifying your key
    motivators and, 12

K

Keirsey Temperament, 14
keywords, 17-19, 70, 83, 94, 107, 121,
    136, 149, 161, 176, 189, 198, 208
keywords for
    accounting, banking, and
        finance career resumes, 70
    administrative and clerical career
        resumes, 83
    government career resumes, 94
    healthcare and social science career
        resumes, 107

hospitality and food service career
    resumes, 121
human resources and training
    career resumes, 136
law enforcement and legal career
    resumes, 149
manufacturing and operations
    career resumes, 161
sales, marketing, and customer
    service career resumes, 176
skilled trades career resumes, 189
teaching and education career
    resumes, 198
technology, science, and
    engineering career resumes, 208

L

law enforcement career resumes,
    148-159
legal career resumes, 148-159

M

manufacturing careers, resumes for,
    160-174
marketing careers, resumes for,
    175-187
Microsoft Word files, 56
mistakes, resume writing, 22
motivators, identifying your key
    interests and, 12
Myers-Briggs Type Indicator, 14

O

O*NET, 14
objective on resume, listing an, 19, 21
operations careers, resumes for,
    160-174

P

positioning, 15
professional experience on your
   resume, 45-48
proficiencies, 14

R

resume
   designs, 32-34
   elements, key, 40-50
   formats, 25-31
   formatting, 25-38
   writing mistakes to avoid, 22
   writing, 7-24
resumes for
   accounting careers, 69-81
   administrative careers, 82-92
   banking careers, 69-81
   clerical careers, 82-92
   customer service careers, 175-187
   education careers, 197-206
   engineering careers, 207-221
   finance careers, 69-81
   food service careers, 120-134
   government careers, 93-105
   healthcare careers, 106-119
   hospitality careers, 120-134
   human resources careers, 135-147
   law enforcement careers, 148-159
   legal careers, 148-159
   manufacturing careers, 160-174
   marketing careers, 175-187
   operations careers, 160-174
   sales careers, 175-187
   science careers, 207-221
   skilled trades careers, 188-196
   social science careers, 106-119
   teaching careers, 197-206
   technology careers, 207-221
   training careers, 135-147
resumes,
   age and, 52-53
   electronic, 56-63
   scannable, 60-61
   Web, 61-62
re-weighting, 9

S

salary information, 22
sales careers, resumes for, 175-187
scannable resumes, 60-61
science careers, resumes for, 207-221
selling, telling vs., 16-17
skilled trades careers, resumes for,
   188-196
skills,
   burnout, 14
   capturing your core, 10
social science careers, resumes for,
   106-119
strategy, 15
supporting documents, 23

T

teaching careers, resumes for, 197-206
technology careers, resumes for,
   207-221
telling, selling vs., 16-17
training careers, resumes for, 135-147
TypeFocus, 14

W

Web resumes, 61-62
working environment, identifying your
   optimal, 11

▶ Arnold G. Boldt

After experiencing his own "downsizing" in 1994, Arnie Boldt explored a number of options before partnering with his wife, Gail Smith Boldt, to form Arnold-Smith Associates, which has helped thousands of job seekers who have found themselves in transition. Since then, he has honed his skills to become recognized as one of the premier resume writers in the country, contributing to more than 30 different books by eight different authors, including numerous titles by *No-Nonsense Resumes* co-author, Wendy Enelow.

In 2004, he was nominated for two prestigious TORI Awards (presented by Career Directors International) in the categories of Best Creative Resume and Best Cover Letter. He has spoken on resume-related topics to groups in the healthcare and manufacturing fields, as well as delivering presentations geared to the older worker and to executives in transition.

Mr. Boldt holds a Bachelor's degree in Technical Communications from Clarkson University and is a Certified Professional Resume Writer and Job & Career Transition Coach. He prides himself on his experience working with the broadest array of clients, ranging from tradespeople and new graduates to corporate executives. A lifelong resident of upstate New York, he makes his home with his wife and two Chihuahuas in a suburb of Rochester.

▶ Wendy S. Enelow

Wendy Enelow is a well-known and well-respected authority in resume writing and career coaching, and has been in private practice for more than 25 years. To date, she has guided more than 5,000 professional, management, and executive clients to achieve their career goals by providing them with best-in-class resumes, cover letters, and job search strategies. In addition, she has authored more than 20 books on resume and cover letter writing, job search, keywords, interviewing, and more.

Ms. Enelow is a frequently requested speaker at national conferences and workshops including the International Career Development Conference, Career Masters Institute Annual Professional Conference, National Employment Counseling Association Annual Conference, President's National Hire Veterans Committee, Professional Association of Resume Writers Annual Conference, Venture for Enterprising Women, and many more. In addition, she has been interviewed by major media outlets nationwide and has more than 100 articles published on various Internet sites.

Ms. Enelow holds a Bachelor's degree in psychology from the University of Maryland. She is a Credentialed Career Master, Master Resume Writer, Job and Career Transition Coach, and Certified Professional Resume Writer. Ms. Enelow currently resides with her husband and pet menagerie in southwestern Virginia.